Therapeutic Interventions for Families and Children in the Child Welfare System

Sheri Pickover, PhD, LPC, is an associate professor and counselor educator at the University of Detroit Mercy in Detroit, Michigan. She has trained clinical mental health, addiction, and school counselors for 11 years and has published several articles on effective clinical interventions. She also founded and acts as the clinical director of the University of Detroit Mercy Counseling Clinic, a training clinic providing free counseling to primarily court-mandated clients. She provides regular clinical supervision, and as former president of the Michigan Association for Counselor Educators and Supervisors, she co-developed and implemented a 30-hour clinical supervision training program.

She began her career in mental health providing crisis counseling at a runaway shelter. After obtaining her master's degree in psychological services, she worked as an in-home family therapist, specialized foster care worker/therapist, foster home licensor, foster care supervisor, clinical supervisor, and delinquency supervisor over the course of 15 years. She testified in court cases, drafted petitions for termination of parental rights, and drove children in foster care to their doctor appointments. Dr. Pickover lives in Southeastern Michigan and enjoys biking and baking brownies for her students and colleagues.

Heather Brown, MS, LPC, ATR, is an art therapist and child and family counselor in private practice. She started her professional career in Baltimore over 14 years ago and has worked as a therapist, trainer, artist, and program developer in a range of settings including a family shelter, special education, and youth development programs, in-home services, and community mental health agencies. After graduating from Eastern Virginia Medical School with her master's degree in art therapy, Heather moved to Detroit, where she served in a collaborative program providing for the mental health needs of foster children and their families through program development, assessment, treatment planning, advocacy, therapy, parenting classes, and professional trainings.

She happily resides in Detroit with her husband and children. She loves the water, playing, dancing, making things and traveling with her good friends and family.

THERAPEUTIC INTERVENTIONS FOR FAMILIES AND CHILDREN IN THE CHILD WELFARE SYSTEM

Sheri Pickover, PhD, LPC
Heather Brown, MS, LPC, ATR

SPRINGER PUBLISHING COMPANY
NEW YORK

Springer Publishing Company, LLC
11 West 42nd Street
New York, NY 10036
www.springerpub.com

Acquisitions Editor: Stephanie Drew
Production Editor: Michael Fergenson
Composition: S4Carlisle Publishing Services

ISBN: 978-0-8261-2218-6
e-book ISBN: 978-0-8261-2219-3

16 17 18 19 20 / 5 4 3 2 1

The author and the publisher of this Work have made every effort to use sources believed to be reliable to provide information that is accurate and compatible with the standards generally accepted at the time of publication. The author and publisher shall not be liable for any special, consequential, or exemplary damages resulting, in whole or in part, from the readers' use of, or reliance on, the information contained in this book. The publisher has no responsibility for the persistence or accuracy of URLs for external or third-party Internet websites referred to in this publication and does not guarantee that any content on such websites is, or will remain, accurate or appropriate.

Library of Congress Cataloging-in-Publication Data

Names: Pickover, Sheri, author. | Brown, Heather (Heather Beth), author.
Title: Therapeutic interventions for families and children in the child
  welfare system / Sheri Pickover, Heather Brown.
Description: New York : Springer Publishing Company, [2016] | Includes
  bibliographical references and index.
Identifiers: LCCN 2015044630 | ISBN 9780826122186 | ISBN 9780826122193 (e-book)
Subjects: | MESH: Mental Disorders—therapy—United States. | Child
  Welfare—United States. | Foster Home Care—psychology—United States.
Classification: LCC HV881 | NLM WM 400 | DDC 362.73/30973—dc23 LC record available at
http://lccn.loc.gov/2015044630

Special discounts on bulk quantities of our books are available to corporations, professional associations, pharmaceutical companies, health care organizations, and other qualifying groups. If you are interested in a custom book, including chapters from more than one of our titles, we can provide that service as well.

For details, please contact:
Special Sales Department, Springer Publishing Company, LLC
11 West 42nd Street, 15th Floor, New York, NY 10036-8002
Phone: 877-687-7476 or 212-431-4370; Fax: 212-941-7842
E-mail: sales@springerpub.com

Printed in the United States of America by McNaughton & Gunn.

CONTENTS

Part IV: Working With Adults in Child Welfare

PREFACE

The purpose of this text is to provide mental health professionals with an understanding of treatment issues unique to children and families who have become involved in the foster care system or children who have been adopted from the foster care system. This text is written for therapists working in multiple settings, including private practice, school settings, child welfare agencies, community mental health, or even juvenile institutions and prisons. The information pertains to any client who has ever had contact with the child welfare system, from adults who grew up in foster care or adopted children, to families who lost their parental rights, to children currently in foster care. These children and families suffer from a variety of mental health and/or substance abuse issues, and a myriad of resources exist to assist the mental health professional in treatment of these issues. However, a resource has not existed, until this text, that speaks to both the mental health needs of children and families and also how to engage families and other professionals. The goal of this text is to provide therapists with information about the child welfare system, explain the worldview of the client and family, and provide treatment interventions to help these clients.

Written as a guide to understanding how the foster care system works, this text explains how all of the parties involved cope and react and how the therapist can intervene at multiple levels to improve outcomes. Each chapter weaves personal examples, ethical issues, multicultural concerns, and current research into a comprehensive and easy-to-follow guide for providing mental health services for the child welfare participant. Many of the interventions described in this text come from clinical experience, trial and error, and evidence-based research. Not all interventions are appropriate for all clients, and not all interventions will work with all clients. Always use clinical judgment and seek supervisory support when needed.

KALEIDOSCOPE METAPHOR

Humans tend to learn best through the use of a metaphor, painting a picture with words that illustrate a point. In this text, each chapter focuses on treating children in foster care, foster parents, adoptive parents, and birth parents through the lens of a kaleidoscope. Every case involves a complex pattern and ever-changing scene before, during, and after the course of treatment. Each color and shape represents trauma, attachment, development, grief and loss, cultural contexts, ethical issues, crises, and transitions. Each turn brings a different perspective into view, but all of the features still exist within the kaleidoscope. We want to remind therapists that even though one shape or color may seem prominent at the time of treatment, all of the issues remain within the child and family, and one gentle turn of the kaleidoscope brings another concern into view. The therapist must continue to turn the kaleidoscope throughout treatment so that she is always reminded of the mosaic of the child's and the family's life in order to provide attuned intervention.

OUTLINE

The text is divided into four sections. First, in Part One, we explain how children enter the foster care system and how child welfare agencies work so that therapists are able to obtain a solid understanding of how to negotiate the child welfare system. Part Two focuses on the worldview of the parties involved in the child welfare system, including the child, the family, the birth parent, and the foster parent. Part Three provides specific information on how to begin treatment, conduct a strength and needs assessment, and understand the role of medication; it provides specific case studies demonstrating how to treat problems related to trauma and attachment and how to develop workable behavior modification plans. Part Three also provides interventions to help clients cope with their complicated losses and the multiple transitions that are an integral part of the child welfare system.

Part Four focuses on how to engage the birth parent, the foster parent, the child welfare system, and the medical and education systems. An ethical imperative for mental professionals is collaboration with other professionals, but silo thinking and lack of access to information often mean that treatment occurs in a vacuum, and children and families who are already stressed and resource deprived are expected to navigate the labyrinth of professionals to get their needs met. These sections provide specific interventions and strategies to engage adults and address how to negotiate the barriers. The last part of this section addresses how to help therapists become more aware of, and able to cope with, the stressors involved in treating these populations.

MARY AND TOM

I remember driving to the shelter that day hoping that both children would fit in my car. I worked in specialized foster care only, so I rarely had to place siblings, but my boss had picked up the case of two siblings, a 13-year-old girl (Mary) and a 10-year-old boy (Tom), to be placed together. I felt ambivalent about placing these children in this new foster home. Sheryl was an untested foster parent. She seemed nice enough but had never parented children this old.

Mary and Tom entered care after being abandoned by their mother. Mary and her mother engaged in a physical altercation in their home, and Tom tried to stop the fight by standing in between his mother and Mary. By the time the police arrived, Mary and Tom's mother was gone and never returned to ask about her children. The police placed them in the shelter. These were old children for a first-time placement in foster care, and their demeanor struck all the adults who met them. They were both very polite and quiet. They didn't demand anything and followed rules readily. The referee in charge of the case demanded they be placed together and took a personal interest in their well-being. As a therapist, something about their affect struck me as odd. I remember describing the two children as deer caught in headlights. What everyone else saw as well mannered, I assessed as fear and trauma. These children were in shock and going through the motions, hoping not to be hurt any more. Time would show the amount of trauma they were trying to cope with; Mary would wet the bed, Tom would explode in rage at his sister.

The foster parent wanted to help them, but she didn't know how to handle a 13-year-old girl who failed to disclose when she was menstruating and a 10-year-old boy who would threaten people with a broken bottle one moment and clean the house out of guilt the next. I worked with this newly formed family for 2 years, watching Mary struggle with her calm foster parent as she tried to get an emotional reaction from her while also desperately trying to help her brother so they could stay together. I often conducted family therapy sessions with the foster parent and Mary, helping the foster parent understand that her minimal reactions to everyday situations made Mary feel that she didn't care. Mary, used to her violent, effusive mother, couldn't read her foster mother, and so she would escalate her behavior to get a reaction.

Although therapy appeared to help Mary, Tom continued to have violent outbursts, and traditional therapy seemed ineffective. I soon discovered that Tom's father had been convicted of homicide and resided in a mental health prison facility not far from his foster home. Tom finally disclosed that his father, a former factory worker, suffered from a closed-head injury and one day, during an argument with his girlfriend, picked up a handgun and killed her. Tom blamed himself for this incident because he had planned to visit his father that weekend and stayed home to play instead; he was 8 years old at the time. I realized that the most therapeutic intervention for Tom was to see his father so he could allay his fears about his father's well-being. I contacted the prison, determined that his father was functioning well in his environment, scheduled a visit, and drove him to see his father. Luckily, the prison allowed visits in an open area, and the search wasn't too intrusive. John and his father could sit next to each other and hug at the end of the visit. I consider myself a pretty good therapist, and I think I've helped many children and families, but as I look back at my career, the most effective therapeutic intervention I ever utilized was taking this child to see his father. I knew that when he got into my car to leave and stated, "I wish my life were a dream and it could just start over."

This book is dedicated to all the foster children, foster parents, adoptive families, and birth families that cannot start over but, with effective therapeutic intervention, can start anew.

ACKNOWLEDGMENTS

Many individuals helped in the process of creating this text. Four master's level graduate students at the University of Detroit Mercy Counseling Program spent their time finding research and editing information. Thanks to Jessica Elezaj, Namer Zayouna, Christina Arsenault, and Jennifer Schilling for their hard work and dedication to this project. Thanks also goes to Heather and to all the children and families who allowed me into their lives and shared their stories; their courage and resiliency continue to astonish me. Finally, thanks to my family for their support and encouragement.

—Sheri Pickover

I am grateful for Sheri and the many other colleagues I've worked with in child welfare. We have learned from each other and supported one another to do the work we wanted to do. I am thankful for all of the researchers, teachers, and trainers who have worked so hard to pass on invaluable information about how to better understand and help this vulnerable population. I am also grateful to God and my own family for helping me help others, as well as all the families that let me become a part of their lives.

—Heather Brown

PART ONE

THE CHILD WELFARE SYSTEM

CHAPTER ONE

INTRODUCTION TO THE CHILD WELFARE SYSTEM

Every child who enters foster care will have at least one or more substantiated experiences of abuse or neglect. This chapter discusses current statistics on child maltreatment and provides definitions for physical abuse, sexual abuse, and neglect. Next, it describes how children enter the child welfare system and the steps that occur from initial protective services investigation, to foster care placement, to exiting the foster care system.

CHILD MALTREATMENT

In 2013, Child Protective Services (CPS) agencies in the United States received 3.5 million referrals and investigated 60% of those referrals (U.S. Department of Health and Human Services, 2013). Most children who were the subject of the reports were young (under the age of 5) and represented White, Hispanic, or African American ethnicities. Eighty percent of the referrals indicated some type of neglect, and 20% were for some type of abuse (U.S. Department of Health and Human Services, 2013). Fifteen hundred children died from abuse or neglect in the United States in 2013 (U.S. Department of Health and Human Services, 2013). Along with the substantiated incidents, foster care children most likely also experience unreported abuse and exposure to domestic violence and substance abuse (Smith, Johnson, Pears, Fisher, & DeGarmo, 2007).

Physical Abuse

Definitions of physical abuse can include beating; whipping; burning; stabbing; or hitting with hands, feet, and objects (United Nations Children's Fund, 2012). Causing a child intentional physical distress can also be physical abuse, such as forcing a child to hold heavy objects for long periods of time or exposing the child to extreme temperatures or illegal substances (U. S. Department of Health and Human Services, 2014a). Children are also considered abused if they are exposed to domestic violence. Domestic violence exposure means the child witnesses adults either hitting each other or other children, witnesses the use of weapons, witnesses physical or sexual assaults, and/or witnesses violent verbal altercations (U.S. Department of Health and Human Services, 2014b). Children who attempt to stop one adult from hurting another and become injured in the process are also considered abused (Bourassa, 2007; Christian, Scribano, Seidl, & Pinto-Martin, 1997).

Sexual Abuse

Sexual abuse of a child includes many different behaviors and exposure that ranges from neglectful exposure, such as adults engaging in sexual activity or watching pornography with children present, to ritualistic aggressive penetration and degradation. Much of the sexual abuse of children is perpetrated by a loved one or trusted caregiver, such as a relative, parent, sibling, neighbor, or friend. It often occurs in the context of a "playful" and coercive game initiated by the abuser in a manipulative manner, with specific threats aimed at the child about not being believed, being bad, and hurting the child's family if the child tells. Penetration involves a body part or object (such as a toy) being placed inside the child's mouth, vagina, or rectum. Molestation involves nonpenetrating sexual touching. Exposure describes the child witnessing others performing any sexual acts by force or by neglect. Exposure also includes the child being forced to watch or view pornographic material or the child being forced to watch any overtly sexual act between people who are closely related or who perceive themselves as being closely related (as in relationships between in-laws, stepsiblings and stepparents, and close family friends). In addition to physical sexual contact, this can include voyeurism, masturbation in front of the child, suggestive talk, provocative photography, and exposing oneself to the child. Any of these involving two children of differing or the same age is considered inappropriate sexual behavior if both children involved are minors.

Nine percent of children are brought into foster care due to confirmed sexual abuse (U.S. Department of Health and Human Services, 2013), although approximately one in six boys and one in four girls are sexually abused before the age of 18 (Centers for Disease Control and Prevention,

2014). Heterosexual males perpetrate almost all child sexual abuse. Close to two-thirds of all child sexual abuse victims do not tell because they fear being blamed, punished, or not believed (Feiring, & Taska 2005; London, Bruck, Ceci, & Shuman, 2005). Incest, the sexual abuse of a family member, is estimated to occur in 14% of all families (Snyder, 2000).

Neglect

Neglect is a nebulous construct with several definitions. Children often experience multiple types of neglect rather than one specific type. Neglect either involves directly not caring for children's needs or failing to protect them from an abusive adult in the home (Dubowitz, Pitts, Litrownik, Cox, Runyan, & Black, 2005). Eighty percent of children who are subjects of a protective services complaint have experienced neglect (U.S. Department of Health and Human Services, 2015).

Physical neglect refers to the lack of basic needs, such as a lack of clothing; lack of access to heat, electricity, and water; and lack of access to food. Medical neglect refers to the lack of basic medical and dental care, such as failure to receive well-child visits or not getting medical treatment for an injury or illness. These are two primary types of neglect that lead to placement in foster care. Parents may also commit educational neglect, which refers to the parents' refusal to send a child to school, or emotional neglect, which refers to the parent failing to provide nurturing. Often these types of neglect are not actionable.

Another frequent type of neglect is failure to protect. A parent who allows another adult to cause injury to a child without intervening may be charged with this type of neglect. For example, a mother who allows her partner to harm her children and does not intervene to stop the physical abuse will be charged with failure to protect.

Children exposed to physical abuse and sexual abuse also tend to be exposed to emotional and verbal maltreatment, although such maltreatment is greatly underreported and difficult to criminalize. These types of abuse and neglect can appear as insulting and degrading the child (calling him stupid, insulting his looks, etc.), threatening abandonment, teaching a child antisocial behavior, and rejecting a child's efforts to receive affection and closeness. Emotional maltreatment occurs when an adult consciously conveys to a child that she is worthless, flawed, unloved, unwanted, endangered, or only valuable to meet the adults' needs. Studies also show that the repercussions and effects of emotional and verbal abuse and neglect on children are much the same as those resulting from physical abuse (Spinazzola et al., 2014).

Ramifications of Child Maltreatment

The impact of abuse and neglect on children is well documented. Exposure to physical abuse, sexual abuse, and/or neglect impacts several areas, including biological, cognitive, and emotional development (Healey & Fisher, 2011). Depending on the age of the child at the time of exposure, brain development may be affected and result in cognitive distortions or delays (Koenen, Moffitt, Caspi, Taylor, & Purcell, 2003). Children may also suffer from nutritional deficits, which impact their growth and development, or may suffer injuries that cause long-term nerve or bone damage (Block, Krebs, American Academy of Pediatrics Committee on Child Abuse and Neglect, & American Academy of Pediatrics Committee on Nutrition, 2005). Young children may demonstrate failure to thrive, which means they do not grow as expected (Block et al., 2005). Older children may begin puberty early or have physical ailments related to the abuse, including sexually transmitted diseases, somatic complaints, or long-term injuries (Tubman, Montgomery, Gil, & Wagner, 2004). Of greatest concern is the impact of abuse on cognitive development. Cognitive developmental deficits occur both due to the stress reactions in the brain and the inability of children to receive educational stimulation because they do not feel safe or lack nutrition (Block et al., 2005; Hildyard & Wolfe, 2002). Typical milestones such as learning emotional regulation, learning to develop empathy, or even making friends can be affected by abuse (Luke & Banerjee, 2012). The biological ramifications of physical abuse and domestic violence also include increases in cortisol, a hormone associated with the stress response that prevents healthy brain development and prolongs difficulties from physical injuries (De Bellis, Spratt, & Hooper, 2011).

Children exposed to neglect also may display problems with hygiene, including not knowing how to bathe or brush their teeth and not knowing how to handle menstruation appropriately. Depending on the severity of the neglect, brain function and normal development may be altered (Glaser, 2000). Infants who do not receive nurturing or basic needs fail to thrive and in some cases die (Block et al., 2005).

Most children entering foster care also enter with a history of educational difficulty. They may have a diagnosed or undiagnosed learning problem, a history of multiple school placements, or behavioral problems in school. Children may have delayed academic skills or in some cases may be unable to perform age-level grade work. As a result, children entering foster care often enter with a poor relationship with schools and teachers (Hildyard & Wolfe, 2002).

Children entering foster care can also exhibit some form of attachment insecurity, which can manifest itself as either hostility toward a caregiver or avoidance of a caregiver. In some cases, children suffer from having no attachment type and do not have the skills to build a quality relationship with an adult. These children, often diagnosed with reactive attachment disorder per the criteria of the *Diagnostic and Statistical Manual of Mental Disorders*, 5th ed. (*DSM–5*; American Psychiatric Association, 2013), do not demonstrate anxiety around strange adults and also display violent and destructive behavior. Finally, although family and social support issues are not unique to foster children, most foster children come from disrupted families and have witnessed illegal substance use, have often lived with parents who lacked higher education, and did not have access to adequate resources. These children have also witnessed domestic violence. In fact, there is a 30% to 60% overlap between domestic violence and child maltreatment (U.S. Department of Health and Human Services, 2014b).

HOW CHILDREN ENTER THE FOSTER CARE SYSTEM

Initial Abuse/Neglect Report

The information discussed in this section is based on clinical experience and information gleaned from the *Child Welfare Policy Manual* (U.S. Department of Health and Human Services, 2015). Generally, there are two ways a child enters the child welfare system: either through a law enforcement entity or through the state protective services agency. Children enter the child welfare system for a myriad of reasons, and each state has individualized laws and procedures, including decision-making rubrics, that illuminate how placement occurs. Not all children who come to the attention of the child welfare system end up in foster care, but often, once a child comes to the attention of CPS, the parents and child are subject to increased scrutiny.

When law enforcement is involved, usually an incident of abuse or neglect has occurred that is so serious that the child's immediate safety is threatened. The police obtain an emergency court order to remove the child and then call the state CPS worker to put the child in protective custody. When this type of removal occurs, the investigation takes place after the child has been removed from the parent's custody.

The other way a child becomes placed in foster care is through the state protective services agency. This occurs when a mandated reporter or anonymous source reports a suspected abuse and/or neglect allegation to the state agency, and the state agency assigns a caseworker to investigate the veracity of the claim. Investigations should occur within 48 hours of the initial report, but often, due to caseload sizes, the investigation takes longer. This investigation includes speaking to the child; the adult accused of the abuse or neglect; and other parties, such as the reporter, teachers, or neighbors.

Once the complaint has been investigated, protective services either decides to dismiss the allegation, substantiate the allegation and recommend prevention services, or substantiate the allegation and recommend removal. If removal is recommended, the protective services worker must draft a petition for removal and go to court to request that the removal be granted. Ultimately, only the juvenile court system has the power to remove a child from her guardian.

A family may be referred for prevention services prior to removal. These services include requiring the parents to attend parenting classes, obtaining financial support to obtain clean and safe housing, turning on electricity and gas, providing funds for furniture or food, or undergoing intensive in-home counseling services designed to keep the family together and intact. Not all families receive these services, and the decision to use preventative services over removal in most cases depends on the level of risk to the child. If the child is deemed at serious risk, meaning the child's personal safety and life are threatened, then removal occurs. If the threat is less serious, family preservation services attempt to prevent removal.

Families can have contact with a state agency several times prior to removal, or children can be removed on the first allegation. Children can be removed at birth for testing positive for illicit drugs, or, if a parent has had other children removed, some states automatically remove any new children born to that mother even if neglect or abuse has not occurred. Sometimes the court removes only one child from a home if only one child is at risk; other times, all siblings in the home are removed even if only one child is considered the primary victim. Each state and county has its own policies, procedures, and protocols for removing children, and consistency does not exist throughout states or the country. Therapists should learn the laws in their states and counties to understand the culture of the state agency and court system.

As a mandated reporter, all mental health professionals should know the child protection laws in the states in which they practice, including the definitions for physical abuse, sexual abuse, physical neglect, medical neglect, educational neglect, abandonment, and failure to protect. Some states allow many forms of corporal punishment, whereas other states allow only open-handed spanking on a child's bottom. Learn the reason your client entered foster care from the court records, the case manager, and the client. Rather than focusing on the truth, consider the varied reports as multiple pieces of data to add to your assessment. The reasons a child enters care are often numerous and accompanied by differing accounts, all of which might be useful to the therapeutic process. Assuming prevention services are unsuccessful, or the risk to the child is too high to leave the child with his family, a state protective services worker drafts a petition to request removal of the child from the custody of the guardian. Once the petition is approved, the caseworker then transports the child to foster care placement.

Figure 1.1 provides a summary of the ways in which children enter foster care.

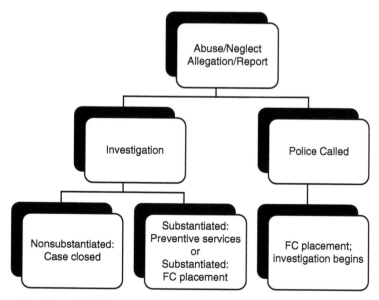

Figure 1.1 *How Children Enter Foster Care*

Initial Placement

Once a decision to remove the child has been made, there are several options available for placement (Table 1.1). First, the state agency attempts to locate a biological family member deemed safe and able to protect the child. Often, grandparents, aunts, uncles, or older siblings are asked to take temporary custody. Recently, federal law also allows placement with fictive kin, meaning a nonbiologically related individual the child and family identify as family, such as a very close friend or neighbor. In all of these cases, the state protective services worker needs to visit the home, ensure the home is safe, and ensure the family member agrees to refrain from using physical discipline on the child. Family members and fictive kin historically have not received financial support for agreeing to care for their relatives beyond health insurance and food assistance, but this process has been changing throughout the country.

If no family member is available, the child is placed in either a foster care home or a temporary shelter. Usually only teenagers are sent to shelters. Typically these shelters are multiple-bed facilities staffed by paraprofessionals who monitor children throughout the day and change shift every 8 hours.

The initial foster home placement could be a temporary placement, meaning it is short term while the agency attempts to locate a more permanent home or approve a family member, or it might be a long-term placement. Almost half of all foster care children placed in the United States return home within 1 year (Child Welfare Information Gateway, 2013), and the median length of stay before replacement is 13.4 months (U.S. Department of Health and Human Services, 2015).

The State and Court Systems

Once a child is placed in foster care, the protective service worker transfers the case to a foster care worker. Every state handles foster care cases

Table 1.1 *Initial Placement Options*

Biological family	Aunts, uncles, adult siblings, grandparents, cousins
Fictive kin	Neighbors, family friends
Shelter	Residential facility
Temporary foster home	10- to 30-day placement
Long-term foster home	90-day to 1-year placement

differently. Some states retain control of the case and assign a state fos-ter care worker to ensure the child's safety, whereas other states con-tract out these services to a private child welfare agency and have a purchase-of-service caseworker who oversees the financial aspects of the case but not the day-to-day progress.

The court system also varies from state to state, but the process is similar throughout the country. Once an initial petition for removal is granted, the court assigns the guardian an attorney (if the guardian cannot afford her own), a prosecutor represents the state, and the court assigns a lawyer to represent the interests of the child. The petition for removal outlines complaints against the parent based on which child welfare law the guardian allegedly violated. The next step is a pretrial hearing in which the court decides if enough evidence exists to proceed the case to trial and continue the child in placement. The next step is a trial. Rarely do these trials result in an actual jury trial, although the par-ent can request one. The judge or referee can also decide the facts of the case, but usually the parents plead no contest to the abuse and/or neglect charges. Unlike in a criminal trial, the parent or parents are not innocent until proven guilty, and the rules of evidence are much more lax. Hear-say testimony is common, and decisions are based on a preponderance of evidence. If the parents are found guilty of the charges, the child is made a temporary ward of the court, meaning the parent retains some custodial rights such as the ability to sign medical consents and make educational decisions, but all decisions can be overridden by the court.

The next hearing is an initial dispositional hearing. The caseworker in charge of the case must draft a plan called a parent/agency agreement (PA) that the parent signs and the court approves. This plan includes all of the steps the parent must take in order to regain custody of the child. The court may order the parent to submit to a psychological evaluation, attend parenting classes, attend individual and family therapy, obtain employment, or refrain from using substances and submit to regular urine testing. The child may also be ordered to undergo a psychological or psychiatric evaluation or participate in individual or family therapy. The agency assigned to the case is responsible for providing referrals and services to the parent to help the parent achieve these goals. During this time, the parents also have structured visits with the child. Initially, visits often occur weekly for one hour, with a caseworker monitoring the visit; they possibly progress to weekly unsupervised visits, either for a few hours or an entire day. If the parent continues to progress, visits move to weekend visits in preparation for family reunification.

The court reviews the case every 90 days, and the caseworker presents a court report on the parents' compliance with the PA agreement. Another dispositional hearing occurs at 180 days, and the court determines if the plan remains reunification or should change to adoption. A permanency planning hearing occurs 360 days after the first dispositional hearing. If the parent has made progress, the court usually either returns the child home and orders in-home services or agrees to give the parent more time to comply with the PA agreement.

If the parent has not complied with the PA agreement, the prosecutor and the agency worker might request a change in plan to adoption. Depending on the state or county, either the state (or private agency) caseworker or prosecutor will draft and file a petition to terminate parental rights. The court sets a trial date, and this trial usually occurs in front of a referee or a judge. The caseworker acts as the primary witness, testifying to the services offered to the parent and how the parent failed to comply with services. Sometimes the parent testifies, and sometimes the child does as well. Unlike in criminal cases, the court needs only a preponderance of the evidence to terminate rights; however, there are two stages to a termination trial: presentation of the evidence and a best-interest hearing. The best-interest hearing, which often occurs with the trial, allows the parent to offer proof that although he didn't comply with the parent/agency agreement, the child's best interest is not served by termination of parental rights. Table 1.2 summarizes the court process.

If parental rights are terminated, the parent no longer has custody and can no longer make any decisions for that child. The child's status changes to a permanent court ward. In most cases, the state no longer allows the child to have any contact with the parent, and the state places the child for adoption. Depending on the age of the child, adoption could take up to a year or longer, or the child may not be adopted. Sometimes

Table 1.2 Court Process

Initial petition/trial	Child returned home
	Child made temporary court ward
Initial dispositional review—30 days after trial	Parent/agency agreement
Dispositional review—every 90 days	Court report on compliance
Permanency planning hearing—360 days	Plan for reunification
	Plan for termination of rights

Table 1.3 *Permanency Planning Options*

Reunification with custodial birth parent	Reunification with noncustodial birth parent
Placement with relative	Termination of parental rights (either or both parents)
Adoption by relative	Adoption by nonrelative
Permanent foster family (14 and older)	Supervised independent living (16 and older)
Independent living (18 and older)	Age out of system

the foster parent adopts the foster child, or a family member adopts the child. According to U.S. statistics, 5% of foster care children age out of the system, never receiving permanent homes (U.S. Department of Health and Human Services, 2013). In cases where the parent has not complied but the child is old enough to request an ongoing relationship with the parent, the child may remain a temporary ward of the court on a long-term basis, with no plan to terminate parental rights, and age out of the system by entering a supervised independent living program, an independent living program (unsupervised), or some type of permanent foster care. Table 1.3 summarizes the permanency planning options.

CHILD WELFARE AGENCIES

A child welfare agency is either a state or private nonprofit agency that takes responsibility for managing the foster care case once a child enters placement. Child welfare agencies are licensed by a state to license foster homes; to provide case management to foster care and adoption cases; and often to provide other services, such as prevention services, mental health services, and supportive services, once the child returns home.

Foster Care Case Management

The foster care caseworker is most often an individual with an undergraduate degree in either social work, psychology, or another mental-health-related field. The caseworker tends to be female, young, and inexperienced; 23% have less than 1 year of experience (Zell, 2006).

Caseworker turnover throughout the United States is very high, with 60% of caseworkers leaving their positions each year (U.S. Department of Health and Human Services, 2013). This turnover can result in negative outcomes for children in foster care (Strolin-Goltzman, Kollar, & Trinkle, 2010), such as increased placement instability (Eggertsen, 2008). Most children will experience at least one incidence of caseworker turnover during their time in care because, as noted, 60% of caseworkers leave their positions within 1 year, and the average length of stay in foster care is just over 12 months (U.S. Department of Health and Human Services, 2013).

A foster care caseworker's caseload is determined by guidelines and state mandates. Some have caseloads as high as 40, whereas others have caseloads of 15. Responsibilities include visiting the foster child in the foster home every month; writing reports on each foster child within 30 days of placement and every 90 days thereafter; drafting the PA; meeting with the birth families to provide referrals and ensure the parent follows the agreement; supervising visits or coordinating day and weekend visits; ensuring the foster care child has bi-yearly dental examinations, yearly medical exams, and up-to-date immunizations; coordinating with all mental health professionals; coordinating treatment with the child's school; obtaining report cards; and attending all school conferences. The caseworker also attends all court hearings and drafts court reports to submit to the court. All of these responsibilities have strict timelines that must be met in order to ensure that the agency keeps its license to place children and for payment to the foster parent to occur. The phrase most often used is that the caseworker will "provide quality-of-care assurance" through these activities. In other words, the caseworker must ensure the safety, permanence, and well-being of the child and family in care. Agencies often employ a quality assurance manager to review files on a regular basis; an independent agency or the state also reviews files at least once every 2 years.

A primary role of a child welfare agency is to recruit, train, and license needed foster parents. Both federal and state laws stipulate who can become a licensed foster parent, and it varies by state. A foster home licensing specialist usually has an undergraduate degree in social work, psychology, or another mental health profession. This individual maintains a caseload of about 30 to 60 homes and has responsibility for visiting each home at least one time per year to ensure the home stays in compliance and for addressing any compliance concerns.

Child welfare agencies recruit foster parents in a variety of ways: through multimedia advertising, through referral from other foster parents, and through individuals seeking adoption. Once recruited, a potential foster parent attends a series of trainings on issues such as behavior management and child abuse or neglect. During this time, the foster parent also submits to an extensive home study. Every member of the family submits to a criminal record check and protective services check. The agency also reviews the family's finances and life history, and obtains marriage certificates, divorce decrees, and any other document to verify the foster parent's claims. The foster parent provides a life story history, and the worker visits the home, measures each bedroom, ensures the home is fire safe, and ensures that a child can access food and the bathroom. Foster parents must agree to never use any form of corporal punishment. A newly licensed foster parent is placed on a provisional license for 6 months; if the parent remains in compliance, the license is renewed for 1 year.

Sometimes during the course of placement, a foster parent violates one or more of the rules she agreed to uphold. This violation might include using physical discipline, refusing to take a child to an appointment, or letting someone move into the home without letting the foster care agency know. When a violation happens, the child welfare agency must file a complaint against the foster parent. The foster care licensing specialist must then conduct an investigation. The investigation involves interviewing all parties involved, visiting the foster home, and drawing conclusions. If the worker substantiates the complaint, the foster parent is either placed back on a provisional license, or the agency can petition to have the foster parent's license revoked. If the agency does not substantiate the complaint, the case is closed. Complaints must be filed any time a child makes an allegation of abuse or neglect, and the report should go to both the state protective services agency and the licensing agency. Anyone can file a complaint against a foster parent, including the child's therapist.

Mental Health Treatment

Some child welfare agencies provide mental health services within the agency itself, but most often agencies contract with other therapists to provide individual, group, and family therapy. In some cases, therapists have dual roles as both caseworker and therapist, providing case management services such as referrals and attending court hearings, while also providing mental health treatment. Therapy can occur in traditional outpatient settings, in the foster home or birth home, or a combination of both. Therapy can be short term or long term. A therapist could provide therapy to only the foster child, to only the birth family, or to both. Therapists also write court reports but might be prohibited from making specific recommendations in case the recommendations do not align with those of the oversight agency. An ongoing challenge for therapists working within the child welfare system is negotiating boundaries. Normal boundaries become difficult to maintain because the client is often the court or the hiring agency, not the child or birth family. The therapist has a duty to the agency that pays for the service, oftentimes the court or a government agency. The parent and child have fewer rights regarding confidentiality because the treatment occurs within the context of a court order. We discuss this issue in depth throughout this text and provide simple but effective strategies to negotiate these ethical issues.

Adoption

An agency will assign an adoption caseworker once parental rights are terminated. Like the foster care caseworker and the foster home licensor, the adoption worker normally has an undergraduate degree in social work, psychology, or another mental health–related field. The adoption caseworker's responsibilities include recruiting an adoptive home for the child, conducting a home study on the potential adoptive home, and filing court paperwork to process the adoption. The adoption caseworker does not take on the foster care caseworker's responsibilities but works alongside the foster care caseworker. Sometimes the foster parent will adopt the child, sometimes a family member adopts the child, and sometimes parents from the community will adopt the child. Each state has different methods to recruit potential adoptive parents. Younger children often obtain adoptive placement more readily than do adolescents.

Residential Treatment

If a foster care child cannot successfully live in a foster home, the child might be placed in a residential treatment facility for short-term treatment. Treatment centers range in the level of restriction placed on the child. Some treatment centers provide 24-hour staff, but children go to a community school and live in a house-like setting, whereas other centers appear more like institutions, with locked doors, 24-hour staff, and mental health professionals on-site. A child might stay in one of these homes for a short time or for years. A standard requirement for placement involves the term "least restrictive community-based placement." Foster care or a family-type home is considered the least restrictive, whereas locked residential treatment is the most restrictive. A child in residential treatment will have a caseworker on-site as well as the foster care caseworker and will interact with different staff throughout the day.

Supervised/Independent Living

The final stage of the child welfare agency service is supervised independent living (SIL) or independent living (IL). When a foster care child reaches age 16 and reunification or adoption appears unlikely, the caseworker will often refer the child to SIL or IL. Designed to help youth in foster care transition to adulthood, these programs involve allowing a child to rent a room from a home provider or placing a child in an apartment setting with other youth in foster care. Each child receives meals, a monthly stipend to pay rent and utilities, and has a curfew; many obtain and maintain employment and attend school. The Fostering Connections to Success and Increasing Adoptions Act extended eligibility for Title IV-E payments for youth in foster care to age 21 (U.S. Department of Health and Human Services, 2013), so youth in foster care may now choose to stay a dependent ward until age 21. Some universities and colleges have instituted support programs for youth in foster care, and some tuition funds exist to support youth in foster care through either community college or a traditional 4-year college.

REFERENCES

American Psychiatric Association. (2013). *Diagnostic and statistical manual of mental disorders* (5th ed.). Washington, DC: Author.

Block, R. W., Krebs, N. F., American Academy of Pediatrics Committee on Child Abuse and Neglect, & American Academy of Pediatrics Committee on Nutrition. (2005). Failure to thrive as a manifestation of child neglect. *Pediatrics, 116*(5),1234–1237.

Bourassa, C. (2007). Co-occurrence of interparental violence and child physical abuse and its effect on the adolescents' behavior. *Journal of Family Violence, 22*(8), 691–701. doi:10.1007/s10896-007-9117-8.

Centers for Disease Control and Prevention. (2014). *Adverse Childhood Experiences (ACE) study.* Retrieved from http://www.cdc.gov/violenceprevention/acestudy

Child Welfare Information Gateway. (2013). *Foster care statistics 2012.* Washington, DC: U.S. Department of Health and Human Services, Children's Bureau.

Child Welfare Information Gateway. (2014a). *Definitions of child abuse and neglect.* Washington, DC: U.S. Department of Health and Human Services, Children's Bureau. Retrieved from https://www.childwelfare.gov/pubPDFs/define.pdf

Child Welfare Information Gateway. (2014b). *Domestic violence and the child welfare system.* Washington, DC: U.S. Department of Health and Human Services, Children's Bureau. Retrieved from https://www.childwelfare.gov/pubPDFs/domestic-violence.pdf#page=3&view=Scope of the problem

Christian, C. W., Scribano, P., Seidl, T., & Pinto-Martin, J. A. (1997). Pediatric injury resulting from family violence. *Pediatrics, 99*(2), 1–4. doi:10.1542/peds/99.2.e8

De Bellis, M. D., Spratt, E. G., & Hooper, S. R. (2011). Cutting edge technologies: Neurodevelopmental biology associated with childhood sexual abuse. *Journal of Child Sexual Abuse: Research, Treatment, & Program Innovations for Victims, Survivors, & Offenders, 20*(5), 548–587. doi:10.1080/10538712.2011.607753

Dubowitz, S. C., Pitts, A. J., Litrownik, A. J., Cox, C. E., Runyan, D., & Black, M. M. (2005). Defining child neglect based on child protective services data. *Child Abuse & Neglect, 29*, 493–511. doi:10.1016/j.chiabu.2003.09.024

Eggertsen, L. (2008). Primary factors related to multiple placements for children in out-of-home care. *Child Welfare, 87*(6), 71–90.

Feiring, C., & Taska, L. S. (2005). The persistence of shame following sexual abuse: A longitudinal look at risk and recovery. *Child Maltreatment, 10*(4), 337–349. doi:10.1177/1077559505276686

Glaser, D. (2000). Child abuse and neglect and the brain—a review. *Journal of Child Psychology and Psychiatry, 41*(1), 97–116.

Healey, C. V., & Fisher, P. A. (2011). Children in foster care and the development of favorable outcomes. *Children and Youth Services Review, 33*(10), 1822–1830. doi:10.1016/j.childyouth.2011.05.007

Hildyard, K. L., & Wolfe, D. A. (2002). Child neglect: Developmental issues and outcomes. *Child Abuse & Neglect, 26*, 679–695. doi:10.1016/S0145-2134(02)00341-1

Koenen, K. C., Moffitt, T. E., Caspi, A., Taylor, A., & Purcell, S. (2003). Domestic violence is associated with environmental suppression of IQ in young children. *Development and Psychopathology, 15*(2), 297–311.

London, K., Bruck, M., Ceci, S. J., & Shuman, D. W. (2005). Disclosure of child sexual abuse: What does the research tell us about the ways that children tell? *Psychology, Public Policy, and Law, 11*(1), 194–226. doi:10.1037/1076-8971.11.1.194

Luke, N., & Banerjee, R. (2012). Maltreated children's social understanding and empathy: A preliminary exploration of foster carers' perspective. *Journal of Child and Family Studies, 21,* 237–246. doi:10.1007/s10826-011-9468-x

Smith, D. K., Johnson, A. B., Pears, K. C., Fisher, P. A., & DeGarmo, D. S. (2007). Child maltreatment and foster care: Unpacking the effects of prenatal and postnatal parental substance use. *Child Maltreatment, 12*(2), 150–160.

Snyder, H. N. (2000) *Sexual assault of young children as reported to law enforcement: Victim, incident and offender characteristics.* U.S. Department of Justice; Office of Justice Programs. http://www.bjs.gov/content/pub/pdf/saycrle.pdf

Spinazzola, J., Hodgdon, H., Liang, L.-J., Ford, J. D., Layne, C. M., Pynoos, R., ... Kisiel, C. (2014). Unseen wounds: The contribution of psychological maltreatment to child and adolescent mental health and risk outcomes. *Psychological Trauma: Theory, Research, Practice, and Policy, 6*(1), S18–S28. doi:10.1037/a0037766

Strolin-Goltzman, J., Kollar, S., & Trinkle, J. (2010). Listening to the voices of children in foster care: Youths speak out about child welfare workforce turnover and selection. *Social Work, 55*(1), 47–53. doi:10.1093/sw/55.1.47

Tubman, J. G., Montgomery, M. J., Gil, A. G., & Wagner, E. F. (2004). Abuse experiences in a community sample of young adults: Relations with psychiatric disorders, sexual risk behaviors, and sexually transmitted diseases. *American Journal of Community Psychology, 34*(1), 147–162.

United Nations Children's Fund. (2012). *Child maltreatment: Prevalence, incidence, and consequences in the East Asia and Pacific Region.* Bangkok, Thailand: UNICEF EAPRO. Retrieved from http://www.unicef.org/eapro/Child_Maltreatment.pdf

U.S. Department of Health and Human Services, Administration for Children and Families, Administration on Children, Youth and Families, Children's Bureau. (2013). *Implementation of the Fostering Connections to Success and Increasing Adoptions Act of 2008. Working document.* Retrieved from http://www.acf.hhs.gov/programs/cb/resource/implementation-of-the-fostering-connections

U.S. Department of Health and Human Services, Administration for Children and Families, Administration on Children, Youth and Families, Children's Bureau. (2015). *Child maltreatment 2013.* Retrieved from http://www.acf.hhs.gov/programs/cb/research-data-technology/statistics-research/child-maltreatment

Zell, M. C. (2006). Child welfare workers: Who they are and how they view the child welfare system. *Child Welfare, 85*(1), 83–103.

PART TWO

THE CLIENT WORLDVIEW

CHAPTER TWO

THE CHILD PERSPECTIVE

This turn of the kaleidoscope focuses on how children experience being placed in foster care, living in foster care, and leaving foster care.

CASE STUDY 2.1

The first time I watched someone try to explain the experience of entering foster care, I was at a training for new foster care workers. The trainer, an experienced foster home licensor, described how he challenged new foster parents with the analogy of being kidnapped at gunpoint and forced to live with strangers. I also remember a poem I read during my first job in foster care that spoke to the stress of someone coming to take a child with no warning; each time the place was warm and shiny, but at the end of the poem, the child had no home.

CASE STUDY 2.2

On a cold fall day, I transported a 6-year-old client, Kevin, to a sibling visit and was in the process of driving him home. Kevin was a biracial male with 10 other siblings and no memory of living with family. He had lived in several foster homes throughout his young life. We were driving back around lunchtime, and I said, "I'm hungry, let's go get something to eat."

And he replied, "I don't have any money."

This statement shocked me. As a young child, I never thought about who bought my food. If I was with an adult, the expectation

(continued)

CASE STUDY 2.2   *(continued)*

would be that the adult would feed me; it wasn't a worry or a thought. This child had been raised in foster care with foster parents who gave him his allowance and made him responsible for buying his own treats or meals out. This interaction reminded me that children in foster care have a different worldview and concerns that other children often do not.

I replied, "I am going to buy you lunch." He then ate his hamburger.

These anecdotes illustrate the challenges faced by children in foster care and adoptive children that are unique to the foster care experience. These issues include coping with a constant threat of removal, adjusting to varying parenting styles, coping with the separation from family, worrying about money and material possessions, and the constant changing of relationships. This chapter reviews each of these issues to help the therapist understand the myriad concerns facing these children (see Figure 2.1 summarizing these issues in an easy reference format). These issues are discussed in three categories: issues related to the removal, issues related to placement, and issues related to being raised in foster care while waiting for some kind of permanency.

PLACEMENT

First Removal

Depending on how it occurs, the removal itself can be as traumatic as the reason for removal (Bruskas, 2008). Children removed in front of an angry parent by the police might experience flashbacks and ongoing anxiety. Children removed from school with no ability to see the parent or pack their own clothes may experience anger and depression. Children removed after their own reports of abuse may be targeted by parents and siblings for breaking the family apart and may struggle with pervasive guilt and shame. Emotional concerns derived from the removal itself include trauma from the removal from the attachment figure,

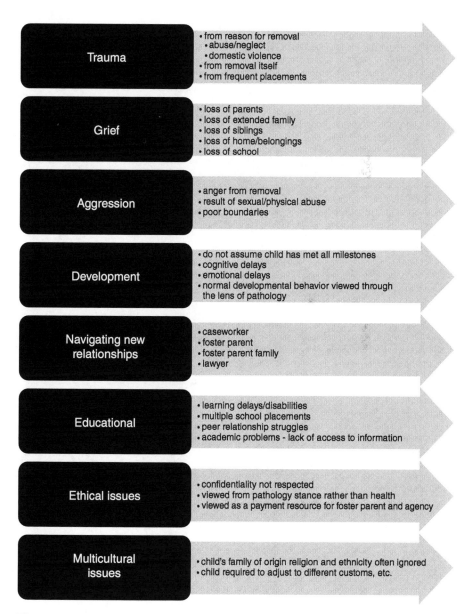

Figure 2.1 *Treatment Issues Unique to Foster Children*

anxiety, depression, and profound grief resulting from the multiple losses (Herrenkohl, Herrenkohl, & Egolf, 2003). Ultimately, the therapist needs to remember that removal results in a sense of helplessness and a profound loss of control that are not usually mitigated by the safety created by being removed from the threatening situation.

Multiple Losses

Children in foster care do not lose only a parent or parents when they are removed from their homes; they lose their homes, their bedrooms, their neighborhoods, their siblings, their extended relatives, their toys and other belongings, their school connections, and their peers and friends. These losses are compounded and overwhelming, especially for a child. Expect children to experience an adjustment disorder and signs of grief and/or complicated grief for several months following the removal (Herrenkohl et al., 2003; Sheperis, Renfro-Michel, & Doggett, 2003; Zito et al., 2008).

Guilt, Blame, and Shame

Children in foster care may quickly withdraw or minimize the allegation after removal for fear of further reprisals or because of a desire to return home. Depending on the reason for removal, a child may also suffer guilt and self-blame for breaking up the family or bear the brunt of the blame from other siblings for disclosing family secrets (Younes & Harp, 2007). Removal causes confusion, and young children often do not understand the reason for removal from their parents. When compounded, the child may feel deep shame over the role the child played in the removal, and although the child is never at fault, adults might send the child the message that the child somehow contributed to the reason for removal. For example, teenagers are often blamed for the abuse they suffer as if it is a result of their behavior, and younger children might be blamed by siblings or parents for not keeping quiet.

Pervasive Fearfulness

Expect a child just placed in care to demonstrate signs of trauma, including not sleeping, having issues with food and eating, experiencing nightmares, and acting out physically and sexually (Landsverk, Burns, Stambaugh, & Rolls Reutz, 2009). For older children, truancy from school and running away from home should be expected, as children try to return to their parents or express outrage at their situation (Landsverk et al., 2009). Children in foster care often do not understand how the foster care system works and may employ several strategies to return home, including acting out in the belief that the child welfare system will surrender and allow them to return home.

TREATMENT ISSUES RELATED TO PLACEMENT

Adjusting to the Child Welfare System

While coping with the reason for removal, children in foster care must also learn to cope with a wide variety of adjustment issues related to the placement itself (see Exhibit 2.1). These issues include learning to cope with different parenting styles; adjusting to new foster siblings; building relationships with new caregivers and caseworkers; building relationships with a new school, new teachers, and new peers; learning a new neighborhood; and learning new house and school rules (Pecora, 2010). Children in foster care must also cope with the change in cultural and religious expectations. Oftentimes the cultural adaption is ignored because of the

CASE STUDY 2.3

Sometimes advocating for children in foster care means arguing with fellow professionals who become blinded by the reality that the system itself creates its own set of problems for the child. Sandra was a 10-year-old Hispanic girl on my caseload who had lived in 15 different foster homes within 3 years. She appeared disinterested in being cared for by adults and appeared oblivious to rules and structure. As she proceeded to disrupt her placement with my agency, I advocated to place her in a residential treatment facility—not because of her behavior, but because she deserved the right to stay in one place for a longer period of time than a month, and the frequent moves appeared to be as abusive as the reason for her initial placement. Her adoption worker refused, insisting she could find an adoptive home. After another failed attempt at locating an adoptive placement, the adoption worker finally relented and allowed Sandra to be placed in a long-term residential treatment facility, where she could stay and not worry about being thrown out.

EXHIBIT 2.1

The fact that adults expect children to make these adjustments in a very short amount of time is absurd, yet it happens. Current research indicates that humans may take over 1 year to fully process grief or adapt to change (Davis, 2001), and the Diagnostic and Statistical Manual of Mental Disorders, 5th ed. *(DSM–5) indicates that adjustment disorders occur within 3 months of the onset of the stressor (American Psychiatric Association, 2013). However, children in foster care are expected to adjust immediately and also live with the constant threat of removal to either a new foster home or a nonfamily structured placement.*

assumption that if foster parents look like the foster child, no cultural barrier exists. Although agencies take steps to ensure a culturally consistent placement, realistically, each family has a unique culture of its own. For example, an African American child placed in an African American foster home might still need to adjust to a different church or family pattern.

Children must adjust to a loss of privacy and confidentiality, because everyone speaks about their issues. They also deal with the new rules of the foster home, including different bedtimes, different religious expectations, different types of foods they may not be used to eating, and different parental expectations. When adults move into new situations, the adults usually negotiate what is theirs and what belongs to the other individuals in the space. They choose what they bring with them and often are asked what makes them comfortable. Children in foster care do not have the luxury of negotiating house rules and struggle to adapt. Children in foster care also must adapt to changes in the family structure, such as sharing a room with a sibling they didn't have before, sleeping alone for the first time, or having new chores they don't know how to perform.

Educational Adjustment

Coping with a new school also presents adjustment issues for a child in foster care (Pears, Kim, & Leve, 2012). Because schools are not consistent in course material by grade level, children in foster care are often behind their peers in knowledge when they enter a new school and struggle to adjust to a new learning environment. Performing well in school both academically and behaviorally is an expectation placed on children in foster care by caseworkers, the court, and foster parents, and children often struggle most with concentrating on school issues while trying to make these multiple adjustments (Zorc et al., 2013).

Instability in Foster Care Placement

Although the optimum plan is for a child to stay in a stable foster home until the child can return to live with her family, such stable homes rarely exist. Children in foster care often move from foster home to foster home, with the length of stay averaging 90 days (Baker, 1989) and decreasing with each replacement. Research also demonstrates that children who are replaced more than one time are at greater risk of more frequent replacements (Courtney & Zinn, 2009). Frequent replacements can account for many of the foster child's ongoing difficulties with adjustment and coping. The child loses not only a home but often also loses clothes; toys; relationships with birth and foster siblings; and relationships with foster relatives and foster parents, school peers, teachers, and a myriad of other individuals. When these losses happen at a repeated pace in a short amount of time, the child may become stuck in the transition process and be unable to cope. The child's sense of safety feels constantly threatened, as the child does not know if the next placement will meet his needs, if food will be available, if the roommate will be violent, or if the rules will match his expectations. Therapists working with foster children need to remember that a foster child used to placement instability exists in a constant state of fear, often unable to focus on basic behavioral expectations such as completing homework or following rules.

The causes of placement instability are numerous and complicated. The majority of research identifies the foster child's behavior as a primary reason for removal (Gauthier, Fortin, & Jéliu, 2004). This behavior can include hitting others, being verbally abusive, or refusing to follow directions (Oosterman, Schuengel, Slot, Bullens, & Doreleijers, 2007). As the caregiving adults increasingly view the child's behavior in a negative way, each negative behavior increases the likelihood of placement disruption (Chamberlain, Price, Reid, Landsverk, Fisher, & Stoolmiller, 2006). Other factors that increase the likelihood of replacement include the age of the child, with older children being at higher risk of replacement

(Courtney & Zinn, 2009), and how the foster care caseworker describes the child to current and potential foster parents. In general, the factor that most predicts future replacement is past replacement (Simmel, 2007). In fact, each foster care move, both planned moves and truancies, increases the chances of subsequent placement disruption by at least 6% (Chamberlain et al., 2006; Courtney & Zinn, 2009).

Placement disruption is mitigated by the amount of training the foster parents receive (Pardeck, 1985) and the foster parents' parenting style. Crum (2010) found that foster parents who adopted a less rigid behavior management style tended to maintain longer foster placements, whereas foster parents who adopted rigid parenting styles had increased placement disruptions.

Consequences of Placement Instability

The deleterious consequences of multiple foster care placements are numerous (see Exhibit 2.2). Each replacement results in an increased likelihood of distrust in case workers, the foster care system, future foster parents, and, tragically, more replacements (Crum, 2010; Simmel, 2007). For therapists providing treatment to foster children, understanding the emotional toll placement instability takes on a foster care child will help the therapist increase rapport and focus on the quality of the relationship.

Children who have multiple placements almost always lose material items from move to move, including clothes and toys. Children often see their belongings stuffed into trash bags for the move, and this metaphorical meaning is rarely lost on the child: Others view them as trash, and they often view themselves as trash. Later in this text, specific strategies are given to increase foster parent empathy for the child, as well as specific strategies to help children cope with the frequent replacements. However, keep in mind that the child, no matter how severe the behavior, should not take the blame for the disrupted

EXHIBIT 2.2

Children who experience multiple placements exist in a constant state of threatened safety and therefore may be unable to do therapeutic work around the abuse or neglect because the present situation causes too much anxiety.

CASE STUDY 2.4

I had the misfortune of having to replace children on my caseload many times. In my long career in child welfare I acted sometimes as both caseworker and therapist, and that dual role meant I had to pick up the child and move him to a new home. The children always expressed anger and blamed the system. I had to let them. I would pick up children with their belongings in garbage bags. Often the move was unplanned, and they couldn't say good-bye to their friends or even finish out a school week. Despite the constant threat of being replaced, many children on my caseload would continue acting out over and over again. One child stated, "I know what I'm doing is wrong, but I'm not going to stop until they let me go home." This statement hit me hard; these children just wanted to be allowed to get on with their lives.

placement. The child did not ask to be removed from the birth home or placed in the system. Children may be held accountable for behavior, but no child should have to earn a safe place to live.

Constant Sense of Danger

The main point for the therapist to realize is that a child in foster care exists in a world where his sense of safety is constantly threatened. Children in foster care often wonder what bed they will sleep in or what school they will attend from day to day. This constant anxiety means that, regardless of all of the other concerns facing children in foster care, the threat to their safety remains their primary concern. The foster child's world is fraught with danger and fear. The child walks on eggshells, worried about when a new threat will surface. Some children cope by acting out in order to make the danger arrive; they cannot tolerate the waiting. Other children withdraw. Feeling safe comes with time, consistent messages, and consistent adult behavior. The therapist provides some measure of stability but in a limited form, and the therapist should remain cognizant that it is rare to find a child in foster care who does not worry about the next placement or when she can go home, and living in this state of flux causes anxiety and depression that is not easily alleviated, because the state of flux is ongoing.

LONG-TERM FOSTER CARE

Unfortunately, many children in foster care reside in foster care or residential settings without finding a permanent placement. Ten percent of children in foster care age out of the system (U. S. Department of Health and Human Services, 2013). Some grow up in the child welfare system, whereas others wait several years to find a permanent home or adoptive family. Children in foster care tend to be examined through the lens of their cases, not their emotional, biological, and cognitive development. Children in foster care end up in a kind of developmental stasis. Normal milestones such as dating, making decisions, joining teams, and beginning identity development become frozen as the child copes with multiple placements and an ongoing crisis mindset. Children in foster care often cannot have the freedom needed to grow because of restrictions from the agency or foster parents, and frequent moves make commitments to school, teams, and clubs difficult. They either suffer from having to grow up under a microscope, with every developmental task and stage scrutinized from a pathological perspective, or, in many cases, their developmental issues are not addressed at all. The only concerns that get addressed as issues are related to the reason for placement.

For example, a 5-year-old child needs to learn to develop perspective taking, empathy, and a sense of self at this age. The child is in the preoperational stage of cognitive development and needs to use fantasy and pretend play to explore the world. Children of this age often create imaginary friends to begin building a bridge between their sense of reality and the reality of the world. But for a child in foster care, the focus might be just on the reason for removal, and opportunities to play and grow might be overlooked while the system focuses on reunification. Having an imaginary friend becomes considered a pathology needing mental health treatment rather than a normal part of development.

This problem is most obvious for adolescents in foster care, who miss out on the needed experiences that facilitate formal operations development, group and individual identity, cultural identity development, and sexual identity development. Adolescents growing up in foster care usually do not receive information on puberty or have opportunities to join sports teams or engage in school activities due to frequent moves or residential placement (Emerson & Lovitt, 2003). The focus on treatment is almost solely on behavior and academic success, leaving the

CASE STUDY 2.5

Marcus was 11 when I met him, and he had been in foster care since the age of 4. His caseworker never filed for termination of parental rights, and he languished while moving from foster home to foster home. He could only read at a second-grade level, but he could sing and wanted to join a choir. His foster parent signed him up for a youth choir, but he couldn't attend because of another replacement. His foster parent had lied about who lived in her home, and he had to be moved again.

social aspects of development on the wayside. Similarly, normal adolescent behavior such as drug experimentation or embarking on romantic relationships is viewed through the lens of pathology. Children in foster care are often not allowed to be children. The expectations for their behavior are higher due to scrutiny from the court system and the child welfare system. Every foible becomes an issue and topic for discussion and treatment. This constant pressure often results in a foster care child refusing to engage in activities or pulling away from society to avoid the ongoing judgment.

RELATIONSHIPS

Ongoing issues of relationships and attachment are primary concerns for this population. Children in foster care often experience multiple relationship losses when placed for long periods of time, including changes in therapists, caseworkers, lawyers, foster parents, and other adults who intervene in their lives. As a result, their ability to trust adults is severely limited, and they often shun new adults (Strolin-Goltzman, Kollar, & Trinkle, 2010). Keep in mind that a therapist may be one of many mental health professionals this child has seen, often not by choice, and the task of building rapport will not be easy.

Another issue unique to children in foster care is the struggle to maintain familial relationships. Children usually cannot visit parents or siblings without court and/or caseworker consent (Mapp, 2002). Parent visitation may be impacted by the parent's ability to follow court mandates, the parent's own history of mental illness and substance abuse, or economic issues such as lack of transportation or social support. Children either visit parents in a supervised setting, at the parent's home, or at the home of another relative, depending on the perceived risk to the child. Visits can be sporadic and inconsistent.

Sibling visits are left up to the whim of the sibling's foster parent or case manager, and even when a visit is scheduled, if a foster parent fails to bring a child for the visit, nothing is guaranteed to happen in order to enforce the visit. Sometimes communication is stopped by foster parents or caseworkers who view the sibling as a "negative influence."

Relationships with other relatives are also problematic. Children in foster care are often tasked with locating their own relatives, including

CASE STUDY 2.6

I was assigned the case of a 14-year-old Caucasian boy, Chet, who was living in his fourth foster home since the age of 6. He had been referred to treatment for acting out in school and at home. Before I could schedule my first session with him, I learned that his father had been killed in a workplace accident. As his therapist, the caseworker came to me to ask me how to handle it. I learned that Chet had a younger brother in residential treatment, and the caseworkers were discussing allowing Chet and his brother to attend the funeral. Chet had not seen his father since the age of 5, and his father's parental rights had been terminated. As I sat with the foster care supervisor for my agency, I listened to her arguments against letting him attend the funeral. She stated that he wouldn't know his family, that his family might behave badly and upset him, and that he might act out more if allowed to attend. After she finished, I told her that her arguments made sense, but there was one problem: We didn't have to live with the consequences of her decision, he did. I told her I didn't think we had the right to tell this child that he couldn't bury his father and say good-bye one last time. If he acted out, then, as adults, we needed to deal with it. She allowed him to go, but the agency responsible for his younger brother did not allow that child to attend the funeral.

aunts, uncles, and grandparents, in order to maintain these relationships. If the child moves frequently, or an adult (foster parent or case manager) does not ensure contact, the child often loses these relationships.

As a therapist, knowing the importance of family to the child and acting as an advocate to ensure visits occur will be as therapeutic as any treatment intervention.

CULTURAL VALUES

As a child in foster care moves from placement to placement, his unique cultural identity becomes altered and possibly lost. Culture derives from heritage and from family of origin, but when children are required to adjust to different family cultures and sometimes different family-of-origin cultures, their own views of culture become muddled. A child in foster care struggles with his own identity and usually does not have adults who attempt to maintain the child's sense of culture. For example, rarely will a foster parent allow the child to attend the same church he previously attended. Likewise, the values of the foster family and the

CASE STUDY 2.7

A graduate student in one of the classes I taught, who was working with a 16-year-old child in the foster care system who had been placed in residential treatment, asked me for advice about how to help the teenager. She would frequently run away from the treatment facility to go home and take care of her sick mother. With each truancy, the child welfare system would increase its punishment, viewing her behavior as criminal in her refusal to follow rules. The student told me that she informed the young woman to "think about herself" and to stop worrying about her mother. I used this story to illustrate to my student that this is an example of putting values on the child by telling her that what she values—caring for her mother—is not as important as ensuring that she follows the rules. This example illustrates how professionals can take away values from someone and impose values that do not fit with the individual's culture or heritage.

child welfare system as a whole are foisted upon children in foster care. These values can clash with those of their families of origin, and children struggle to maintain a foot in both worlds.

Beginning treatment with a child in foster care requires multiple turns of the kaleidoscope, and although we have touched on several concerns in the last two chapters, each child has her own unique worldview and experience. The texts in the following list represent a jumping-off point to begin learning about the world of the foster child. Read these texts and this chapter, but remember that the best expert on the experience of the child in foster care is the child himself.

Beam, C. (2014). *To the end of June: The intimate life of American foster care*. New York, NY: First Mariner Books.

Desetta, A. (1996). *The heart knows something different: Teenage voices from the foster care system*. New York, NY: Persea Books.

REFERENCES

American Psychiatric Association. (2013). *Diagnostic and statistical manual of mental disorders* (5th ed.). Washington, DC: Author.

Baker, J. N. (1989). Therapeutic foster parent: Professionally or emotionally involved parent? *Child and Youth Services Review, 12*, 149–157.

Bruskas, D. (2008). Children in foster care: A vulnerable population at risk. *Journal of Child and Adolescent Psychiatric Nursing, 21*(2), 70–77.

Chamberlain, P., Price, J. M., Reid, J. B., Landsverk, J., Fisher, P. A., & Stoolmiller, M. (2006). Who disrupts from placement in foster and kinship care? *Child Abuse & Neglect, 30*(4), 409–424. doi:10.1016/j.chiabu.2005.11.004

Courtney, M. E., & Zinn, A. (2009). Predictors of running away from out-of-home care. *Children and Youth Services Review, 31*(12), 1298–1306. doi:10.1016/j.childyouth.2009.06.003

Crum, W. (2010). Foster parent parenting characteristics that lead to increased placement stability or disruption. *Children and Youth Services Review, 32*(2), 185–190. doi:10.1016/j.childyouth.2009.08.022

Davis, G. F. (2001). Loss and the duration of grief. *JAMA: Journal of the American Medical Association, 285*(9), 3051–3057.

Emerson, J., & Lovitt, T. (2003). The educational plight of foster children in schools and what can be done about it. *Remedial and Special Education, 24*(4), 199–203.

Gauthier, Y., Fortin, G., & Jéliu, G. (2004). Clinical application of attachment theory in permanency planning for children in foster care: The importance of continuity of care. *Infant Mental Health Journal, 25*(4), 379–396. doi:10.1002/imhj.20012

Herrenkohl, E. C., Herrenkohl, R. C., & Egolf, B. P. (2003). The psychosocial consequences of living environment instability on maltreated children. *American Journal of Orthopsychiatry, 73*(4), 367–380. doi:10.1037/0002-9432.73.4.367

Landsverk, J. A., Burns, B. J., Stambaugh, L., & Rolls Reutz, J. A. (2009). Psychosocial interventions for children and adolescents in foster care: Review of research literature. *Child Welfare, 88*(1), 49–69.

Mapp, S. (2002). A framework for family visiting for children in long-term foster care. *Families in Society, 83*(2), 175–182.

Oosterman, M., Schuengel, C., Slot, N. W., Bullens, R. A. R., & Doreleijers, T. A. H. (2007). Disruptions in foster care: A review and meta-analysis. *Children and Youth Services Review, 29*(1), 53–76. doi:10.1016/j.childyouth.2006.07.003

Pardeck, J. (1985). A profile of the child likely to experience unstable foster care. *Adolescence, 20,* 689–696.

Pears, K. C., Kim, H. K., & Leve, L. D. (2012). Girls in foster care: Risk and promotive factors for school adjustment across the transition to middle school. *Children and Youth Services Review, 34*(1), 234–243. doi:10.1016/j.childyouth.2011.10.005

Pecora, P. J. (2010). Why current and former recipients of foster care need high quality mental health services. *Administration and Policy in Mental Health, 37,* 185–190.

Sheperis, C. J., Renfro-Michel, E. L., & Doggett, R. A. (2003). In-home treatment reactive attachment disorder in a therapeutic foster care system: A case example. *Journal of Mental Health Counseling, 25*(1), 76–88.

Simmel, C. (2007). Risk and protective factors contributing to the longitudinal psychosocial well-being of adopted foster children. *Journal of Emotional & Behavioral Disorders, 15*(4), 237–249.

Strolin-Goltzman, J., Kollar, S., & Trinkle, J. (2010). Listening to the voices of children in foster care: Youths speak out about child welfare workforce turnover and selection. *Social Work, 55*(1), 47–53.

U.S. Department of Health and Human Services, Administration for Children and Families, Administration on Children, Youth and Families, Children's Bureau. (2013). *Implementation of the Fostering Connections to Success and Increasing Adoptions Act of 2008.* Working document. http://www.acf.hhs .gov/programs/cb/resource/implementation-of-the-fostering-connections

Younes, M. N., & Harp, M. (2007). Addressing the impact of foster care on biological children and their families. *Child Welfare, 86*(4), 21–40.

Zito, J. M., Safer, D. J., Sai, D., Gardner, J. F., Thomas, D., Coombes, P., . . . Mendez-Lewis, M. (2008). Psychotropic medication patterns among youth in foster care. *Pediatrics, 121*(1), e157–e163. doi:10.1542/peds/2007-0212

Zorc, C. S., O'Reilly, A. L. R., Matone, M., Long, J., Watts, C. L., & Rubin, D. (2013). The relationship of placement experience to school absenteeism and changing schools in young, school-aged children in foster care. *Children and Youth Services Review, 35*(5), 826–833. doi:10.1016/j.childyouth.2013.02.006

CHAPTER THREE

THE ADULT PERSPECTIVE

This turn of the kaleidoscope focuses on the worldview of the adults in the child welfare system. Birth parents, extended family members, and foster and adoptive parents enter treatment with their own group of concerns.

TREATMENT ISSUES UNIQUE TO BIRTH PARENTS

Parents who lose their children to the child welfare system come to treatment with a unique worldview. They have been convicted of committing a crime against their children and society and suddenly find every aspect of their lives scrutinized and judged (see Exhibit 3.1). This section provides information on the worldview of birth parents as it concerns their interactions with the child welfare system. Of course, each individual enters treatment with a unique set of needs and strengths, but birth parents as a whole may experience concerns specific to being involved in the child welfare system.

CASE STUDY 3.1

About 10 years into my career, I worked with a married couple who had lost all their children to the foster care system. The children ranged in age from 7 to 17, and despite multiple foster homes and years of placement, the children remained close to their parents. The parents had been unsuccessful in finding work, clean housing, or following any other court requirements, but they attended every visit and often spoke about getting their children back. After providing family therapy for months, I finally realized that the mother and father had no desire to change the way they lived, but it didn't mean they didn't love their children.

Issues That Led to Removal

There are many reasons that parents lose temporary or permanent custody of their children. Most children are removed for neglect (U.S. Department of Health and Human Services, 2013). For example, the reason for removal can be because of a failure to pay the electricity or water bill, because of lack of food in the home, or because the home is unkempt. Birth parents who lose their children because of neglect often suffer from unemployment, lack of education, lack of access to resources, lack of familial support, and display poor decision making when confronted with stressors (Bass, Shields, & Behrman, 2004; Dowdell & Cavanaugh, 2009) Birth parents may also suffer from a substance abuse disorder that aggravates the neglect, a mental illness (diagnosed or undiagnosed) that contributes to the issue, and/or a developmental disability (Dowdell & Cavanaugh, 2009; McNichol & Tash, 2001). Birth parents may have a lack of access to health care and mental health care as well and may be suffering from physical ailments that prevent gainful employment, such as high blood pressure or diabetes (Hansen, Lakhani Mawjee, Barton, Metcalf, & Jove, 2004).

Birth parents may also have committed an act of physical or sexual abuse or domestic violence that led to the removal or have failed to protect a child from an act of abuse or domestic violence. Birth parents who engage in physical abuse often struggle with emotional regulation or may be repeating a cycle of abuse from their own childhoods (Child Welfare Information Gateway, 2013a). Birth parents often identify themselves as past victims of abuse or neglect, with poor communication and levels of trust with their own families of origin (McWey, Pazdera, Vennum, & Wojciak, 2013). Clearly, as a therapist working with the child and/or family, one cannot address all these issues and will most likely need to collaborate with several professionals during the course of treatment.

EXHIBIT 3.1

Having empathy for the adult perpetrator is often the greatest challenge for therapists, and failing to have empathy can lead to lack of engagement and unsuccessful treatment.

Ambiguous Loss/Grief

Therapists must be mindful of the grief parents suffer when they lose their children to foster care. The loss is ambiguous, meaning the parents know the children are alive, but they have limited access to the children and no longer have control over the children's welfare (Mapp & Steinberg, 2007). Birth parents are often angry, defensive, and confused regarding the reasons for removal (Lewis, 2011). Individuals who suffer an ambiguous loss display behaviors consistent with other types of grief, including feeling numb, having a sense of disbelief, feeling depressed, and expressing anger. Because the loss is viewed as the fault of the parents, they usually receive little support over this loss (Gerring, Kemp, & Marcenko, 2008). When first working with birth parents, remember to validate and empathize with the grief they feel over the loss of their children. Despite the fact that the parents may be responsible for the reason for removal, the grief is nonetheless real.

Loss of Parental Control

Parent/Agency agreements (PAs) often include demands that tax birth parents who lost custody because of their inability to manage everyday life. Along with functioning under the threat of never seeing their children again, they are instructed to attend parenting classes, participate in therapy, find employment, and secure safe housing, all within 6 months. Birth parents become easily overwhelmed and require as much empathy and support as their children but often do not receive it as they are viewed as the perpetrator and not deserving of empathy or support (see Exhibit 3.2).

Birth parents also must learn to cope with losing control of parenting decisions. Before being thrust into the child welfare system, the parents made decisions regarding when their children went to bed, what they wore to school, when to cut their hair, and all the house rules and behavioral expectations. When children are removed, the parents lose all these

EXHIBIT 3.2

As a therapist, keep in mind that a parent who feels safe and respected is always a better parent than a parent who feels threatened and judged.

controls and are rarely asked for feedback or consulted on the needs of their children. The implication is that the parents have failed completely as parents, so all decisions are removed from their control. The parents must cope with having to answer to many adults regarding the welfare of their children, including foster parents, caseworkers, judges, and the parents' attorneys. Parents struggling with access to resources or education lack the ability to navigate these challenges and therefore drop out of the process. They must cope with having a stranger view and critique their every interaction with their children. Foster children are often asked to report on their parents' behavior during unsupervised visits, leaving the birth parents in a constant defensive position, unable to parent their children. Children who act out during a visit might threaten the parent with "telling on them" and thus avoid punishment, leaving the parents feeling helpless. Sometimes agencies or the courts require the therapist to supervise visits in order to make recommendations regarding reunification. This stressor also becomes an issue for birth parents.

Birth parents are rarely consulted on matters such as schoolwork or punishments handed out by foster parents. Although laws are specific about not removing a child from his culture, the child might be exposed to differing religious or spiritual traditions, experience differing techniques or expectations for hair care, or be allowed or denied items against the parent's wishes. Some examples of these include taking the child to a different church, allowing the child to eat sweets when the parent does not allow the child to do so, or cutting the child's hair without the parent's permission. When parents complain, their grievances are viewed as a nuisance rather than a request to have their wishes respected.

Another common issue is the infantilization or role reversal of the birth parents. Because of the issues related to removal, the child welfare system tends to treat birth parents like children and take away their parental and adult authority. This process can be as obvious as not referring to the parents by their last names, referring to them as "the mother" or "the father" rather than their given names (which sends a message of dismissal—the person only exists in relation to the child), or disregarding their concerns regarding their child.

Sometimes the birth parent must face the reality that the child is given more power to make decisions regarding her role in the family, which upsets the family balance. For example, a child may be asked if she wants to go home, even if the parent is in compliance with court-ordered treatment, and the child's decision is followed. The child is asked to report on the parent's behavior after visits, which places the child in the role of authority. These issues make reunification very challenging, as the parent may feel reluctant to make parenting decisions for fear the child will be removed again.

Strengths

Once birth parents enter the child welfare system, they, like their children, are viewed from a place of pathology. Even though attempts are made to encourage caseworkers and therapists to identify strengths, the PA and court system come from a deficit-focused model. Birth parents, however, do have many personal strengths. Although most strengths are specific to the individual parent, any parents able to cope with and manage the stressors associated with the interaction with the child welfare system have coping-skill strengths. Birth parents may have resiliency and protective factors, such as community resources, strong bonds with their children, and the ability to cope with adversity (Child Welfare Information Gateway, 2013b; Voydanoff & Donnelly, 1998). In most cases, they love their children and usually do the best they can with what they have (Bowyer, 2009).

TREATMENT ISSUES UNIQUE TO FOSTER AND ADOPTIVE PARENTS

Many other texts that examine children in foster care fail to address the treatment issues faced by foster or adoptive parents. For the purpose of this section, the term *foster parent* refers to either the traditional idea of a foster parent (a nonrelative adult who takes a child in and provides care), a relative placement (a related adult who takes the child in and provides care), or a parent adopting a child from the foster care system. The assumption in the literature and in the child welfare system is that these parents are colleagues in the hierarchy of child welfare, and child welfare professionals expect them to cope with the multiple issues they face with minimal support and basic training. There are several issues that are unique to this population, including training to cope with children in foster care, amount of experience, loss of parental control and control over the home, unrealistic expectations, ambiguous loss and grief, attachment to the foster child, anger at the birth family, and inability to cope with the difficulties of the child welfare system (Geiger, Hayes, & Lietz, 2013).

Attachment and Loss

Foster parents are tasked with an odd job: take in a child with little preparation and begin parenting this stranger, only to have the child leave,
sometimes with little warning (Khoo & Skoog, 2014) or time to plan or
grieve. Although this temporary relationship exists from the beginning, it
is still unusual and often difficult to handle. The job demands that the parent build a quality relationship with the child, who often displays odd or
difficult behaviors and may be wary of adults, and then terminate the attachment. The child welfare agency also asks foster parents to go through
this process multiple times, with little time in between placements due to
the ever-present need for more foster homes. The irony of being a good
foster parent is that the better the foster parent, the more placements she
receives, and the greater the risk of emotional exhaustion and burnout.
Child welfare agencies place a great deal of pressure on foster parents
to take children before they might be emotionally ready for a new placement and expect foster parents to live with a difficult child, sometimes for
months, with minimal support. Foster parents must cope with the constant threat of loss because they have almost no control regarding when a
child is returned home or adopted out of the home.

The desire to care for an abused or neglected child can often result
in foster parents feeling a need to "rescue" the child from the birth parents (Edelstein, Burge, & Waterman, 2001). Although the foster parent
often is expected to work with a birth parent who has committed abuse
and neglect against the child, the foster parent rarely receives training on

CASE STUDY 3.2

I worked with many foster parents who struggled with the need
to rescue the foster care child from the birth parents. For example,
I worked at an agency where foster parents followed the birth father
to catch him lying about his job, and I worked with other foster
parents who hired their own attorney, claiming that their foster care
children were sexually abused by their father and demanding that
rights be terminated. I heard foster parents blame me or the agency
when they decided to request removal because of the pain involved
and wanting to keep the child.

how to separate himself from the situation and justifiably sides with the child over the birth parent, maybe even sending negative messages to the child. Watching a child in pain every day is emotionally exhausting and may make the foster parent angry, sad, and reluctant to help the reunification process. Chapter 11 discusses interventions to help foster parents cope with these issues.

Vicarious Trauma

Foster parents are exposed daily to a litany of stories and behaviors that illustrate the amount of trauma their charges have faced. They hear stories of sexual abuse, physical abuse, domestic violence, and neglect, and they witness the consequences of this trauma, such as night terrors, fear responses, tantrums, and physical aggression. This constant exposure, termed *vicarious trauma*, refers to secondary exposure to traumatic events. Exposure to vicarious trauma often results in the individual feeling overwhelmed, exhausted, depressed, and anxious (Dane, 2000). The foster parent may feel held hostage by the story, unable to intervene and helpless to address the pain (Dane, 2000). Although research exists for therapists regarding exposure to working with traumatized victims, little work has been done on the impact on foster parents.

Lack of Support and Training

Foster parents receive training prior to their first placement and then are required to obtain ongoing training every 2 years. These trainings often occur at the foster care agency and are taught by social workers who are rarely trained in how to teach adult learners (Gerring et al., 2008). Some agencies follow specific training models, such as the PRIDE training program (Dorsey et al., 2008) or Parent Child Interaction Therapy (PCIT), which involves providing treatment to foster parents of foster children displaying behavioral difficulties (Vanschoolandt, Vanderfaeillie, Van Holen, & De Maeyer, 2012). Foster parents receive little day-to-day support. Whereas birth parents and foster care children receive therapeutic services, foster parents often do not. Some foster parents mentor each other or participate in support groups. Foster parents, however, can easily be overwhelmed by the behaviors and emotional issues traumatized children and their families present, and may not receive needed support from the case manager, the

---

CASE STUDY 3.3

I worked as a therapist in a foster care agency that, like most agencies, licensed new foster parents and provided training by bachelor-level foster home licensing specialists. I began working with two toddlers (one boy and one girl) who had just been placed with foster parents, Angela and Bob, who had never had a placement before. Angela came into the agency one day asking for respite (asking for the child to be removed for a weekend to provide a break for the foster parents) because the male sibling was throwing violent tantrums, including hitting Angela and pulling out Angela's hair. Angela appeared emotional and distraught, unable to help the child or stop the tantrums. Despite the fact that the toddler was in therapy, the foster parent felt that she needed more help. When she asked the agency for respite, the licensing supervisor stated that she needed time to find someone on her own. After receiving guidance from another foster parent in a mentoring role, Angela demanded the respite more assertively. The agency supervisor responded by removing both children from her care. Ironically, 1 year later, the children became eligible for adoption, and Angela and Bob fought to adopt both children, which they did.

---

foster care agency, or the rest of the child welfare system. Foster parents are expected to take in the child and handle the tribulations on their own. Foster parents also may receive minimal training on how to work with birth parents or how to handle their feelings toward birth parents, which can cause problems during visitations and court proceedings.

Case Study 3.3 illustrates the struggles foster parents face from agency workers who are not empathetic to the challenges of coping with difficult and often traumatized children. In-home therapy services exist to provide treatment for foster children, but foster parents are often not provided in-home family therapy as a supportive measure. The mental health needs of the foster parents remain unaddressed.

Foster parents may also be pressured into taking children inappropriate to their parenting ability because of foster home needs. In an optimal world, foster homes that meet the needs of a specific child would always exist, but, more likely, a child enters care in a crisis situation and a foster home with an empty bed receives the call. For example, a foster parent may want to take children under 10 years old, but if a 15-year-old boy comes into care and the foster parent has an open bed, the agency may pressure the foster parent into taking the child. Attempting to parent children when they have received little information or training on how to handle the needs of children in foster care is a primary reason foster parents identify for placement disruption (Khoo & Skoog, 2014). Finally, foster parents may have their own personal history of abuse or trauma that becomes triggered by the presence of the child.

Loss of Parental Control

Like birth parents, foster parents must relinquish considerable control over their parenting decisions and home autonomy. Some agencies treat foster parents like colleagues, but more often foster parents are treated like subordinate employees and given assignments with little input. Foster parents struggle with the parenting restrictions placed on them by licensing, including the inability to use physical discipline. Foster care children can have power over the foster parent through complaints to the case manager or their parents. As a result, foster parents may express that they feel hopeless and helpless to effect change, and, as a result, they defer to the case manager or therapist to make decisions. This lack of control often results in the decision not to continue to provide foster care (Geiger et al., 2013). They also may display rigid decision making, such as separating finances and making the child responsible for his own food and clothes, and may even keep toys and clothes once the child leaves. The opposite may happen as well, with foster parents taking a lackadaisical approach to parenting, giving the child no structure for fear that the children might complain. Foster parents often struggle with birth parent visitations as well. Just like children of divorce, a foster care child becomes torn between the two parents, and the foster parent, seeing herself as the child's protector, might encourage the child to avoid visitations, or might build a wedge between the birth parent and child. Building this wedge might be driven by the foster parent's need to save the child.

Unrealistic Expectations

For therapists, the most frustrating issue of working with foster parents is the perceived unrealistic expectations foster parents have toward treatment and toward the child. Foster parents may appear to have a lack of empathy toward the child, focusing solely on the child's behavior and expecting the child to adjust to the foster parents' rules quickly and with little complaint. Foster parents also sometimes display a lack of understanding of appropriate developmental behavior and needs (Gamache, Mirabell, & Avery, 2006). For example, one foster parent who had never raised adolescent males often complained about how much they ate. She did not understand the amount of calories growing boys need and viewed their eating habits as bad behavior.

Foster parents may also appear to have a lack of empathy toward the birth parents, appearing judgmental and harsh. Often foster parents are viewed as the "better" parents, but they often have their own parenting foibles that may be just as ineffective as those of the birth parents. For example, foster parents, like birth parents, may react emotionally to behavior, use less-than-effective behavior management techniques, and become just as frustrated as birth parents. A foster parent may appear to expect the mental health therapist to "fix" the foster child with little input or work on the part of the foster parent. The foster parent may expect the child to be grateful to be in the foster parent's home and feel angry and hurt that the child isn't more thankful. Reminding the foster parent that no one would be grateful to lose his home and family will help.

Foster Parent Strengths

Foster parents have a myriad of strengths that can easily be lost in the everyday struggle to maintain placement. They often come with a desire to help, a sense of commitment, and the ability to cope with constant change. Like birth parents, foster parent strengths are often unique to the individual but should be identified and mentioned frequently throughout the placement process. Foster parents who demonstrate personality characteristics described as happy-go-lucky and emotionally stable are usually the most effective types of foster parents (Redding, Fried, & Britner, 2000).

Engaging in the child welfare system, either by choice or by court mandate, leaves adults with a sense of powerlessness, and strengths are often overlooked. Just as the best understanding of the perspective of children in foster care comes from the children themselves, birth parents, foster parents, and adoptive parents are the best sources for understanding their unique perspective.

REFERENCES

Bass, S., Shields, M. L., & Behrman, R. E. (2004). Children, families, and foster care: Analysis and recommendations. *The Future of Children, 14*(1), 4–29.

Bowyer, S. (2009). The experiences of birth parents. *Community Care, 1791,* 24–25.

Child Welfare Information Gateway. (2013a). *Long term consequences of child abuse and neglect.* Washington, DC: U.S. Department of Health and Human Services, Children's Bureau.

Child Welfare Information Gateway. (2013b). *Parental resilience.* Washington, DC: U.S. Department of Health and Human Services, Children's Bureau.

Dane, B. (2000). Child welfare workers: An innovative approach for interacting with secondary trauma. *Journal of Social Work Education, 36*(1), 27.

Dorsey, S., Farmer, E. M., Barth, R. P., Greene, K., Reid, J., & Landsverk, J. (2008). Current status and evidence base of training for foster and treatment foster parents. *Children and Youth Services Review, 30*(12), 1403–1416. doi:10.1016/j.childyouth.2008.04.008

Dowdell, E. B., & Cavanaugh, D. J. (2009). Caregivers of victimized children: Differences between biological parents and foster caregivers. *Journal of Psychosocial Nursing, 47*(6), 29–36.

Edelstein, S. B., Burge, D., & Waterman, J. (2001). Helping foster parents cope with separation, loss, and grief. *Child Welfare, 80*(1), 5–25.

Gamache, S., Mirabell, D., & Avery, L. (2006). Early childhood developmental and nutritional training for foster parents. *Child and Adolescent Social Work Journal, 23*(5), 501–511. doi:10.1007/s10560-006-0053-x

Geiger, J. M., Hayes, M. J., & Lietz, C. A. (2013). Should I stay or should I go? A mixed methods study examining the factors influencing foster parents' decisions to continue or discontinue providing foster care. *Children and Youth Services Review, 35*(9), 1356–1365. doi:10.1016/j.childyouth.2013.05.003

Gerring, C. E., Kemp, S. P., & Marcenko, M. O. (2008). The connections project: A relational approach to engaging birth parents in visitation. *Child Welfare, 87*(6), 5–30.

Hansen, R., Lakhani Mawjee, F., Barton, K., Metcalf, M. B., & Jove, N. (2004). Comparing the health status of low-income children in and out of foster care. *Child Welfare, 83*(4), 367–380.

Khoo, E., & Skoog, V. (2014). The road to placement breakdown: Foster parents' experiences of the events surrounding the unexpected ending of a child's placement in their care. *Qualitative Social Work: Research and Practice, 13*(2), 255–269. doi:10.1177/1473325012474017

Lewis, C. (2011). Providing therapy to children and families in foster care: A systemic-relational approach. *Family Process, 50*(4), 436–452.

Mapp, S. C., & Steinberg, C. (2007). Birth families as permanency resources for children in long-term foster care. *Child Welfare, 86*(1), 29–51.

McNichol, T., & Tash, C. (2001). Parental substance abuse and the development of children in family foster care. *Child Welfare, 80*(2), 239–256.

McWey, L. M., Pazdera, A. L., Vennum, A., & Wojciak, A. S. (2013). Intergenerational patterns of maltreatment in families at risk for foster care. *Journal of Marital and Family Therapy, 39*(2), 133–147.

Redding, R. E., Fried, C., & Britner, P. A. (2000). Predictors of placement outcomes in treatment foster care: Implications for foster parent selection and service delivery. *Journal of Child and Family Studies, 9*(4), 425–447. doi:10.1023/A:100941880913

U.S. Department of Health and Human Services, Administration for Children and Families, Administration on Children, Youth and Families, Children's Bureau. (2015). *Child maltreatment 2013*. Retrieved from http://www.acf.hhs.gov/programs/cb/research-data-technology/statistics-research/child-maltreatment

Vanschoolandt, F., Vanderfaeillie, J., Van Holen, F., & De Maeyer, S. (2012). Development of an intervention for foster parents of young foster children with externalizing behavior: Theoretical basis and program description. *Clinical Child and Family Psychology Review, 15*(4), 330–333.

Voydanoff, P., & Donnelly, B. W. (1998). Parents' risk and protective factors as predictors of parental well-being and behavior. *Journal of Marriage and the Family, 60*(2), 344–355.

PART THREE

THERAPEUTIC INTERVENTIONS

CHAPTER FOUR

BEGINNING THERAPY

CASE STUDY 4.1

I received a new client referral for Brandon, which described a wide range of behavior concerns. Brandon was barely passing seventh grade despite being bright. Almost weekly, he got into fights and cussed out teachers. He was moody and disagreeable in his foster home. His foster parents felt like they could not connect with him or trust him and were leaning toward requesting his removal from their home. School personnel recently found a large rock in Brandon's backpack, and his foster father found a hammer under his mattress. Brandon had not made any direct threats and offered no explanation when confronted about the items. He kept his clothes and belongings packed in black plastic bags carefully stacked in his closet. His birth mother lost her parental rights when he was an infant due to her struggle with alcoholism, and his adoptive grandmother had reportedly been physically and verbally abusive to him, leading him to run away. His foster care worker had referred him to therapy and described him as a "liar" and manipulative because she had trouble getting straight answers from him and doubted his reports of being victimized by his grandmother.

The first time I met Brandon, he came to the session by himself, and although he was only 12, he appeared more like a 16-year-old. He acted grumpy at first, not saying much. I introduced myself warmly, complimented him on his hat, and invited him to my office. He walked beside me with his head down. Once in the office, I offered him a choice of seats. Before launching into my assessment, I took a few minutes to explain who I was and what kind of help I offered the kids who came to see me. I pointed out that the pictures

(continued)

CASE STUDY 4.1 *(continued)*

and poems decorating my walls were made by kids in foster care who were trying to deal the best they could with all the changes, workers, foster parents, and courts in their lives. "I learned from all these kids that being in foster care is definitely no visit to the candy store," I said as I sat relaxed in my chair pulled up next to him. I noticed he cracked a small smile but remained silent. I went on, "Or Disney World or a water park or the mall. . . ."

He interjected, "I get it. It sucks." Pause. "And I don't like to go to the mall anyways."

Regardless of his demeanor, Brandon did not miss a beat. However, he barely understood himself and his life and felt like adults did not understand or know how to help him. When I showed him that I was interested and ready to hear, empathize, and help him figure things out, he kept opening up. When the foster care worker threatened him with group homes and the foster parents threatened him with removal from their wonderful home in response to his confusing behaviors, I kept myself safe and accessible. He knew I would not support him hurting others or himself, but he also knew that I genuinely cared.

Before the therapist can view the changing scene and complex patterns the child's kaleidoscope reveals, the therapist must hold it steadily in her hands. This may seem simple enough, but it brings many questions to mind: Who gives the therapist the opportunity or even the right to hold it—the worker, the birth parent, the foster parent, or the child? Should the therapist just take it without permission? What if the child does not want the therapist to see it? How can a therapist support overwhelmed foster parents, give the court updates on treatment progress, and prevent a replacement when the child does not actively engage in the session?

Beginning therapy with a child in care can become complicated quickly. There is no doubt that parents and workers play a major role in sharing their concerns about the client. But no matter how the therapist breaks it down, it is still the client who must give the therapist access to her inner world in order to effect real change.

The therapist must be given the kaleidoscope to see willingly. In order to keep a steady turning view, the client has to allow the therapist to look. It is difficult to observe the shifting intricacies of a turning design when the kaleidoscope is being tugged on or snatched back. This chapter emphasizes the importance of creating and maintaining a working therapeutic relationship with a youth in the child welfare system by exploring its challenges, breaking down specific ways to build and rebuild it, and troubleshooting the resistance that often occurs.

THE CHALLENGE OF BUILDING RAPPORT

Any child or teen in foster care has had his trust and belief in adults tested, stressed, or obliterated. Every child deserves to be safely cared for and understood by able and willing caregivers. Youth in care have had these basic rights violated, sometimes severely, and many times repeatedly—first by their birth parents and then possibly by adults in the foster care system who did not help the youth or their parents. For many children, the adults to whom they finally reported their fears about what was happening in their homes may be seen as the traitors, either because the information led to their removal or because it did not. Sometimes the professionals who carried out the act of the actual removal are perceived to be violators as well. Police, protective services workers, and other adults whose responsibility it is to keep children safe may be perceived as perpetrators of the child's fears. Even the foster care worker may be perceived as confusing or useless in understanding the child's plight or effecting the changes in the family that are so desperately needed.

By the time the child comes to therapy, the therapist will be seen through the lens of the child's cumulative experiences with adults who say they are there to help (Oetzel & Scherer, 2003). The therapist working with youth in child welfare must be aware of this dynamic and avoid assumptions and judgments about the "helpful" or "trustworthy" adults in the child's life, including oneself. Seeing adults through the eyes of each client will result in both a truer sense of empathy and more realistic expectations for the outcomes of therapeutic interventions.

With that being said, it is impossible to provide effective treatment with this population without some semblance of trust and rapport (Oetzel & Scherer, 2003). This task can be a tall order for therapist and client alike. A youth may balk or lash out at any attempts by the therapist to

Table 4.1 *Distrust Shown in Different Extremes*

Extreme Avoidance	Extreme Superficial Engagement
Refuses to enter therapy room	Instantly physically affectionate
Refuses to talk or make eye contact	Idealizes therapist ("Best ever!" "Will you be my mom?")
Verbally or physically aggressive	Inauthentic; only aims to please

interact. Others may engage with superficial ease, even calling the therapist "Mom" or "Dad." Table 4.1 summarizes the distrust often shown in these extremes. Many will fall somewhere in between: cautious, guarded, attentive, but disconnected. The therapist working with this population will be hard pressed to find a child or teen who is not ambivalent at best about opening up to a therapist and working collaboratively to change himself. Accept that these reactions to therapeutic engagement are protective efforts on the client's part. One of the therapist's first challenges is to face the child with empathic regard rather than frustration and judgment. Start by better understanding and honoring these efforts, as they are adaptive ways to survive confusing and harmful adults, which is a goal to be supported, not undermined.

As a child therapist, the immediate and primary task is to provide a corrective opportunity for the child to experience a safe, caring, consistent adult who understands the child and is responsive to the child's needs—within healthy boundaries in the context of the relationship. The need to protect oneself to survive is primarily activated in youth in care, so the therapist's efforts to engage a client must balance with the client's need to not get close to another adult while actually allowing the therapist to become close. This can be a delicate and sometimes lengthy endeavor but is absolutely foundational to providing effective treatment. In fact, some might argue that rapport building in itself is the primary intervention of the effective therapist (Gurland & Grolnick, 2008).

Beyond the child's irreconcilable dilemma of distrusting the adults in control, therapists face many other challenges in the basic factors and pressures of working with foster care children. This population is often referred for therapy because of behavioral problems, and therapists can feel incredible pressure from foster parents and workers to "fix" the child. This leads therapists to jump into treatment too quickly without first building rapport. Even when workers and caregivers truly empathize with the child, their own time, energy, and focus may not allow

CASE STUDY 4.2

Taylor was 11 when I started working with her, and I struggled to build rapport. She could not number the amount of therapists she had met or foster homes she had been in. She tolerated adult interactions without active defiance. However, her foster mom's chief concern was that she "listened" to kids but not adults, which made her an easy target for older siblings and bullies at school. Taylor was constantly getting in trouble for "stupid things" and for "not telling the truth" when confronted about her poor decision making. It was not until I invited her estranged sisters in for a session that I felt like I saw the "real" Taylor, a child who was desperate to return to the familiar and a sense of belongingness rather than try so hard to fit in to other people's worlds. Her animation and level of presence and participation were markedly different. After that, there was a boost of trust in our relationship, but progress in treatment was slow, and gains were inconsistently maintained. I kept my focus on building, maintaining, and, at times, repairing what rapport we had between us, through a failed adoption and a permanent separation from her sisters when their adoptions were completed. One day it hit me: I had become the most consistently present adult figure in her life. The outcomes of treatment may not have been what everyone wanted to see, but I know I worked within her capabilities and within the reality of her world. The last contact I had with her was at a residential shelter for teens waiting for home placements. Taylor reflected on her role in the failed placements without regret. "I wasn't ready to be a part of their families," she explained, "but I know there are adults who want me and will help me. I'm not giving up."

them to be patient and attentive enough to benefit the child (Gurland & Grolnick, 2008). Also, unlike adults who will talk and tell their stories, children, in general, even if not in foster care, are often reluctant to share information. Children and teens do not process information or communicate like adults. Many of their responses to questions are based on telling the adult what they think the adult wants to hear, not what the "truth" is (Lutz, Hock, & Kang, 2007).

HOW TO BUILD RAPPORT

The task of building rapport begins the moment the therapist lays eyes on the case information or the actual child, whichever occurs first. It can be surprisingly easy for the therapist to acquire detailed personal information about children in foster care before ever meeting them (Gurland & Grolnick, 2008). If the therapist learns part of the child's story before meeting the child, she must delay forming speculations about the kaleidoscopic view until live contact occurs.

There is much relevant literature about how to create psychological safety, hold the space, and make therapy a "safe container" for clients of all ages. In order to engage a youth in treatment, therapists should strive to make themselves, their space, and all communication safe, accessible, reliable, and transparent (Gurland & Grolnick, 2008; Lee et al., 2006). The following discussion highlights multiple ways to do so.

Nonverbal Communication

Much research has been done about the power and influence of nonverbal communication. Communication is composed of 7% actual words used, 38% tone of voice, and 55% nonverbal/body language (Oetzel & Scherer, 2003). For younger children, children with insecure attachments, and children in trauma, the percentage for nonverbal is even higher (Oetzel & Scherer, 2003). Therapists working with children in care are foolish to not intentionally use warm, open, and nonthreatening body language in every interaction with the child. Therapists must also be aware of and attentive to how their nonverbal communication may be unintentionally perceived by the child. For some children, a bright affect and large smile may be experienced as overwhelming and intolerable, or the way the therapist tucks her hair behind her ears may trigger a trauma response (Lutz et al., 2007).

Beyond maintaining an awareness of the sheer power and impact of the therapist's own nonverbal communication, the child's body language and nonverbal cues are also major avenues for communication. Children are constantly showing adults what they feel and how they are doing through nonverbal communication (Lutz et al., 2007). The tendency of adults, therapists included, is to negate or minimize what the child is "saying" through nonverbal communication because "using words" is prioritized. Teaching a child to use language to communicate his wants and needs can be done more effectively when the therapist is able to receive and respond to the nonverbal language the child is using as well (Lutz et al., 2007). The effective therapist uses both with ease, in conjunction and interchangeably.

A simple application of this involves making efforts to engage in warm, welcoming eye contact with the child. Notice if the child avoids eye contact and, if so, when. Staring is intrusive, but glancing and calmly checking is comforting and accessible. Making eye contact at the same level as the child invites connection, and getting below her eye level shows that you are not a threat. Do not underestimate the value of eye-to-eye contact in combination with body language with a child or teen, even when it means bending down, being on the floor, or sitting side by side, rather than across a desk (Freire, Eskritt, & Lee, 2004).

Simple Interactions

Following are several examples of simple interactions that can be incorporated in engagement and treatment to build a trusting therapeutic relationship.

When a person consistently uses a child's name, it innately implies recognition and supports self-efficacy (Freire et al., 2004). Accurately pronouncing, spelling, remembering, using, and recounting playful associations with a child's name throughout beginning sessions and far into treatment is a simple and clear way to show the client that he or she matters to you (Freire et al., 2004). Similarly, do not be afraid of gentle touch. Healthy, appropriate physical contact between adults and children is a natural and normal part of childhood that enhances child development. Balking at or rejecting their bids for appropriate physical connection can be damaging. Setting boundaries around touch can limit it to include high-fives, fist bumps, palm-to-palm, or accepting a hug when offered by the child.

Find or create ways to offer the child choices even before the child enters the therapy room. For example, if the child is waiting in the lobby and the therapy office is upstairs, ask whether the child would like to take the stairs or the elevator. Once in the room, offer a choice of seating positions. Ask if the child would like to start with the assessment right away or in 5 minutes. When completing questionnaires or speaking with the parent, offer coloring or clay. As with all helpful choice giving with children, keep in mind that too many choices offered can induce additional anxiety (Fitzgerald, Henriksen, & Garza, 2012). Focus on offering two or three simple, concrete options at a time and not pressuring the child to choose if the child seems ambivalent or unsure. Pay attention to the child's reactions to the choices to gauge whether the amount or nature of choices is empowering or distressing and modify accordingly. For example, if the therapist shows a client a pack of multicolored paper and asks a child to choose a color, the child might express interest and curiosity in perusing and making her choice. Conversely, the child may hesitate and appear unsure about this seemingly simple task. The therapist can help by responding with pulling out two colors and saying, "How about red or yellow?" with a tone of curiosity and warmth.

Use *reflection* and *mirroring* both verbally and nonverbally to respond to the child rather than making interpretations or value judgments (e.g., "Oh, is that you and your mom?" or "What a pretty picture!"). Research on building secure relationships and increasing feelings of safety with victims both indicate that this therapeutic approach reaps much more value for this population than moving directly toward interpretation, cognitive behavioral intervention, and problem solving (Gurland & Grolnick, 2008).

Children in foster care are still children, and both their lives and the world around them do not stop when they enter the therapy room. Incorporate practicality and a sense of presence and realness in your interactions. For example, we know that children and teens' ability to focus differs from that of adults (Lutz et al., 2007). Schedule shorter sessions with younger children or older children who have difficulty sustaining engagement. Also, take opportunities to interact with the child in the present moment. Attention to seemingly irrelevant factors can build rapport and set the tone of the relationship to "keep it real." Notice the weather, the crowdedness of the lobby, the loudness of people in the hall, the temperature of the room, and even the therapist's own blunders, such as dropping a pen or misspeaking. These small interactions humanize both the child's experience of therapy and a helping adult. These are not meant to distract from the session's goal but rather create the norms of therapy: acknowledge, validate, and problem solve comforts and discomforts of life. These are nonthreatening ways to show the client that the therapist can see what she sees and that what people notice matters. What an important step this is to building rapport.

Use simple, fun, and creative rituals to build consistency and connection in therapy sessions. The implementation of predictable interactions and patterns naturally decreases anxiety and distrust (Alvord & Grados,

2005). For example, make actions such as pushing the elevator button, watering the plant, checking out the window, going to the bathroom, holding a soft pillow, setting an intention, or making a wish with a wand a part of beginning and/or ending each session. Consistently celebrate childhood accomplishments such as birthdays and moving up a grade. Use snacks, cards, music, or verbal affirmations expressing the value of both the child's existence and his efforts in the child's everyday life.

Explanations of Therapy and Confidentiality

Take time to gain understanding of the child's experience with, and perceptions of, what therapy is and is not. This can be an invaluable opportunity to better understand the child's worldview and offer corrective information both verbally and nonverbally. For example, if a child states that therapy is for crazy people, respond with curiosity about how the child came to that conclusion along with relevant information about the actual types of people that come to therapy and the kinds of problems those people might have. Offer a story of another child who came to see the therapist that is relatable to the child, or point out drawings hanging on the wall made by other child clients. Many mixed messages about therapy come from both media and the people in the child's life. It will be more beneficial for the therapist to curiously gather information about what the client already assumes before offering more information. Also, the therapist's explanations must always be given in developmentally appropriate language and reasoning. For example, the therapist might tell a 6-year-old that therapists are kind of like teachers, but instead of helping children with writing and numbers, therapists help kids with feelings and family problems. For a 10-year-old, the therapist might add more concrete information about the types of problems that therapists help kids with—such as feeling sad when they miss their moms or scared when adults fight. For a 17-year-old, the therapist might focus more on helping the client identify what she wants and then offering realistic ways the therapist can or cannot help her. For example, a teen might state that all he wants is to have more money to buy certain shoes, and the therapist can respond with a joke about being a nonbank type of therapist but rather a really-good-at-listening therapist who can help him figure out his own ways to get the shoes he wants, as well as other things that are important to him. Keep in mind that many children and teens do not ask the informational questions about therapy that they want to

Table 4.2 *Common Child Questions and Answers About Therapy*

Questions	Answers	Reflections
What does a therapist do?	Help people.	What do you want help with?
Why do I have to come here?	Because some of the adults in your life think it might help you.	Do you think therapy can help you?
What will we do when I come here?	Sit, talk, listen, draw, stand, play, breathe, write, etc.	What do you want to do when you come here?
How often will I come?	Weekly, biweekly, etc.; articulate length of session.	How often would you like to come?
When can I stop coming?	When therapy has helped you, or when the adults in your life decide.	When do you want to be done with therapy? How will you know when you're done?

ask and will benefit from knowing, for a variety of reasons. The amount and nature of the information given depends on the client and should be formulated with the intention of building rapport and setting the stage for the therapeutic space. Table 4.2 captures some of the essential information about therapy that can be beneficial for the client and therapist to reflect on at the beginning of treatment.

Also take time at the very beginning of treatment to explain what confidentiality and mandated reporting are and are not, with both the client and parent together and separately. Inform the child with developmentally friendly vocabulary and reasoning. Break it down into three parts: (a) that the child is allowed to share anything she wants to share about what the therapist says or does with anyone she chooses; whereas (b) the therapist is only allowed to share what the child says or does with the child's permission; unless (c) there is a safety concern, the judge asks the therapist, or the therapist needs help from another therapist to make sure he is doing a good job. For example, say, "If you tell me you're getting hurt, then I have to tell another grown-up." Ask questions to gauge the child's understanding of the information and address any miscommunication or confusion. Respond to a client's disinterest or avoidance of these topics with patience and validation, but do not let go of the discussion—confidentiality and mandated reporting are far too relevant to clients' lives and their therapy experience. Being clear from the beginning about both of these topics can go a long way in establishing trust and prioritizing the child's sense of safety.

Parent Involvement

Depending on the age of the client, the quality of relationship between the child and the caregiver bringing the child to the session, and the goals of therapy, the therapist may work primarily with the caregiver (which may include the foster and/or birth parent, both intermittently and together) before working with the child, work with the parent and child together for all or a portion of sessions, or almost exclusively work with the child individually. The more factual information the therapist can get about the substantiated abuse or neglect and the current court order around birth-family contact, as well as current placement concerns, the better. Sometimes the therapist does not know that there is information she does not have, which can inadvertently end up establishing the therapy space as one of confusion and distress. Additionally, keep in mind that many children in foster care have experienced more than what has been reported or substantiated. This is not to say that children should not talk about abuse or neglect or contact with their families in session. Rather, approach each of these topics knowing the facts and realizing there might be unknowns while seeing the child's worldview.

Gauging the child's separation anxiety and the impact of any parent's participation are major factors to consider when building rapport and considering the level of parental involvement (Suveg et al., 2006). If a child shows separation anxiety when parting from a caregiver for a session, the prioritization of making the transition with ease will be greatly influential to the experience of therapy for the child. If not tended to, the anxious child may either escalate their resistant behavior or may by sitting in session with the therapist for an hour unable to concentrate on the interventions offered and deeply dreading coming to subsequent therapy appointments. Use of transitional objects and showing the child where the parent will be while the child is in the session are useful interventions that take minimal time to help ease such anxiety. For example, the therapist might proactively create a ritual around allowing a child to "check" out the window to see her mom's car in the parking lot at a certain time (or times) before or during the session. For another child, the therapist may request that the parent wait during the session in a location closer than the waiting room or even let the child take the parent's keys into session with her as assurance that the parent will not leave without her. As with many needs of a child, once the therapist finds a way to accurately understand and meet the child's need for comfort in separation, the child will no longer rely on the intervention to be comforted.

Rapport as a Perpetual Goal

There may be times when the therapist's well-intentioned rapport is breached due to the client's reenactment of unhealthy adult–child relationships, the client's perceived actions of deception, or the therapist's actual mistakes. Common causes of damaged trust include both the occurrence of mandated reporting incidents along with the manner in which the therapist handles the incidents with the child; real or perceived confidentiality violations by the therapist; and inconsistent attendance, whether due to therapist cancellations or parents' noncompliance with treatment. Regardless of the reason or who is responsible for the breach, the effective therapist continually prioritizes maintaining and repairing rapport throughout the assessment, treatment planning, crisis management, transitions, treatment, and termination. The therapist can keep a barometer of rapport status at each point of contact and prioritize tending to it when it drops with the use of the rapport-building techniques discussed earlier and those that follow.

TIPS FOR BUILDING RAPPORT BY AGE GROUP

The next few sections illustrate additional techniques for building rapport with children of specific age groups. Please note that each of these techniques may be used in front of birth and foster parents to model effective ways to improve the quality of their trusting relationship with their child.

Children Ages 3–11

Begin treatment with nondirective play or art therapy. Allow the child to choose what they want to play and do in the room. Do not engage with the child unless invited. Comment on the child's actions. For example,

CASE STUDY 4.3

Kayla was a 7-year-old girl who had moved to a new foster home and did not want to participate in therapy. She would not play by herself or with me. To engage her, I picked up a puppet and began saying to the puppet, "I really want to get to know Kayla, but she won't talk to me. Could you ask her to whisper what her favorite ice cream is?" Then I had the puppet ask her. She whispered to the puppet, and then I asked the puppet her answer. I said, "Her favorite ice cream is strawberry?"

Kayla replied, "It's not strawberry. It's chocolate!"

I turned to the puppet, "Why did you tell me the wrong one?"

We engaged in conversation using the puppet, and I learned her favorite food, movies, type of clothes, and toys she liked. This technique sent her the message that I was more interested in who she was than what she did.

say, "I notice you are playing with the doll house," "You are hitting that ball hard," or "You look angry when you hit the ball." Remember to focus on empathy and validation in the first few sessions. If a child says, "I don't want to be here," for example, respond with "It's not fair that you have to come here." For children who do not engage in play or art and want to play a game with you, let the children make the rules of the game. With older children, ask them to teach you the game, even if you know how to play it. The point is to give the child control and to reverse the power in the room. If you want or need to ask questions, try to focus the questions on who the child is as a person rather than why the child is engaging in certain behaviors.

Another technique to build rapport is mirroring the child's actions, with the child's permission. For example, if a child begins to draw, say, "I like what you are doing. Can I copy you?" If the child agrees, continue by asking what colors to use and if the picture is correct. This technique allows the child to have an experience of an adult who views his actions as important and therefore aids in building rapport. Research increasingly shows that mirroring and sometimes narrating in this way with play—making faces, sounds, or body movements—increases brain functions and stimulates neural connections (Oetzel & Scherer, 2003).

CASE STUDY 4.4

In my first session with a 13-year-old girl in foster care who had been to multiple therapists, I stood up and said, "How fed up are you with being dragged to therapy? Fed up to here [I stood on my toes] or here? [I jumped; I'm a short person]"

She jumped above me and said, "To here!"

I responded by stating, "I don't blame you."

From there, we could begin treatment because I conveyed to her my understanding of her worldview.

Adolescents

Both empathy and validation remain key aspects of working with this age group. The therapist should show clear and authentic interest and motivation to see the youth's worldview. When therapists begin treatment by showing understanding of their perspective, adolescents will feel that their experiences are valid and that what they are going through matters.

Take the time to authentically validate and witness the ups and downs of their world. Therapists should allow themselves to be confused, scared, and frustrated as a way to join and normalize before moving to problem-solving interventions. Focusing on who the adolescent is remains a strong way to build rapport. Avoid questions that focus on behavior problems at home or school unless the child brings it up. Therapists working with teens in this population will do well to be conscientious about following through on even small things, such as giving out bus tickets or ending the session on time as indicated to the client.

ADDRESSING COMMON BARRIERS TO TREATMENT

Sometimes it may feel like most of treatment involves dealing with barriers such as inconsistent attendance, constant crises, demanding paperwork and schedules, lack of investment in treatment, and unrealistic expectations, rather than actually providing therapy. The way in which therapists respond to barriers will likely be a major intervention in treatment. Look at barriers as treatment opportunities for intervention, growth, and advocacy. When therapists look closely at the perceived obstacles, they will find the resonant themes of attachment, trauma, developmental concerns, grief, and cultural context in each, meaning that they too are presenting problems readily available for intervention. Following are strategies to view and respond to common barriers in a therapeutic manner.

Continuous Crises

Many therapists default to focusing their treatment attention on simply responding or reacting to the client's, foster parent's, birth parent's, and worker's "crisis of the week." While acknowledging that this population truly does present many real crises, the therapist will be more effective when able to discern the crises' patterns and their driving forces before spending session after session putting out fires. The more often the therapist is able to respond to the need underlying the behavior or crises, the more effective treatment will be, and the more empowered both the therapist and the family will feel. This is easier said than done, but is a win-win nonetheless. A strong case conceptualization will allow the therapist to intervene proactively in regard to the identified underlying needs, triage with other professionals and support staff, create boundaries, and respond to the underlying issue rather than only react to its manifestation. Strive to maintain a clear, empowered therapeutic role rather than becoming part of the disempowering reactive interaction patterns. See the forest through the proverbial trees. Seek supervision when needed. Always attend to safety concerns ethically and immediately with every effort to maintain rapport while doing so. If legitimate safety concerns are the constant crises, the client may be in need of a higher level of care.

Negative View of Therapy

Therapists know that the highest predictor of positive outcomes of treatment involve the client's motivation to receive help and to change. Most children in care do not come to therapy because they asked for counseling. Some have specifically asked not to go. Many are brought to their first therapy session without even being told where they are going. Many have preconceived notions of what therapy is and is not. Beyond explaining what therapy is and is not, take the time to gain understanding of the client's view of therapy and what the client wants and does not want help with. Remember, clients are showing their worldviews through what they are saying, through what they are not saying, and through other nonverbal communication. Validate and normalize the child's viewpoint regardless of how far from ideal or realistic it is.

In general, remember that children and teens do not want to be viewed as needing treatment. They may be embarrassed about attending counseling. Also, depending on the child, they may not want to be identified as a foster child, and anything associated with that label, such as therapy, will be automatically resisted. A major part of child development is evolving a sense of self-competency and self-efficacy. The experience of foster care by nature erodes these normal emotional and cognitive developments. It is normal for children to want to try to handle their issues alone. It is also natural for them to experience an increased sense of helplessness in the child welfare system. Use validation and empathy as the starting point of all interventions. If therapists fail to do this, they will fail in treatment.

A negative view of therapy is not the only cause for inconsistent attendance at scheduled sessions. Other reasons include changes in placement, transportation issues, and scheduling conflicts. When attendance issues emerge as barriers to effective treatment, work to identify the underlying cause or causes, and address them from the root through rapport and collaboration with other professionals. Do not avoid the larger issues or engage in punitive threats to close the case.

Unrealistic Outcomes

There is no magic-cure treatment for this population. Child welfare places significant responsibilities and challenging timelines on all involved parties, from therapists and workers to parents and children. Beyond offering individual and family interventions, therapists also engage in court reports, case conferences, collaboration, and transition crises that can easily overload a therapist's balance of time and professional responsibilities. Insurance-driven paperwork with this population can result in a high percentage of sessions being filled with completing required paperwork and tracking down signatures of adult parties. Just as in any profession, advocate for employee needs, and strive to maintain a work–life balance. Professionally, choose to accept and even make friends with the demands rather than fighting or being enveloped by them. Find ways to use the "demands" as a parallel process–based intervention and model empowerment, advocacy, and compassion with clients and colleagues. For example, when completing reams of questions with a client, validate the sometimes frustrating nature of following rules that cannot be chosen or changed. Empathize and problem solve out loud, demonstrating the self-talk that the client will benefit from having while actually implementing the same in oneself.

When the therapist develops a strong case conceptualization and identifies clearly what can and cannot be accomplished in therapy, she can more energetically focus on realistic goals during the therapeutic session. This is a vulnerable, needy, and gut-wrenching population for many compassionate helpers, which can lead to a myriad of nontherapeutic dynamics. By making realistic sense of the conflicting demands of the mix of parents, workers, court, child, and oneself, the therapist can choose to bite off only what is manageable. Asking, expecting, or demanding more of the client and related parties than they are able to safely give is a surefire way to lose a client and any opportunity to provide genuinely effective intervention. Consider how it takes many adult clients years of therapy to unravel layers of childhood trauma and family dysfunction in efforts to better their lives and relationships.

HANDLING RESISTANCE

Therapists working with this population can expect, and respect, some level of resistance to therapy by both caregivers and clients in one form or another (VanFleet, 2000). It may come actively with defiance such as physically or verbally lashing out, complaining, disrespecting, or literally running away (Sommers-Flanagan, Richardson, & Sommers-Flanagan, 2011). It may be more passive, such as refusing to talk, play, or even walk into the office. Other presentations of resistance to the therapist's efforts to help include pervasive lying, avoidance or denial of the circumstances or events of the clients' own lives, and acting falsely agreeable or pleasing rather than authentic (Mahalik, 1994). Following are several specific pointers on how to understand and effectively respond to resistance in treatment. Keep in mind that patiently taking even the smallest steps to building rapport, as mentioned earlier in this chapter, is a proactive effort that will aid in decreasing resistance to treatment (Davis & Hollon, 1999).

Reframe Resistance

See the resistance in terms of its defensive purpose rather than naming it as a barrier to treatment. Resistance is a form of self-protection. Form ideas about where the resistance is coming from and how it is serving the client from the client's worldview. Instead of wondering "Why is she doing this? Can't she see I'm trying to help her?" or thinking "What a pain this child is to work with," use more sophisticated reasoning that considers the nuances of distrust, protection, intention, and fear. Pursue exploration of such questions as, "What is it like for me, a stranger, to ask her these personal questions? What am I doing or saying that feels so threatening to her? What has her experience been thus far of adults offering to help her?" Typical motivating factors for resistance to helping professionals in this population include the need for control and protection centered around fears of being hurt, hurting others, rejection after closeness, increasing confusion, causing more problems, or making existing problems worse by letting themselves experience how scared, angry, hurt, or depressed they really are (Davis & Hollon, 1999; Fitzpatrick & Irannejad, 2008; Mahalik, 1994).

Additionally, there are many behaviors that can easily be labeled as resistance to treatment that are actually involuntary protective measures of the client. This means that the same behavior, such as refusing to enter the therapy room, may be consciously chosen by the client as a way to avoid something or may be a developmental or trauma-based neurological response to a perceived threat. The client may be avoiding allowing yet another adult to take control in her life, and her decision to refuse to enter the room is based on asserting her need for autonomy (Fitzpatrick & Irannejad, 2008; Sommers-Flanagan et al., 2011). Conversely, the client may be actively triggered in a sensory manner—perhaps by the gait of the therapist or the color of the walls—causing her to reexperience a traumatic memory and freeze on the spot or run away. Some resistant behaviors involve a combination or sequence of both. For example, stopping in the hall may start as an effort for the client to assert herself but may turn into a trauma response when the therapist changes the tone of his voice or uses gestures that activate a traumatic memory. Recognizing these differences can be a key to generating effective responses. The assessment of the client's presenting needs and history will offer clues about the nature of the resistance. Familiarity with how trauma, attachment, and development function and interact with one another will also aid the therapist in being able to recognize and differentiate the processes behind the behavior.

CASE STUDY 4.5

Casey could cuss out the best of them but gave me some slack because she liked doing art and getting out of school to come to therapy. She had "oppositional" written all over her every move, and I thought I had her authority-fighting, control-starved case conception down. That was until a few months into treatment when I accidentally grazed her knee when reaching for a marker across the floor. She literally jumped at my touch. I was taken aback. Her reflexive flinch showed me more than weeks of hearing about all she hated and did not care about. I had missed her underlying and profound trauma driving the rebellious behavior. The world's view of Casey, including my own, was skewed to focus on her difficult behaviors rather than her experiences of brutal deception and abuse for most of her life.

Balance Control and Safety

One clear and readily available way the therapist can empower the client in the relationship and the therapy space is to offer simple, concrete options. These types of interventions can quickly ease some resistance. For others, it may magnify it because the idea of doing anything the therapist suggests may be too threatening in itself. Taking a patient and affirmative stance to this type of resistance may be needed. Prolonged silences and awkward positions may be what is needed. The therapist can continue to create or take opportunities, however small, to show that the client has control and has options in the moment. Veer away from using logic to convince the client that he should not do what he is doing, because that implies judgment and tells the child that he is "wrong" (Sommers-Flanagan et al., 2011; VanFleet, 2000).

With that being said, the therapist cannot passively accept or allow aggressive or unsafe behavior from the client toward himself or others, including the therapist. If therapy is to be a safe space, there must be limits to the nature and extension of resistant behaviors. Also, a therapist should not be expected to effectively handle an aggressive or unsafe client in isolation. Clear understanding of the agency's or employer's policies and procedures for crises, and training in nonviolent crisis intervention will be assets to therapists working with this population due to the increased likelihood of unsafe behaviors. Triage, collaboration, and working closely with parents and professionals, especially in the office area, are necessary (VanFleet, 2000).

Because resistance is likely to be strongest in the beginning of treatment, it can be a major barrier to the assessment process. The therapist may be building an understanding of the client and the client's resistance while actively dealing with the client's resistance. This dilemma will naturally lead a therapist to engage the client with a form of "trial and error." Maintain a level of consistency with the client while being adaptable with

CASE STUDY 4.6

Before I even met Christopher, eight different professionals from his school, child welfare case, and foster placements sat in my office describing the complex history and distressing current status of this 7-year-old boy. He was a "runner" at school and a "screamer" at home: inconsolable, un-directable, and unpredictable. Needless to say, I was not the first therapist he had seen. He was not the first impervious client I had worked with either; however, he would prove himself as one of the most memorable. It took five sessions for him to actually come into the therapy room for the entire session. Much of our time together before that was spent sitting or standing in the hallway. After numerous different attempts to engage him, he latched on to a ritual of feeding the fish in a tank around the corner from my office. It was a safe "access" point for him to nurture and allow nurturance. After several mostly silent sessions, he wrote a note to the stuffed animal lion I was using to engage him, saying, "Dear Mr. Lion, Please stop talking to me and just leave me alone. Thanks, Christopher."

I wanted to show him that I accepted his distrust and his desire not to engage, so I beamed with pride and thanked him. He kept coming to therapy, found ways to feel safe and secure in his confusing world, and gradually, through six different foster and adoptive placements across four years, his "resistance" waned. The running turned into an honor roll performance and the screaming changed into a dry sense of humor with an embrace of the predictability and routine in his home and church. At the end of therapy, he smiled about how he "used to be."

intervention approaches to try different ways of engaging and responding to the client (Sommers-Flanagan et al., 2011). The way the therapist
approaches the client, both verbally and nonverbally, may change quite
a bit from the beginning of treatment when creating a therapeutic flow
and finding safe connecting points with the client that reframe and ease,
rather than bolster, the client's resistance.

Be a Therapist

It is not a therapist's job to be a parent to the client, regardless of the child's
need for parenting. When a therapist corrects or punishes a client's resistance as unwanted behavior, the therapist is widening the power imbalance
in the relationship and telling the child they are wrong for trying to protect
themselves, thereby disempowering the client. Instead, the therapist must
validate, normalize, and respect a client's efforts to resist a relationship with
the therapist and the help being offered. Resistance is a form of coping and
must be understood and accepted as the client's best choice in the moment.
Empowering the client's sense of choice and increasing the number of via-
ble options for the client to cope with fears and threats are the ultimate goals
of the therapist. Parents may have the same goals, but parents' responsibilities to the child are far more extensive than those of the therapist (VanFleet,
2000). Therapists cannot and should not be all the things a child needs.

Every caring and consistent interaction that the therapist gives
the child is therapeutic in itself. When the therapist reflects the client's
value and personal power, the client will feel better and stronger. Ultimately, a mindful, empathic therapist is the most effective intervention
to reduce resistance. Focus on being present and accepting what the
client is bringing to the moment without judgment or anxiety (Kelly,
Smith Hall, & Miller, 1989). Even therapists must learn from mistakes
and own their decisions and efforts, regardless of the result. When the
therapist models flexibility and empowerment, the client will be one
step closer to being able to do and feel the same.

REFERENCES

Alvord, M. K., & Grados, J. J. (2005). Enhancing resilience in children: A proactive
approach. *Professional Psychology: Research and Practice, 36*(3), 238–245. doi:10
.1037/0735-7028.36.3.238

Davis, D., & Hollon, S. (1999). Reframing resistance and noncompliance in cognitive therapy. *Journal of Psychotherapy Integration, 9*(1), 33–55.

Fitzgerald, K., Henriksen, R. C., Jr., & Garza, Y. (2012). Perceptions of counselors regarding the effectiveness of interventions for traumatized children. *International Journal of Play Therapy, 21*(1), 45–56. doi:10.1037/a0026737

Fitzpatrick, M. R., & Irannejad, S. (2008). Adolescent readiness for change and working alliance in counseling. *Journal of Counseling and Development, 86*(4), 438–445.

Freire, A., Eskritt, M., & Lee, K. (2004). Are eyes windows to a deceiver's soul? Children's use of another's eye gaze cues in a deceptive situation. *Developmental Psychology, 40*(6), 1093–1104. doi:10.1037/0012-1649.40.6.1093

Gurland, S. T., & Grolnick, W. S. (2008). Building rapport with children: Effects of adults' expected, actual, and perceived behavior. *Journal of Social and Clinical Psychology, 27*(3), 226–253. Retrieved from

Kelly, K., Smith Hall, A., & Miller, K. (1989). Relation of counselor intention and anxiety to brief counseling outcome. *Journal of Counseling Psychology, 36*(2), 158–162.

Lee, B. R., Munson, M. R., Ware, N. C., Ollie, M. T., Scott, L. D., & McMillen, J. C. (2006, April). Experiences of and attitudes toward mental health services among older youths in foster care. *Psychiatric Services, 57*(4), 487–492.

Lutz, W. J., Hock, E., & Kang, M. J. (2007). Children's communication about distressing events: The role of emotional openness and psychological attributes of family members. *American Journal of Orthopsychiatry, 77*(1), 86–94. doi:10.1037/0002-9432.77.1.86

Mahalik, J. (1994). Development of the client resistance scale. *Journal of Counseling Psychology, 41*(1), 58–68.

Oetzel, K. B., & Scherer, D. G. (2003). Therapeutic engagement with adolescents in psychotherapy. *Psychotherapy: Theory, Research, Practice, Training, 40*(3), 215–225. doi:10.1037/0033-3204.40.3.215

Sommers-Flanagan, J., Richardson, B. G., & Sommers-Flanagan, R. (2011). A multi-theoretical, evidence-based approach for understanding and managing adolescent resistance to psychotherapy. *Journal of Contemporary Psychotherapy, 41*(69), 69–80.

Suveg, C., Roblek, T. L., Robin, J., Krain, A., Aschenbrand, S., & Ginsburg, G. S. (2006). Parental involvement when conducting cognitive-behavioral therapy for children with anxiety disorders. *Journal of Cognitive Psychotherapy, 20*(3), 287–299.

VanFleet, R. (2000). Understanding and overcoming parent resistance to play therapy. *International Journal of Play Therapy, 9*(1), 35–46.

CHAPTER FIVE

ASSESSMENT

The kaleidoscope is the therapist's case conceptualization in motion. Assessment involves recognizing all of the colors and shapes in the kaleidoscope while making sense of the interconnected patterns as it turns. There are countless resources and diverse formats for completing 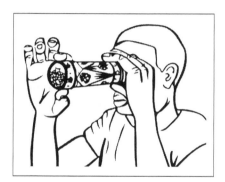 assessments, and many therapists use the standardized assessment tools mandated by employers, insurance providers, municipalities, or a combination thereof. This chapter offers in-depth guidance and targeted resources for the assessment process focused on building an attuned case conceptualization to determine effective treatment interventions.

HOW TO APPROACH ASSESSMENT IN CHILD WELFARE

Assessments of children in foster care are anything but straightforward and clear. The complexity of history and current circumstances for this population can be overwhelming to everyone involved. Child welfare best practices focus on three goals: safety, permanency, and well-being (Golden, 2000). In returning to the kaleidoscope metaphor, colorful figures in every child's treatment represent their developmental status, attachment patterns, grief, and exposure to trauma. Effective assessments will prioritize the therapist's culturally conscious understanding of these evolving and interrelated features and how they drive the child's plethora of social, emotional, behavioral, relational, and academic concerns. The following points outline key features of how the therapist can approach assessment accurately and efficiently.

Assessment as an Intervention Process

Approach assessment as a process rather than a product. It is not the "snapshot" of the therapist's peek through the kaleidoscope that will steer effective treatment, but rather the encompassing continual rotation. When a child is in foster care, there is an overwhelming amount of instability in the child's life that can make a definitive and thorough assessment nearly impossible. Whether the therapist chooses to turn the kaleidoscope or not, being in child welfare means being in constant change. The same colors and shapes may be there, but how they appear and affect one another will evolve as time passes on. The therapist must continue to rotate his own view as well. Turn the kaleidoscope with gentle, intentional control rather than jumpy, crisis-driven jerks.

An effective assessment will be conducted as a series of interventions, not a reactive gesture to a child in emotional turmoil. Because there is no guarantee on how many sessions a child may attend, include rapport building during the first meeting to reinforce the positive experience of therapy. This will positively influence the child's future encounters with yourself as well as therapists in general. Balance information-gathering-only efforts with empathic witnessing of the client's worldview. For example, if a new client cannot or will not answer a slew of assessment questions, the therapist may safely assume that the child is experiencing the assessment as a threat or a risk not worth taking. Like adults, children communicate many things through their silence, and not all silences mean the same thing. Increase the focus on building rapport and establishing safety in the therapeutic relationship while increasing understanding of the client and any lack of verbal participation. Accept the information given and document the lack of participation, even if it results in a less than optimal original assessment. Account for any scarcity and contributing factors in the case conceptualization. Keep in mind that with a nonresponsive client, much information gathering can be completed with the help of social workers, birth parents, foster parents, and other influential people in the child's life.

Not every need identified in the assessment is able to be met in a child's therapy, and many influencing factors are far out of the therapist's control. Identifying which problems are beyond both the child's and the therapist's control is a pivotal component of conducting an excellent assessment and providing realistic treatment. Referrals for additional services may be made, especially when safety concerns are present, and additional testing by other professionals will increase understanding of the client's present concerns.

Child therapists cannot be all things to all people. Being an effective child therapist includes having a heightened awareness of the parent, family, and systemic needs and concerns affecting the client, as well as becoming an expert at differentiating what will be addressed in therapy and what must be delegated to additional services. Depending on the level and current impact of family dysfunction, the child therapist should refer the family to see a separate therapist for family therapy rather than offer it in conjunction with individual therapy. Training, experience, and supervision in family therapy are necessary to provide any type of family intervention (Gouze & Wendel, 2008).

Merging of Multiple Viewpoints

The therapist must assess the client with consideration of multiple viewpoints: the client's, the caseworker's, and the families': birth, foster, and possibly adoptive too. When a child is a part of the child welfare system, different parts of the system tend to see only parts of the child. To gain a fuller understanding of the child, as well as capitalize on the internal and external resources a youth has at his disposal, it is necessary to extend the assessment beyond the child and the adult bringing the child to your office.

The older the child, the more capable she is of verbally reflecting on herself and what she sees and wants. When the child does not have the verbal or cognitive skills to answer even developmentally appropriate questions, use observation and contact with multiple figures in the child's life. Keep in mind that older siblings may have the most accurate information describing a younger client. For clients of all ages, assessment information will be most effectively gathered through a combination of direct observation of the client, the client's responses and interactions, and information from others. Always articulate the source of documented assessment information.

It is not uncommon for a child in foster care to have already seen multiple therapists due to both the high turnover rates of professionals and the child's changes in placement. Best practice for therapists involves acquiring and reviewing all previous records as part of the assessment process, with the understanding that the client's presentations and circumstances in the past may or may not align clearly with the present (Romanelli et al.,

2009). Avoid accepting previous diagnoses and recommendations blindly without updating screenings. Also, screen for potentially missed treatment needs, as the child's world and responses to it are constantly changing.

ASSESSMENT: STRENGTHS AND CONCERNS

EXHIBIT 5.1   BOAT IN THE STORM

Picture this: You're out fishing on a boat and a flash storm appears. Whether you saw it coming or not, it's here, and it's bad. There's no way

for you to outrun it. It's already starting to pour. The wind and waves are kicking up fast. You're stuck, whether you like it or not.

What do you do? Panic? Cling for dear life? Scream for help? Fight through it?

Now picture what advice you would give to someone else in this circumstance—as expert storm-goer. No one can make a storm go away, but there are things that can be done to increase the likelihood of survival.

A good place to start is by tallying up what you have to work with and using your equipment and skills in a way that's helpful. What about a rain poncho, life vest, flares? Does your boat have a cabin you can go in to wait it out? Are there leaks? Do you have a repair kit? Buckets to throw out excess water? Can you row or sail your boat? If it's motorized, how much gas do you have? Is there anyone available to come on board to help? Anyone you trust that actually knows something about surviving a storm? Or are the people around you just as scared as you?

You also need to recognize your capabilities and what's beyond your control. Are you even able to stand up in the boat to get that life jacket on the other side? Is it raining too hard to see the directions for safely setting off your flare? Or are you too terrified to even let go of the helm? Is it even safe to let go? Are you able to think straight, or are you shutting your eyes up tight and waiting for it all to disappear?

When a child in foster care walks into therapy, that child is already in the storm (see Exhibit 5.1). The therapist's job is to start what will be an ongoing assessment of the child's strengths and support resources, capabilities, survival-based efforts (both adaptive and maladaptive), and needs in order to use the best interventions at the right time to help the child weather through this part of his life. There are many things these children can do and not do that can make their situations worse. There are also tools and strengths that they may use. These may be overshadowed by the danger around them, but they are still there. For example, it is easier to notice the uselessness of a child beating the waves with oars out of anger than to recognize the strength and energy in the child's swings as a potential for paddling to safety. Help children to find and capitalize on what they have, and learn how they can use it to help themselves while gaining the perspective that this storm too will pass.

Step 1: Identify Strengths

From the point of first contact, begin a tally of the client's strengths and supports that will help keep the client safe and survive the chaos and danger around him. A strong assessment will not limit itself to only capturing the long list of vulnerabilities and reactions of a very vulnerable population. Therapists are actively empowering clients by building on their internal and external resources, starting at the beginning of treatment (Alvord & Grados, 2005).

There is an outpouring of research around resiliency and protective factors and their ability to mitigate the harmful effects of loss, trauma, and other adverse childhood experiences in terms of the client's strengths, supports, and experiences (Gil, 2006; Sieta, Mitchell, & Tobin, 1997). Resiliency describes a child's ability to bounce back or recover from difficult experiences with minimal lasting negative reactions (Alvord & Grados, 2005). Protective factors identify the specific characteristics, experiences, and supports of the child, the child's family, and the child's community that boost resiliency (Afifi & MacMillan, 2011). Children in foster care, like all children, range in their possession of both of these factors. Assessing the presence of protective factors and signs of resiliency will aid in providing strength-based interventions and making effective referrals for additional supports and services.

Tables 5.1 and 5.2 summarize a range of both internal characteristics and interpersonal experiences that have been shown to increase children's ability to effectively weather the storms of their lives as both children and adults (Alvord & Grados, 2005). Use these lists to start a basic tally of what the child has to work with. It will provide direction for strength-based interventions as well as increased perspective and attunement to the child's worldview.

Table 5.1 *Individual Signs of Resiliency and Protective Factors*

Adaptable temperament	Strong verbal and communication skills	Engages with talents, hobbies, and interests	Cooperative/gets along well with others
Positive self-worth	Self-awareness and self-acceptance	Positive self-care (hygiene, dress, etc.)	Able to self-regulate emotions and behavior
Problem solves	Sense of humor	Optimism	Good health
Strong cultural connection/identity	Positive school experiences	Positive and realistic sense of who they are	Comfortable asking for and receiving help
Internal locus of control	Ability to build relationships	Average to above-average IQ	Adaptable coping skills

Table 5.2 *Family and Community Signs of Resiliency and Protective Factors*

Safe/clean living environment	Stable, nurturing caregiver	Stable, nurturing extended family	Adults model and expect prosocial behavior
Adults use effective coping skills	Clear family roles and responsibilities	Caregivers understand child development	Adults make decisions while recognizing child's interests and goals
Traditions and celebrations	Daily routines	Positive social and/or religious affiliations	Consistent rules and structure
Strong cultural connection/identity	Education support	Financial stability	Comfortable asking for and receiving help

Step 2: Identify Presenting Concerns

Focus the assessment of presenting concerns on (a) keeping a broad perspective and (b) making sense of driving factors for behaviors. There will be many colors in the kaleidoscope, and there are many negative features of raging storms. Go beyond identifying what they are to understanding *why* they are. Effectively surviving high winds involves knowing whether they are coming from a rainstorm, a hurricane, or a tornado. Avoid focusing on one central concern without considering the backdrop of context and contributing factors. Remember that many child misbehaviors represent their best efforts to cope with stress. They may or may not be effective coping tools, but the child is doing the best he can. Assessment begins the process of understanding and sorting out children's efforts to cope in order to teach, assist, and redirect them to be more effective rather than further damaging themselves and those around them.

The next section describes how to assess concerns most relevant to children in foster care. We understand that the following concerns are often strongly interrelated and that each must be attended to for a comprehensive assessment: safety, current environment, relationship, development, abuse and neglect, attachment, grief and loss, trauma, and addiction. Because attachment, trauma, and grief are primary treatment issues for this population, they are introduced in this chapter and further explored in separate chapters.

Safety Concerns

Assess for safety at the first point of contact. Research indicates that 35% of youths in foster care are likely to demonstrate one or more behaviors or tendencies that make them dangerous to themselves or others (Stewart, Baiden, Theall-Honey, & den Dunnen, 2014). Assess the imminence and severity of danger in order to effectively prioritize treatment interventions and continue the assessment. Depending on the severity of the safety concern, the assessment process may need to be interrupted in order to focus on safety planning or immediate triage, following the policies and procedures of the employer.

Table 5.3 identifies common forms of self-harm and harm to others.

If the safety concern does not require immediate psychiatric attention, continue the assessment process to (a) building an understanding of the driving force(s) for dangerous behavior and (b) starting safety planning in conjunction with the assessment process.

Table 5.3 *Dangers to Self and Others*

Danger to Self

Scratching/picking (leading to infections)	Hair pulling
Cutting (superficial or deep)	Suicidal ideation, gesture, or plan
Drug use	Promiscuity
Truancy from home	Truancy from school

Danger to Others

Verbal assault	Physical aggression/violence
Sexual perpetration	Psychotic with loss of control/ intent to harm

Current Environmental and Relational Concerns

Adjusting to abruptly living under a stranger's care, no matter how responsible, nurturing, and similar in appearance and culture the new caregiver is, can be psychologically jarring for individuals of any age. Assess the client's current level of adjustment and comfort in his placement to identify both placement strengths and concerns for treatment through genuine curiosity and dismissal of assumptions.

Best practice in child welfare involves placement of children in homes that mimic the cultural, ethnic, sexuality, racial, and religious characteristics of their birth family. This does not always occur, and differences can cause additional identity concerns for the child as well as exacerbate other presenting concerns. In assessment, identify differences between birth and foster homes, school, and community around these features, and assess for both positive and negative impact on the child's sense of identity from the child's worldview as well as those of the foster and birth parents. For example, the foster parent may not know how to help the child take care of her hair, may have values that clash with the child's family of origin (e.g., cooking styles, music preferences, attending church), or may celebrate holidays in a different manner.

When a child enters care, he is given another identity: a foster child. The associations with this identity are almost all negative and range from pity to disdain. For these children, coming to terms with this part of their identity, what it means to them and to the world around them, is part of being in child welfare. Children and families can vary greatly in their comfort level with discussing being in foster care and what it is like. Assess the child's current level of comfort or discomfort with this identity and varying experiences of the identity in different places (e.g. school versus foster relatives). Therapists should model understanding and accepting both the reasons for the child coming into care as well as the difficulties related to being in foster care.

Beyond their temporary caregivers, children in care will likely have some type of significant interpersonal relationship concern with caregivers, siblings, peers, school staff, or other professionals involved in their lives. Assess patterns and specific areas or types of relationships that seem to be most gratifying and the most difficult for the child. View the identified relationship concerns in the context of the child's current level of developmental functioning as well as being descriptive of their attachment type(s), trauma responses, and grieving process.

When assessing a child's family concerns, be sure to distinguish which identified concerns are attributed to birth, foster, or adoptive families, or a combination thereof. For some children, there will be very distinct worldviews in each of the different families, whereas others will maintain a more broad perspective of family in general. The child's perspectives on families may be wrought with ambivalence and contradictions. Sometimes the family members whom a client believes are most helpful are not accessible or may be hurtful. Be wary of assumptions and projecting your own values and wishes on the client's view of birth versus foster family.

Be sure to gather information about the amount and quality of the client's relationships with younger, same age, and older peers, noticing any discrepancies. Look for patterns or labels that the client may have, or may have been given, in the world of his peers as well. Relational concerns with child welfare staff may also be present. Some children project their needs for nurturance and comfort on their foster care workers. Others distrust or disdain their workers to the extent that cooperation and participation in even minimal communication is problematic.

Developmental Concerns

Every youth in care is in the midst of actively developing, yet the child welfare system often focuses more on the child's physical safety than on the child's developmental concerns (Zeanah, Shauffer, & Dozier, 2011). Effective therapists working with children and teens are familiar with key developmental frameworks. Complete a basic assessment of the client's current developmental functioning and concerns in the psychosocial, physical, cognitive, moral, and affective areas to aid in maintaining realistic expectations, driving appropriate treatment intervention, supporting effective parenting and behavior management techniques, making appropriate referrals, and advocating for the client.

Therapists can utilize any area of healthy development as a protective factor and strength on which to build effective treatment interventions. Simply interacting with a child in her accurate current developmental stage will be an intervention in itself to bolster the child's self-worth and affirm her age-appropriate ability to cope with the distress in the child's life.

Part of the therapist's developmental assessment will include preliminary screening for delays in any area of development as well as unidentified developmental disabilities. Referrals may be made for psychological testing to screen for learning disabilities or cognitive delays, neurological testing to test for brain functioning, speech and language assessment for communication concerns, and occupational therapy evaluation for sensory concerns.

Table 5.4 offers an integrative developmental timeline by age according to established developmental theories, including Erikson's psychosocial stages, Piaget's theory of cognitive development, Kohlberg's moral development theory, and Maslow's hierarchy of human needs. Development of affective abilities, sexuality, and racial or ethnic identities is also included.

Abuse and Neglect Concerns

Upon intake, every child in foster care will have at least one substantiated experience of abuse or neglect. The therapist must gather as much factual information as possible about the incident from the parents and workers before meeting with the child so that the assessment process can be focused on understanding the child's worldview and reactions. Children's perceptions of being maltreated are often very different from what is documented by involved professionals. Additionally, it is not uncommon for youth to enter foster care with more experiences of unreported or unsubstantiated maltreatment in their birth or foster homes (Kochanska, Aksan, & Carlson, 2005). Therefore, during the assessment, therapists are recommended to (a) identify the substantiated maltreatment with the purpose of gaining the child's perspective and reactions and (b) ask directly about, and watch out for signs of, any additional abuse or neglect occurring in the past and present. Keep in mind that because therapists are mandated reporters, all unreported incidents discovered during assessment must be reported to protective services.

Table 5.4 *Developmental Timeline (Newman & Newman, 2014)*

Age	Cognitive	Physical	Emotional
Infancy: Birth to 1	• Developing senses • Object permanence—toys do not disappear when covered • Learns verbal language • Unable to categorize ethnic differences	• Crawling, walking, grabbing • Sitting up, holding head up • Using voice to communicate	• Attachment—connects to and trusts caregiver • Trust versus mistrust
Toddlerhood: 1½ to 3	• Learns to control impulses (e.g., can wait for a cookie) • Vocabulary of about 500 words • Creates sentences to meet needs • Fantasy-based thinking (e.g., thinks people are inside the television) • Tend to see people as individuals, not parts of racial or ethnic groups	• Bladder control and toilet training • Walking, running, improved gross motor skill • Begins to make representational drawings • Beginning masturbation	• Autonomy ("I can do it") versus shame and doubt • Learns self-control and exists apart from parents • Feels shame and doubts abilities if not allowed to try

(continued)

Table 5.4 *Developmental Timeline (Newman & Newman, 2014) (continued)*

Age	Cognitive	Physical	Emotional
Early School Age: 4 to 6	• Morality based on parent reaction • Perspective taking—"Other kids don't think like I do" • Imaginary friends • Identification with parents • Categorizes people with similar hair and skin color and reflects adults' attitudes toward race and ethnicity	• Improving fine and gross motor skills • Toileting accidents • Nightmares	• Gender identification • Group play/socialization • Feels sympathy and empathy/learns to share • Initiative versus guilt—"I want to do it" or "I tried, failed, and didn't live up to my standards"
Middle Childhood: 7 to 12	• Concrete operations development • Accurately uses race/ethnicity to identify self and others as well as social cues/stereotypes (e.g., "She acts White")	• Growth spurt • Improves gross and fine motor skills, plays sports, etc. • Becomes awkward with body	• Makes same-sex friends • Team play • Industry versus inferiority—"I am capable" versus "I am not capable"
Adolescence: 13 to 18	• Formal operations development—conceptual then hypothetical thinking • Can plan for future and career • Separates from parents • Ethnic identity—conformity, dissonance, resistance, immersion, introspection, articulation	• Puberty: girls develop breasts, widening of hips; boys develop lower voices, have regular erections, grow facial hair • Sexual feelings begin • Requires more calories and sleep	• Group identity versus alienation—"What group do I belong to?" versus "Am I alone, not part of anything?" • Identity versus role confusion—"Who am I?" versus "I don't know who I am" • Transitions, leaving home

Therapists should recognize the substantiated incident(s) of abuse or neglect in the initial assessment; however, in-depth assessment of reactions should be based on the client's interest and ability to tolerate discussing this information. Such interactions have the potential to promote healing and safety or further traumatize the child and damage the therapeutic relationship. Follow the client's lead. Stop questioning about maltreatment if the child is saying or showing you that he is unwilling or unable to continue. Continue by focusing both verbal and nonverbal communication to validate fears, affirm courage, value and prioritize safety, and set the stage for therapy to safely discuss anything that matters to the child, no matter how bad, confusing, or scary it may be. Further assess the child's avoidance through the lens of development, attachment, trauma, and grief to better understand its source and protective purpose.

Always use developmentally appropriate language and reasoning when asking youth whether or not they have been abused or neglected. Particularly with younger children, be conscientious of how they may label body parts or describe actions in nonadult language. If the therapist feels unsure about the child's understanding of abuse or neglect but suspects possible victimization based on other presenting concerns, the therapist should use drawing or dolls to have the child show the therapist what he has seen or experienced. Remember that therapists are not investigators of abuse or neglect. Processing past substantiated incidents is different than revealing new incidents for the first time in session.

Depending on the developmental age of the child and the child's ability to clearly understand and answer questions about abuse and neglect, therapists may choose to use basic psychoeducation about what sexual abuse, physical abuse, domestic violence, and neglect are and are not. This is a prime example of how assessment can also be used as an intervention to increase the child's safety skills and sense of empowerment. For example, upon learning that the physical and verbal abuse a young boy experienced from his stepfather was wrong and in fact against the law, the boy's sense of power shifted, leading him to declare, while face-to-face with his father in the next visit, that what his dad did was not okay and that his dad was not allowed to do it anymore. This empowered behavior was a striking contrast to the client's typical cowering and withdrawal during family visits.

Include as much of the following information as possible in the initial assessment. Identify the nature and number of incidents of direct physical abuse, sexual abuse, neglect, and witnessing of domestic violence or abuse of family members. Note the corresponding age(s) of the child and the length of the incidents and whether they were chronic or acute and isolated in nature. Also ask about whom the abuse involved beyond the child and the perpetrator, including both household members and unrelated individuals.

Child and teen victims of sexual abuse are least likely to disclose this type of abuse, and it is extremely uncommon for children and teens to lie about being sexually abused (London, Bruck, Ceci, & Shuman, 2005). Additionally, many children in foster care disclose sexual abuse long after they have been in placement and not at initial removal when questioned (London et al., 2005). With these points in mind, the therapist must still directly ask about each child's experience(s) of sexual abuse. If sexual abuse is denied by the child but strongly suspected, the therapist must focus on building rapport and increasing safety skills while remaining ready to respond to disclosure whenever it may occur.

Common reactions to child sexual abuse across all ages include difficulty sleeping, heightened anxiety or fearfulness, negative self-worth, shame or guilt, withdrawal, somatic complaints, rage, aggressiveness, and age-inappropriate sexual behavior. Signs of trauma may also be present, along with fire setting and other high-risk behaviors, especially in older children and teens.

The reactions of youth who have been directly physically abused mirror those who have witnessed domestic violence or physical abuse of family members—adult and children alike. Assessment should include the current reactions as well as factual information about the nature, context, and length or patterns of the violence. For example, determine if the abuse came from one or multiple family members; was correlated with substance use, mental illness, or other adult concerns; occurred in context of "punishment"; and whether it was patterned, ritualized, or unpredictable (Levenson & Morin, 2006).

Common childhood reactions to both physical abuse and domestic violence include any combination of the following: generalized anxiety; difficulty managing anger; withdrawal and depression; horseplay; bullying; aggression; violent touching; regressed or delayed development; poor social and safety skills; low self-worth; trauma responses; and insecure, or absence of, attachment patterns.

For children who were neglected, identify likely source(s) of the neglectful parent's maltreatment of the child, which may include a combination of the following: mental illness, trauma, unresolved grief, addiction, poverty, and lack of family or community support. When assessing for signs of neglect, remember that the fact that parents have neglected their children in one area of life or during a certain time period does not mean that all of the child's needs went unmet for the child's entire childhood. Also, when more than one parent, relative, or caregiver is involved, the form and severity of neglect may vary greatly between them. Incidents of neglect may result in traumatization of the child, and insecure attachment patterns are strongly associated with neglectful relationships. Table 5.5 summarizes signs of neglect according to type.

Table 5.5 *Signs of Neglect According to Type*

Type of Neglect	Examples of Child Reactions
Emotional	Poor adult–child boundaries, distrust of adults, reliance on other children for help or direction, sleeping difficulties, lack of understanding of cause–effect relationships
Physical and Environmental	Parental behaviors, hoarding food, stealing/taking without asking from others or stores, toileting issues, poor hygiene, destruction of property, lack of interest in receiving or having possessions taken away, fighting, truancy/running away
Medical	Unidentified health concerns such as allergies, asthma, vision, hearing, and so on; somatic complaints; not bringing injuries to parent's attention (e.g., cuts for cleaning and bandage); fear of medical interventions
Educational	Unidentified or unaddressed learning or cognitive disabilities, working behind grade level due to missing school

Attachment Concerns

Attachment is descriptive of the relationship between the child and the child's primary caregiving adults; it is not a feature of the child (Kochanska et al., 2005). The first step to assessing the foster care child's attachment style begins with observation. When possible, watch how the child interacts with her birth and foster parent(s). Also observe how the child chooses to engage with the therapist and other professionals such as foster care workers and teachers. Behaviors that indicate attachment problems vary according to the type of insecurity and the age of the child.

The likelihood that a foster care child will have some type of attachment insecurity is high. The attachment insecurity may result from previous abuse and neglect, difficulties relating to the foster parent, or both (Kochanska et al., 2005). When assessing for attachment patterns, be sure to identify current examples or memories of the child's healthy connections, experiences, and perceptions of adults or places in the child's life. These connections are protective factors that can be built upon for effective intervention.

There are four major attachment patterns (Table 5.6). These include secure attachment and three different forms of insecure attachment; these three forms of insecure attachment correlate with patterns of caregiver behavior (McWey, 2004). Assessing the caregiver's parenting style will help with assessment accuracy. Successful foster parents will be pros at engaging children in secure attachment patterns.

Table 5.6 *Attachment Patterns*

Attachment Pattern	Parent's Behavior	Child's Behavior
Secure	Responsive, consistent, attuned to child's needs	Anxious when left with a stranger, seeks comfort from caregiver, able to tolerate separation when older, enjoys and cognitively benefits from exploration
Anxious Avoidant	Emotionally rejecting, distant, dismissing of child's needs because of lack of attunement	Avoids caregiver, expects rejection, maintains proximity in case caregiver is available
Anxious Ambivalent	Inconsistent, intrusive, preoccupied with personal emotional state	Clingy, uncertain, expresses anger at caregiver, yells at/hits caregiver
Disorganized/ Unattached	Frightening, confusing, fearful, stuck in unresolved trauma or grief	Does not show preference for one caregiver, ambivalent toward caregivers, the need to seek comfort and the fear of caregiver lead to confusion and inconsistency

Children in foster care who have attachment disorders may receive a diagnosis of Reactive Attachment Disorder, code 313.89 in the current version of the *Diagnostic and Statistical Manual of Mental Disorders* (5th ed.; *DSM–5*; American Psychiatric Association [APA], 2013). This disorder, listed under trauma and stressor-related disorders, includes seven criteria a child must exhibit. These criteria include behavior consistent with an Anxious Avoidant or Disorganized/Unattached attachment style and are more common in children who have had a history of emotional neglect and/or multiple inconsistent caregivers (APA, 2013). According to the *DSM–5*, the disorder is rare, but therapists working with this population may see many children with this diagnosis (Hall & Geher, 2003).

Grief and Loss Concerns

Every child in foster care has experienced multiple losses, most of which are related to his removal and any replacements. A loss can be anyone or anything of value that the child is deprived of or that is currently unrecoverable by the child (Table 5.7). Many adults think of loss in permanent terms, but the separations and changes in family and home may be experienced as permanent or temporary depending on the child's developmental levels and trust in the adults telling the child otherwise. Revisit the child's developmental ability to understand object permanence and think hypothetically.

Table 5.7 *Types of Loss*

Common Losses

People	Contact with parents, siblings, relatives, friends, community, school
Possessions	Bedding, toys, books, photos, electronics, hobbies
Places/space	Room, home, yard, school, community activities, landscape
Traditions/routines	Holidays, birthdays, sayings, songs, dancing, cooking, smells, bathing, bedtime routines

Assessment of grief should focus on identifying the nature of the losses the child has experienced and the way that they currently affect the child. Include losses unrelated to being in foster care, such as the death of a grandparent, whether before or after the child's removal. Also assess for anticipated losses, such as the school year ending or a petition to terminate parental rights. Be sure to differentiate between grief and traumatic grief.

Grief does not always occur as solely a clear, uncomfortable emotional reaction. Grief can also be confusing, ambiguous, and unresolved. For example, when an ill, elderly parent dies, the adult caregiver will feel grief and also feel relief from the burden of care. The relief does not negate the need for the adult or child to grieve. Unresolved grief can trouble a child throughout the rest of his life. Focus on both identifying specific losses that are causing dysfunction as well as the child's overall ability to grieve the myriad of losses he is experiencing (D'Antonio, 2011). Be readily familiar with the common stages or signs of grief. These may include shock or disbelief, denial, guilt, anger, despair, blaming, and bargaining ("if only . . . " thinking). Grief can be experienced and acted out emotionally, physically, socially, and spiritually (D'Antonio, 2011).

A loss can either be traumatic or not traumatic. This is determined by assessing the child's responses to the loss, not by the nature of the event itself. There are several ways to differentiate grief from traumatic grief. Sadness drives grief, whereas fear drives trauma responses. Traumatic grief may encompass grieving, but grief can stand alone. Clients tend to be more capable of verbalizing thoughts, feelings, and memories around grieved losses, whereas traumatic losses are often more difficult for children to talk about. Grief involves regrets, whereas trauma involves self-blame. The experience of anger in grief tends to be emotional but not destructive or harmful, whereas traumatic anger often becomes assaultive (D'Antonio, 2011; Steel & Raider, 2009).

Trauma Concerns

Every child in foster care has been exposed to at least two potentially traumatizing events: (a) removal and (b) abuse or neglect leading to removal. This does not mean that every child in foster care will have a diagnosis of post-traumatic stress disorder (PTSD). By definition, PTSD according to the *DSM–5* involves both exposure to a threatening experience *and* demonstration of a specific series of emotional, behavioral, and cognitive reactions (APA, 2013). Undoubtedly, all children in foster care meet the first criteria, but each will require thorough assessment and ongoing observation before diagnosing and treating them for PTSD. Therapists working with this population should complete an evidence-based trauma screening for every child, to both identify potentially traumatic experiences and thoroughly assess the child's current trauma responses. It is important to understand that a child can still experience trauma responses or symptoms but not meet the full criteria for PTSD, meaning that the child demonstrating some trauma responses will still benefit from trauma-informed assessment and care.

An evidence-based trauma assessment tool will aid clinicians in determining whether the child meets the criteria for PTSD as well as any trauma responses that may not warrant the full diagnosis (Hawkins & Radcliffe, 2006; Portnova, 2007).

According to the *DSM–5*, there are four main diagnostic criteria for PTSD in children, with some differences noted between children under and over 6 years old: re-experiencing, avoidance, negatively altered thoughts and feelings, and hyperarousal (APA, 2013). Children in foster care will likely demonstrate behaviors in one or more categories. Likewise, some children's trauma responses will fall more heavily in one area than another and may change with time, intervention, and additional traumatic exposures. Similarly to how each child's response to a potentially traumatic situation is highly individualized, so are the combination and intensity of the child's responses. Thorough assessment, monitoring, and reassessment as needed of the child's trauma responses are greatly beneficial in providing effective treatment.

When assessing each symptom category, the therapist should understand that each criterion describes a set of observable reactions that came into existence as the child's most effective survival strategy at that time but does not stop when the traumatic incident is over. Trauma responses are neurologically based, meaning that the child did not think through or have conscious control over the responses. These trauma responses are results of humans' automatic and neurobiological coping mechanisms for survival that can become impairing when the child is no longer facing the imminent threat (Bonanno & Mancini, 2012).

Children who demonstrate *re-experiencing* trauma responses are involuntarily reliving emotions and sensations related to the trauma. Re-experiencing is most often triggered by a sensory-based feature of the child's current environment that may or may not have an obvious relation to a traumatic incident.

A child experiencing *avoidance* makes efforts to stay physically and/or psychologically away from reminders of the traumatic event, especially ones that may lead to increased re-experiencing or arousal. Some youth may describe feeling emotionally "numb" or be observed to completely dissociate at times.

Negatively altered thoughts and feelings can encompass a broad range of emotional patterns and belief systems that are characteristic of a victim mindset, such as low self-worth; anxiety and depression; decreased interest in once-pleasurable activities; feeling distrust of self, others, and the

CASE STUDY 5.1

Five-year-old Mark, 9-year-old Katie, and 15-year-old Jeanine are siblings who were removed from their parent's care after multiple allegations of domestic violence, abuse, neglect, and incest. Every night, Mark waits until his foster parents are in bed and then wanders the house, often eating and playing (arousal), whereas Katie goes to sleep easily but wakes up sweating from nightmares (re-experiencing). Jeanine will only fall asleep on the floor so she can feel anyone approaching (arousal) and starts to panic if her bedroom door clicks shut—after years of being locked in the basement to be sexually abused (re-experiencing).

When asked about what happened in their home, Mark says everything was great (avoidance), whereas Katie tells confusing, disjointed stories of abuse in the third person (avoidance). Jeanine worries about her siblings hating her for "breaking up the family" because she is the one who confided in her school counselor about what was happening at home (negatively altered thoughts/feelings).

Mark tends to play violently with his toys and is very destructive (re-experiencing). His teacher says he cannot sit still at school and is constantly disrupting other students (arousal). Katie is bright but continues to not hand in her completed homework almost daily and shrugs off any concern expressed by teachers or her foster parents about not living up to her potential (negatively altered thoughts/feelings). Jeanine is promiscuous and engages in high-risk behaviors with peers (re-experiencing).

In therapy, Mark starts running the halls every time the therapist raises her hand to give him a high five or points while redirecting his destructive behavior (arousal and re-experiencing). Katie repeatedly draws pictures of herself as gross, covered in feces. She describes feeling like a piece of trash and tells her foster mother that she would be better off dead (negatively altered thoughts/feelings). Jeanine stays late at school and "forgets" her weekly appointment because the glasses her therapist wears remind her of her dad's (avoidance).

world in general; pervasive guilt or shame for causing or not preventing the traumatic event; feeling detached or separate from life; and impaired ability to feel positive emotions.

Children experiencing *hyperarousal* and *reactivity* may become hypervigilant and demonstrate heightened startle responses. They may have difficulty concentrating; have difficulty falling or staying asleep; show increased irritability; and display anger outbursts that are overreactive, reckless, or harmful. Arousal and reactivity as trauma responses can have a very similar presentation to features of attention deficit-hyperactivity disorder, oppositional defiant disorder, and conduct disorder.

The most beneficial time to assess a child in foster care for trauma symptoms is at the time of initial removal and again 6 weeks after being in the foster placement (Van & Seedat, 2013). This way the therapist can attempt to acquire information about potential trauma responses to abuse or neglect with input from the birth family, as well as additional or compounded trauma responses to the removal and subsequent separations. Assessment at initial removal involves many potential barriers, particularly the child and family members being unwilling, unavailable, or unreliable in reporting information for a range of reasons (Webb, 2006). However, efforts to gather this information will often be worthwhile and should always be made.

Finally, trauma assessments are solely deficit-based evaluations. Although the information gathered is imperative to understanding the child's needs, it lacks direction regarding what will help the child. Research on resilience and trauma indicates that in order to effectively help the traumatized child, the therapist must also identify certain strength-based factors, which will become the child's resources for healing (Steel & Raider, 2009).

Addiction Concerns

Every assessment should include a screening for addiction concerns. Screen both the client and the parents in the child's life. Parents include adults in their current placement as well as their birth parents or caregiving relatives. This information can be gathered from the client as well as from the parents and workers. Foster care professionals should already be aware of any addiction concerns of both foster and birth parents. If there are any new concerns, be sure to share them with the assigned worker.

Addictions can involve a substance, such as alcohol and/or drugs, or can involve a process or activity such as gambling, spending, or eating. Gather preliminary information about how often the substance or activity is engaged in, for how long, and who else in the family engages in similar patterns. For children and teens without known addictions, ask about experimentation and addictive activity in peer groups. Identify the client's patterns and volume of use or activity, any negative impacts on the client's well-being and daily living, the client's purpose for the addictive behavior, and the client's motivation or desire, if any, to decrease the behavior. Gauge the client's perceived level of control around the potential addiction. Find out from the client's perspective what other adults, including workers and parents, are aware of regarding the addictive behavior. This screening information will drive both treatment goals and potential referrals for substance abuse, eating disorder treatment support, or other forms of support (Aarons et al., 2008). Treatment for addiction concerns must come from a counselor who is trained and experienced in working with addictions.

CONCLUSION

Once the therapist has identified goals that accurately address underlying needs, there can be confusion about "where to start." For much of this population, treatment goals and their priority can feel like a moving target because of additional losses and exposures to traumatic experiences. Additionally, beyond these tragedies, life outside of foster care goes on. Both foster and birth family members and friends face illness, injury, divorce, bullying, heartbreak, deployment, incarceration, and death. Community violence takes place. Car accidents happen. The domestic violence, mental health, and substance abuse issues with birth parents may continue and worsen, or similar problems may surface in the foster placement.

Returning to the imagery of the kaleidoscope, the effective therapist will see and work with what is in view at the moment, while continuing to intentionally turn it in order to keep a more full perspective of the pieces. For example, if a client is being replaced, this must be the primary focus in sessions. The client will benefit from the therapist "meeting where the client is at" in the present moment of the session while also guiding the client toward interventions aimed at the goals that are known to be present and are interrelated, as opposed to choosing and working through one goal at a time.

Remember that assessment of youth in foster care is a process, and even the initial formal assessment may take several sessions at the start of treatment. Triage from the beginning with a focus on safety concerns, needs for additional testing, substance abuse concerns, and therapy referrals for family members. Prioritize understanding the child's perspective while gathering information from multiple sources beyond the client, including current caregivers and caseworkers and participating birth parents. The central purpose of assessment of youth in foster care is for the therapist to make sense out of the client's presenting concerns in order to drive effective and targeted interventions.

REFERENCES

Aarons, G. A., Monn, A. R., Hazen, A. L., Connelly, C. D., Leslie, L. K., Landsverk, J. A., . . . Brown, S. A. (2008). Substance involvement among youths in child welfare: The role of common and unique risk factors. *American Journal of Orthopsychiatry, 78*(3), 340–349. doi:10.1037/a0014215

Afifi, T. O., & MacMillan, H. L. (2011). Resilience following child maltreatment: A review of protective factors. *Canadian Journal of Psychiatry, 56*(5), 266–272.

Alvord, M. K., & Grados, J. J. (2005). Enhancing resilience in children: A proactive approach. *Professional Psychology: Research and Practice, 36*(3), 238–245. doi:10.1037/0735-7028.36.3.238

American Psychiatric Association. (2013). *Diagnostic and statistical manual of mental disorders* (5th ed.). Washington, DC: Author.

Bonanno, G. A., & Mancini, A. D. (2012). Beyond resilience and PTSD: Mapping the heterogeneity of responses to potential trauma. *Psychological Trauma: Theory, Research, Practice, and Policy, 4*(1), 74–83.

D'Antonio, Jocelyn. (2011). Grief and loss of a caregiver in children: A developmental perspective. *Journal of Psychosocial Nursing & Mental Health Services, 49*(10), 17–20. doi:10.3928/02793695-20110802-03

Erikson, E. H. (1964). *Childhood and society* (2nd ed.). Oxford, England: W. W. Norton.

Gil, E. (2006). *Helping Abused and Traumatized Children.* New York: NY: Guilford Press.

Golden, O. (2000). The federal response to child abuse and neglect. *American Psychologist, 55*(9), 1050–1053. doi:10.1037/0003-066X.55.9.1050

Gouze, K. R., & Wendel, R. (2008). Integrative module-based family therapy: Application and training. *Journal of Marital and Family Therapy, 34*(3), 269–286.

Hall, S. E. K., & Geher, G. (2003). Behavioral and personality characteristics of children with reactive attachment disorder. *Journal of Psychology, 137*(2), 145–162.

Hawkins, S., & Radcliffe, J. (2006). Current measures of PTSD for children and adolescents. *Journal of Pediatric Psychology, 31*(4), 420–430.

Kochanska, G., Aksan, N., & Carlson, J. J. (2005). Temperament, relationships, and young children's receptive cooperation with their parents. *Developmental Psychology, 41*(4), 648—660. doi:10.1037/0012-1649.41.4.648

Levenson, J. S., & Morin, J. W. (2006). Risk assessment in child sexual abuse cases. *Child* Welfare, 85(1), 59–82.

London, K., Bruck, M., Ceci, S. J., & Shuman, D. W. (2005). Disclosure of child sexual abuse: What does the research tell us about the ways that children tell? *Psychology, Public Policy, and Law, 11*(1), 194–226. doi:10.1037/1076-8971.11.1.194

McWey, L. M. (2004). Predictors of attachment styles of children in foster care: An attachment theory model for working with families. *Journal of Marital and Family Therapy, 30*(4), 439–452.

Newman, B.M. & Newman, P.R. (2014). *Development through life: A psychosocial approach.* Belmont, CA: Wadsworth Publishing.

Portnova, A. A. (2007). Typology of post-traumatic stress disorder in children and adolescents. *Neuroscience and Behavioral Physiology, 37*(1), 7–11. doi:10.1007/s11055-007-0142-0

Romanelli, L. H., Landsverk, J., Levitt, J. M., Leslie, L. K., Hurley, M. M., Bellonci, C., & Jensen, P. S. (2009). Best practices for mental health in child welfare: Screening, assessment, and treatment guidelines. *Child Welfare, 88*(1), 163–188.

Seita, J.R., Mitchell, M., & Tobin, C. (1997). Connections, continuity, dignity and opportunity: Essential ingredients for creating our village: Reclaiming children and youth. *Journal of Emotional and Behavioral Problems, 6*(1), 45–47.

Steel, W., & Raider, M. (2009). *Structured sensory intervention for traumatized children, adolescents and parents (SITCAP): Evidence based interventions to alleviate trauma.* Lewiston, NY: The Edwin Mellen Press, Ltd.

Stewart, S. L., Baiden, P., Theall-Honey, L., & den Dunnen, W. (2014). Deliberate self-harm among children in tertiary care residential treatment: Prevalence and correlates. *Child & Youth Care Forum, 43*(1), 63–81. doi:10.1007/s10566-013-9225-y

Van, D. H., & Seedat, S. (2013). Screening and diagnostic considerations in childhood post-traumatic stress disorder. *Neuropsychiatry, 3*(5), 497–511. doi:10.2217/npy.13.61

Webb, N.B., Ed. (2006). *Working with Traumatized Youth in Child Welfare.* New York: NY: Guilford Press.

Zeanah, C. H., Shauffer, C., & Dozier, M. (2011). Foster care for young children: Why it must be developmentally informed. *Journal of the American Academy of Child & Adolescent Psychiatry, 50*(12), 1199–1201. doi:10.1016/j.jaac.2011.08.001

CHAPTER SIX

DIAGNOSIS, MEDICATION, AND CHILD WELFARE

This turn of the kaleidoscope focuses on diagnosing to identify and treat mental health concerns with psychotropic medications in children within the child welfare system. Although every child's kaleidoscopic pattern does not necessarily include a "diagnosis" or "medication" colored shape, a large percentage will, and each facet is highly relevant to the therapist's assessment, treatment, and advocacy of the client's presenting concerns.

A majority of children in foster care are provided mental health services through managed care. This means that treatment is driven by a *Diagnostic and Statistical Manual of Mental Disorders* (5th ed.; *DSM-5*; American Psychiatric Association [APA], 2013) diagnosis unless the caregiver is seeking (and privately paying for) alternative treatment or nonparticipating providers, which is the extreme minority. Gaining a more complete understanding of current common practices, including their strengths and deficits, will benefit the therapist in providing the most effective treatment for the child in care. This chapter offers information on current trends in diagnosis and medication, how diagnoses and medication are used, dangers of inaccurate diagnosing and ineffectively medicating, and ways to overcome common barriers to giving an accurate diagnosis for clients.

DIAGNOSIS

Common Diagnoses

Research shows that the most common diagnoses given to youth in foster care are, in order of frequency: attention deficit hyperactivity disorder (ADHD), separation anxiety, oppositional defiant disorder (ODD), and conduct disorder (CD). Elimination disorder, major depressive disorder, generalized anxiety disorder, and posttraumatic stress disorder (PTSD) tend to be secondary diagnoses that are given less frequently (Linares, Martinez-Martin, & Castellano, 2013).

Children in foster care receiving mental health treatment are also likely to be given more than one diagnosis, typically with ADHD as the primary diagnosis (Linares et al., 2013; Ruben et al., 2012). One study found that nearly 10% of the children were given five or more diagnoses (Linares et al., 2013).

In practice, therapists can expect all youth in foster care to experience an adjustment disorder and signs of grief for several months following the removal from the birth home and after additional transitions or re-placements once in care, including adoptive placements and reunification (Zito et al., 2008). The diagnosis of PTSD related to the youth's multiple threatening experiences of abuse and/or neglect and removal encompasses a range of behavioral and mood-related criteria that overlap those of ADHD, ODD, major depressive disorders, anxiety disorders, and other mood disorders. The symptoms of reactive attachment disorder also have crossover with these diagnoses and, although it does not encompass or describe the entire foster care population, given the known attachment insecurities related to abuse and/or neglect as well as removal, this diagnosis must be considered as well (Levy & Orlans, 1998).

Accurate Diagnosing

Because treatment is driven by diagnosis, it is imperative to diagnose accurately, as effective treatment may differ greatly depending on what's being treated. Many children in foster care spend years in therapy being treated for symptoms related to one diagnosis when the presenting concerns were actually driven by another. As mentioned previously in this text, accurate assessment, and in turn diagnosis, is an ongoing process.

In reality, the results of the assessment, including the diagnosis, greatly depend on who attends the assessment, what they share, and what they do not to share—whether intentionally or due to a lack of knowledge. Initial diagnoses are typically made at an intake appointment by a master's or doctoral-level licensed mental health practitioner. As in other types of assessment, diagnoses are given based on the information presented by those attending the appointment. Ideally, assessments for this population will be completed with multiple caregivers and professionals present, including the current foster parent(s) or residential care provider(s), the birth parent(s), and the primary foster care worker(s) assigned to the family. The assessor's understanding of the child welfare system, level of effort in gathering information from multiple sources, and ability to incorporate multiple and potentially contradicting descriptions of a child effectively will also greatly impact what diagnoses are given at intake (Cantos & Gries, 2010).

Some youth in foster care are referred for further evaluation of behavior and mental health concerns. Psychiatrists may complete a separate evaluation focused on assessing accurate diagnosis and/or providing recommendations for treatment, including use of psychotropic medication. Children may also complete psychological testing to assess mental health, learning disabilities, cognitive functioning, and personality dynamics to make additional treatment recommendations for parents, therapists, and schools. Neuropsychological testing may be completed to determine if any of the presenting behaviors are accounted for by brain damage or developmental deficits in brain functioning.

Mental health diagnosing is notoriously nonuniform, and disagreements between professionals are likely to occur (Jensen-Doss & Weisz, 2008). Some primary care physicians may diagnose and prescribe psychotropic medications, although this is not best practice (Pidano, Kimmelblatt, & Neace, 2011).

There are several key differential diagnoses therapists working with this population must be especially aware of. Therapists are recommended to look at the source of the child's behavioral concerns and not simply engage in criteria matching. This can be done in part during the diagnostic process. For example, although the criteria of ODD, CD, or ADHD may be truly descriptive of the child's current functioning, if the related behaviors occur in the context of trauma or developmental delays, then PTSD and/or a developmental disorder must be considered for the primary diagnosis in order to drive effective treatment. Additionally, the primary behavioral and emotional concerns of many children in foster care are related to grief and attachment concerns that are not encompassed in *DSM–5* diagnoses, or their symptoms are trauma related but do not meet the full criteria for PTSD.

Table 6.1 presents examples of several common overlapping criteria that warrant close attention when diagnosing or reassessing clients.

Table 6.1 *Symptoms and Associated Diagnoses*

Common Symptoms	Potential Diagnoses	Potential Source
Difficulty paying attention; fidgety; often interrupts; trouble listening and following directions	Hyperarousal in PTSD ADHD Adjustment disorder	Trauma exposure Insecure attachment Anxiety related to grief
Irritability; not "caring"; argumentative; "incentives" don't seem to matter; quick to anger	Avoidance and negative cognitions in PTSD MDD ODD Adjustment disorder	Trauma exposure Despair, denial, and anger related to grief Insecure attachment Instable home and parenting
Abrupt mood changes; incongruent affect; confusing or aggressive behavior responses; does things "out of nowhere"	Re-experiencing in PTSD Mood disorder Adjustment disorder	Trauma exposure Insecure attachment

Please note that each of the symptoms listed could also indicate a possible neurological developmental disorder.

Diagnosing children in foster care can both drive meaningful change for the child and the child's family and can further disempower an already vulnerable, disenfranchised population. Sometimes therapists forget the great meaning that children and families give to the diagnoses given to them. Diagnoses become labels that the adults, peers, and the child can use for understanding and growth or for negative connotations and prescriptive judgment. Diagnosis has an important place in building understanding, advocating for needs, and coordinating treatment interventions. However, given the gravity and breadth of colors and shapes in a child's kaleidoscope, how can one or two mental health labels sum up the complicated catastrophe that is the child in foster care's reality? It is unrealistic and unproductive to place such weight on a diagnosis, but far too often that is exactly what is done. "He's ADHD and bipolar" should never be the primary descriptor for a child, whether to a judge, case manager, or prospective adoptive or foster parent.

When careful diagnosis is done with the child's encompassing story in full consideration, the therapist is then able to use the description of

CASE STUDY 6.1

Wayne spent 4 years receiving outpatient therapy and medication management for multiple diagnoses of ADHD, bipolar disorder, and ODD. When I received his case after his previous therapist left the agency, I was astounded by the years of steady attendance without progress. Sitting before me were an adoptive mother and a 13-year-old boy who were tired of trying to get the help they knew they needed. Within a few sessions of reviewing records and clarifying presenting problems and the history of their concerns, I completed a PTSD screening and observed the tenuous nature of their insecurely attached interactions. Wayne met the full criteria for PTSD related to witnessing domestic violence in a foster home and subsequently losing the placement and all contact with his primary attachment figure. I immediately shifted the direction of treatment to a combination of evidence-based trauma treatment and attachment interventions. Within 6 months, he was off of almost all of his medications with the psychiatrist's support and was suspension-free for the first time in his academic life.

the diagnosis to the child and family as an intervention to increase their understanding of the child and what that label means for effective treatment and support by all involved. Therapists should not give diagnoses that they cannot explain or educate both the child and parents on in a way that provides increased empathy and direction.

MEDICATION

Children in foster care are 2 to 3 times more likely to be prescribed psychotropic medication than are children who are not in care. Depending on the state of residence, anywhere from 14% to 50% of children in foster care are prescribed psychotropic medication (Abdelmalek, Adhikari, Koch, Diaz & Weintraub, 2011; Solchany, 2011). A study of youth in treatment foster care showed that 59% took psychotropic medications, with nearly two-thirds of those children taking two or more medications (Brenner, Southerland,

Burns, Wagner, & Farmer, 2014). About 5% of children in foster care across the country are prescribed three or more psychotropic medications (Rubin et al., 2012).

The most commonly prescribed psychotropic medications are, in order, atypical antipsychotics, stimulants, and antidepressants (Linares et al., 2013). Stimulant prescriptions are tied with high rates of ADHD, antidepressants with depression, and atypical antipsychotics with their "off-label" uses for a number of emotional and behavioral concerns, including behaviors related to ADHD, anxiety, mood instability, depression, sleep difficulties, and eating disorders. Thus, this is by far the most prescribed category of medication for the foster care population (Rubin et al., 2012; Salahi & Diaz, 2011).

Antipsychotics were initially designed to treat schizophrenia and bipolar disorder. "Off label" indicates that the drugs are being used for purposes other than what they are approved for, meaning that the vast majority of children in foster care taking these medications are not diagnosed with either schizophrenia or bipolar disorder. Studies have found that not only are many youth in foster care being treated in this risky fashion, but the doses of these medications tend to be much higher than the maximum level approved by the Food and Drug Administration (FDA); in fact, youth in foster care have been found to be 9 times more likely than youth not in care to be prescribed medication for which there was no FDA-recommended dose (Abdelmalek et al., 2011). There are many known serious side effects of antipsychotic medications, such as altered metabolism, weight gain, increased risk of diabetes, tremors, muscle spasms, restlessness, and tardive dyskinesia (Solchany, 2011). To date, there have been no long-term safety studies for the prolonged use of antipsychotics in children (Abdelmalek et al., 2011).

Disturbingly, the use of psychotropic medications, particularly atypical antipsychotics, varies greatly across states (Rubin et al., 2012; Solchany, 2011). A foster child in one state may be 53 times more likely to be prescribed five or more psychotropic medications than if that child resided in another state (Abdelmalek et al., 2011)

An additional disturbing trend in psychotropic treatment of children in foster care involves the medicating of infants, toddlers, and preschoolers. For this most vulnerable age group, one study found that foster children were nearly twice as likely to be prescribed a psychiatric drug as compared with nonfoster children (Narendorf, Bertram, & McMillen, 2011).

CASE STUDY 6.2

I was once subpoenaed to testify as an expert witness and treatment therapist for multiple siblings in a large set during a termination trial in which the parents were charged with multiple counts of neglect, incest, and physical abuse. The children had each been carefully assessed, and all showed predominant symptoms of PTSD. My ability to educate the court about the nature of trauma and each of the specific criteria of the disorder in the context of the family offered substantial ground to a complicated and shaky case in which the children were in great danger of being returned to further harm. I was asked to speak to the differential diagnoses of psychosis, ADHD, and even ODD when the defense made efforts to undermine some of the children's testimony of the abuse by viewing the children as being in the midst of overactive and defiant delusion rather than pure terror and unfathomable hurt.

Lack of clear, consistent oversight of medicating this population; high rates of significant emotional and behavioral distress; and a sense of urgency to keep removed children calm and well behaved combine to create a sort of perfect storm of unsafely overmedicating this population. "Kids get aggressively diagnosed and sometimes we look for the easy solution, which is a pill over psychotherapy or better parenting" (Abdelmalek et al., 2011, p. 3).

When a child is inaccurately diagnosed, the child is at risk for being medicated unnecessarily. For example, many children in foster care spend years in therapy being treated with stimulants and behavior modification unsuccessfully because their identified symptoms are related to trauma. Careful diagnosing, especially around internalizing disorders related to symptoms of anxiety and depression, may decrease the demand for psychotropic medications (stimulant and atypical antipsychotics).

OVERCOMING BARRIERS TO ACCURATE DIAGNOSING

There are many significant barriers to providing accurate mental health diagnoses for youth in foster care. Therapists must anticipate these

CASE STUDY 6.3

I was working in a group home for emotionally impaired children as a clinical supervisor. One day, the team leader called me in a panic. A foster care agency had transferred a client into our group home but had given us little information on him. The 16-year-old White male, Rudy, came during the day when the other boys were at school. He was a tall young man with facial hair. I came into the cottage and found him watching *Rugrats* videos and dancing. He was wearing a long-sleeved dress shirt despite the warm weather and had trouble engaging in eye contact. When I examined his file, I discovered that he had been in foster care since the age of 4, at which time a case manager had decided he was not autistic because he "liked to get hugs." A psychiatric evaluation listed his diagnosis as a developmental delay, not otherwise specified, and his educational diagnosis was emotionally impaired. He had been in foster care with older foster parents for years but was removed after he became physically aggressive toward the foster mother. I was astounded. How could this child have been in foster care for so many years and clearly have been misdiagnosed by psychiatrists, educational professionals, and social work professionals? I arranged for him to have a neuropsychological exam in order to obtain an accurate diagnosis of autism, which he received. I could then work on getting him placed in a proper foster home with plans for long-term placement where he could stay once he reached adulthood.

barriers and be proactive in addressing them. Accurate diagnosing will always increase efficient and effective treatment, medication management, referrals, and advocacy, resulting in better outcomes for the stability, safety, and well-being of the child and family. Unknown, inaccurate, unavailable, and contradictory information regarding the child's history and course of presenting problems are the most significant barriers to accurate diagnosing.

The following are common barriers to gathering such information:

- Unavailable or uncooperative parents (birth or foster) who provide inaccurate information or withhold information

- Lack of records from schools and previous caregivers
- Inconsistent child welfare record keeping due to staff changes
- Child withholding information or providing inaccurate information

Additional barriers may be related and include time constraints, difficulty in gathering records, and absence of consents to release/obtain information about the client. Scheduling conflicts and transportation, although relatively trivial, can be challenging as well. Even with all of the time and resources in the world, barriers involving complex losses, safety concerns, and severe trust/fear issues can be the most difficult to navigate effectively.

Many youth in foster care are given multiple and changing diagnoses during their wardship. These changes may be due to emerging symptoms, progress in treatment, and changing dynamics in their placement or court case, which affect their mental health. However, changes in diagnosis may also be related to a change in the treatment provider responsible for diagnosing the child. Turnovers in staff and changes in the treatment agency due to replacement are the main causes for change in the child's assigned therapist. This can contribute to the change in diagnoses, whether moving toward more or less accuracy, and greatly influences the course of the child's treatment. Maintaining a consistent treatment provider throughout a child's placement has the potential to eliminate a significant number of barriers related to lack of, or inaccurate reporting of, mental health concerns and strengths.

Although it is clear that thorough and accurate information should be gathered from multiple sources, actually doing so can be daunting. Fortunately, treating a child in foster care means that therapists are one among several professionals working at the same task. Licensing, foster care, adoption, and protective services personnel have already gathered a vast amount of information about the child, the birth parents and home, allegations and substantiated abuse and/or neglect, schooling, and the foster parent and home. Therapists will benefit from building relationships and accessing records across these disciplines. Reviewing records and gathering current perspectives from both the client and caregivers will provide a rich and detailed account of the child's life thus far. Additional contact should include birth parents, previous placements, previous mental health providers, school personnel, and the primary physician. This clinical information must be shared with any treating psychiatrist in order to effectively advocate for the client

CASE STUDY 6.4

I received Casey's case as a transfer. At age 12, she had been in four different treatment facilities and six different schools and had recently been adopted by her aunt after staying in three different foster homes. Making sense of her case file was confusing, as it was full of contradictions. It seemed she had been given nearly every diagnosis possible for her age at one point in time or another. Her aunt's anger about the past and anxiety about her future minimized her ability to speak clearly to Casey's presenting concerns without rage and blame. If her aunt wasn't present in session, Casey still barely spoke. Even her current foster care worker avoided involvement, citing the pending dismissal of wardship due to adoption as grounds for her lack of participation.

and address any conflicting diagnosing with clarity to support collaborative, complementary treatment. Seeking out convergences as well as discrepancies in mental-health-related concerns across parties will aid in a clear case conceptualization, as further delving into the child's world can become overwhelming, even for a well-educated, emotionally stable therapist.

In terms of the necessary time commitment, treating a client in foster care is at least equal to two comparable cases in the general population due to the sheer amount of parties intricately involved in the child's life. It is difficult to "only do therapy" with this population for multiple reasons, the foremost being that the proverbial parent is not one but three or more separate and often discordant entities: birth family, foster and possibly adoptive family, and foster care worker. Additionally, substitute multiple residential or shelter staff for foster placement if applicable, and add additional caregivers if placement stability is an issue.

Advocate to limit the number of cases in foster care or overall caseload size when working as a therapist solely with this population. Document the range and significance of coordination and conferencing aside from direct contact with the client. Stability and consistency in supportive connections are key aspects of effective treatment with this population.

REFERENCES

Abdelmalek, M., Adhikari, B., Koch, S., Diaz, J., & Weinraub, C. (2011, November 30). *New study shows U.S. government fails to oversee treatment of foster children with mind-altering drugs.* Retrieved from http://abcnews.go.com/US/study-showsfoster-children-high-rates-prescription-psychiatric/story?id=15058380

American Psychiatric Association. (2013). *Diagnostic and statistical manual of mental disorders* (5th ed.). Washington, DC: Author.

Brenner, S. I., Southerland, D. G., Burns, B. J., Wagner, R., & Farmer, E. M. (2014). Use of psychotropic medications among youth in treatment in foster care. *Journal of Child and Family Studies, 23,* 666–674. doi:10.1007/s10826-013-9882-3

Cantos, A. L., & Gries, L. T. (2010). Therapy outcome with children in foster care: A longitudinal study. *Child and Adolescent Social Work Journal, 27,* 133–149.

Jensen-Doss, A., & Weisz, J. R. (2008). Diagnostic agreement predicts treatment process and foster care. *Pediatrics, 121,* e157–e163.

Levy, T. M., & Orlans, M. (1998). *Attachment, trauma, and healing: Understanding and treating attachment disorder in children and families.* Arlington, VA: CWLA Press.

Linares, L. O., Martinez-Martin, N., & Castellano, F. X. (2013, January). Stimulant and atypical antipsychotic medications for children placed in foster homes. *PLoS ONE 8*(1): e54152. doi:10.1371/journal.pone.0054152.

Narendorf, S. C., Bertram, J., & McMillen, J. C. (2011). Diagnosis and medication overload? A nurse review of the psychiatric histories of older youth in treatment foster care. *Child Welfare, 90*(3), 27–43.

Pidano, A. E., Kimmelblatt, C. A., & Neace, W. P. (2011). Behavioral health in the pediatric primary care setting: Needs, barriers, and implications for psychologists. *Psychological Services, 8*(3), 151–165. doi:10.1037/a0019535

Rubin, D., Matone, M., Huang, Y., DosReis, S., Feudtner, C., & Localio, R. (2012). Interstate variation in trends of psychotropic medication use among Medicaid-enrolled children in foster care. *Children and Youth Services Review, 34*(8), 1492–1499. doi:10.1016/j.childyouth.2012.04.006

Salahi, L., & Diaz, J. (2011, December 1). Antipsychotics for foster kids: *Most commonly prescribed meds.* Retrieved from http://abcnews.go.com/Health/Wellness/foster-children-commonly-prescribed-antipsychotics/story?id=15056937

Solchany, J. (2011). *Practice and policy brief: Psychotropic medication and children in foster care.* Retrieved from http://www.americanbar.org/content/dam/aba/administrative/child_law/PsychMed.authcheckdam.pdf

Zito, J. M., Safer, D. J., Sai, D., Gardner, J. F., Thomas, D., Coombes, P., . . . Mendez-Lewis, M. (2008). Psychotropic medication patterns among youth in foster care. *Pediatrics, 121*(1), e157-e163. doi:http://dx.doi.org/10.1542/peds/2007–0212

CHAPTER SEVEN

TREATING ATTACHMENT

In this chapter, we turn the kaleidoscope toward the way children view their relationship with adults. We review the basic underpinnings of attachment theory, discuss how attachment theory applies to children and families in the child welfare system, and provide specific treatment recommendations for working with children with attachment problems. This chapter is an overview and is not meant to provide all the information needed to provide attachment-focused treatment.

CASE STUDY 7.1

This first time I met Susan she appeared small for 7 years old. I picked her up to be placed in a new foster home, and she turned to the shelter staff and demanded her money. She put out her hand and stomped her foot. The shelter staff replied "You're not grown" and handed me the money in an envelope instead. Susan had been in foster care for a little over a year, and I became her foster care worker/therapist after her adoptive placement was disrupted. Susan had assaulted her 2-year-old brother, and they could no longer be placed together. Her initial placement occurred due to domestic violence in her home when she was 4 years old. Her mother's boyfriend assaulted her mother and broke Susan's arm during the assault. Susan never saw her mother again. Susan initially appeared friendly and charming, with a good vocabulary and adult-like demeanor. After her placement, I soon realized that she hated adults and found them to be mostly a nuisance. She rarely asked for help and appeared artificially friendly and polite but refused to follow house rules and insisted on making adult decisions. Attempts to engage her in traditional ways fell flat; she would not engage in play therapy and appeared disinterested in anything I had to offer. She met all the criteria for a child with an insecure attachment or even unattached, and I realized I had to get creative if I was going to reach her.

ATTACHMENT THEORY

Human beings are the most helpless of all animals at birth. Although born with some reflexes such as breathing and sucking, human infants are completely reliant on their caregivers for a longer period of time than are other mammals (Moriceau & Sullivan, 2005). From the onset of birth, the human infant's reliance on a caregiver to meet biological and emotional needs remains a central process to survival. Bowlby (1969), trained in a traditional psychoanalytic theoretical approach, developed attachment theory to explain how the infant instinctively strives to meet these emotional and physical needs and how these instinctive behaviors persist throughout human development.

Bowlby (1969) theorized that attachment behavior is instinctive and that human infants are preprogrammed to develop in a socially cooperative way. The child engages in a number of behavioral strategies for which proximity to the mother is the predicted and desired result. As the child strives to seek and maintain proximity to the caregiver, the child forms an attachment to the individual (Bowlby, 1988).

Bowlby (1988) theorized that attachment occurs as a central nervous system process, and the attachment behavior allows the child to eventually tolerate distance and inaccessibility through increasingly sophisticated methods of verbal and nonverbal communication. The behavior begins as a response to pain, fatigue, and fear, and is ultimately a survival response for protection from predators (Bowlby, 1988). In fact, when faced with a stranger, it is the actual physical distance from the primary caregiver rather than the caregiver's reaction to the strangers that leads to distress (Ainsworth, 1992). Attachment behavior includes, but is not limited to, crying, smiling, babbling, and, with the advent of increased verbal skills, calling to the caregiver. But any form of behavior that results in attaining or maintaining proximity to an individual who appears able to cope with the world and meet the child's needs is construed as attachment behavior (Bowlby, 1988). All these behaviors initiate with the ultimate goal of proximity to the caregiver and the meeting of needs.

Once activated, attachment behavior results in a systemic homeostatic relationship between infant and caregiver. As the caregiver responds to the attachment behavior, the infant's central nervous system marks the responses and maintains the behavior that proved most effective (Bowlby, 1988). Attachment then takes on biological, emotional, and cognitive components. The activation of the attachment system and resulting proximity with the primary caregiver leads the child to be able to tolerate distance and therefore begin exploration, which is necessary for cognitive growth. This concept is referred to as a secure base, a stable buoy that the child can rely on to alleviate fear and pain and therefore can venture into the world (Bowlby, 1988). This secure-base relationship depends on experience. The child becomes attuned to the responses of the caregiver and, as the child ages, the child incorporates new experiences into the attachment system (Waters, Hamilton, & Weinfield, 2000). The attachment system is a living system, constantly shifting and changing as the child ages and incorporates new life experiences that challenge the child's sense of safety.

In the ninth month of life, children develop object constancy, an emotional and cognitive process that allows the child to hold an image in her mind. The child holds the image of the parent in her mind, and if the parent is missing, the child searches for the parent. The child also develops an image of self, based on how the caregiver reacts to the child. If a secure attachment exists, the child holds the image of self as someone who is worthy of care and holds the image of the parent as someone who is kind and consistent. The child then develops a working model for all potential caregivers and peers as individuals who will meet expectations (Bowlby, 1969). Like attachment itself, these models also evolve over time as the child adjusts the attachment system to react to new environmental challenges (Waters et al., 2000). A child with a secure attachment system internalizes a model of others as responsive and caring and internalizes a model of self as worthy (Bowlby, 1988).

Infants with a secure attachment style receive tender and affectionate care from their caregivers, who also respond quickly to their cries (Ainsworth, 1992). A child with a secure attachment system knows that her needs will be met and can decrease the amount of proximity to the caregiver in order to feel safe (Bowlby, 1988). However, children with an insecure attachment style have no confidence that their attachment figures will be accessible and responsive when needed. The anxious-ambivalent child develops an attachment style that ensures the child close proximity to a caregiver in order to assure the parent's availability (Bowlby, 1973). Anxious-ambivalent children view their caregivers as rejecting, but the rejections are often intermittent and inconsistent. The children do experience some experiences of love from their parents and, as a result, their anxiety that rejection will occur again results in often hostile and angry interactions designed to force the caregiver into an interaction. Anxious-ambivalent children seek close proximity to the caregiver and protest loudly in the hope that needs will be met (Bowlby, 1980). Children classified as anxious avoidant have little confidence that when in need they will receive help, and as a result, they expect rejection (Bowlby, 1988). These children avoid their caregivers (while in the same room) and rarely demonstrate emotion when the caregivers attempt to engage. This strategy allows the child to maintain proximity to the caregiver while ensuring that rejection does not occur (Bowlby, 1973).

Disorganized attachment occurs when the child cannot develop a specific attachment system with a caregiver and as a result does not respond to a caregiver in a consistent manner. These children may appear either avoidant, ambivalent, or closed off, or respond with a complete inability to tolerate stress (Main & Cassidy, 1988). Disorganized attachment often occurs due to multiple inconsistent caregivers, neglect, trauma suffered by the infant or mother, or abuse.

Although each attachment system exists on a continuum, the styles become entrenched in a cycle of interaction that perpetuates the attachment (Bowlby, 1988). This perpetuation appears to continue beyond infancy and has a profound effect on human development (Sroufe, 1988). Children who enter foster care usually exhibit some type of insecure attachment style or develop one as a result of ongoing placements.

How Attachment Impacts Development

Although attachment is the first developmental task of human beings, the process of attachment continues throughout the life span (Sroufe, 1988). Bowlby's theory predicts that secure base use and attachment styles are significantly stable across time and yet are open to change in light of significant attachment-related experiences (Waters, Merrick, Treboux, Crowell, & Alberersheim, 2000). "The idea of working models means both that such models are active constructions forged over time and they are subject to change" (Sroufe, 1988, p. 22). Therefore, attachment patterns appear to be a fundamentally living system, both enduring and always changing.

As the infant grows, the working model of attachment may become firmer but with the understanding that the child begins to take more control over her environment and relationship choices (Sroufe, 1988). As the child begins to choose how she attaches to others, the child becomes an active force in her own development and an active force in maintaining or adjusting her attachment system. Therefore, children with a secure attachment system move toward their developmental tasks with the ability to explore their environment and the belief that they can adapt to new situations (Sroufe, 1988). However, they move toward these goals with the reality that the attachment system can change due to any internal or external factor.

Attachment variations act as the conduit for development, and although attachment has a strong predictive value, later factors, including environment and the changes in the attachment relationship, affect development as well (Sroufe, 2002). Attachment can be seen as the foundation of developmental adaptation, and each subsequent developmental stage builds on the child's ability to adapt to the developmental changes that lay ahead (Erickson, Sroufe, & Egeland, 1985). The construct of attachment has been established as a dynamic phenomenon. As attachment models evolve with the primary caregiver, the nature of attachment theory is that the attachment process may also apply to other significant relationships in the life of a child. This fact is an important consideration for therapists when working with attachment issues in children and families. The child may develop a different kind of attachment system with a foster parent or therapist than the child uses with her parent, and each attachment system requires attention.

Early primary relationships predict major domains of later adaptation better than any other assessments from infancy (Sroufe, 2002). The attachment system helps the infant learn to successfully express and modulate affect, which allows the child to successfully engage other adults and peers as the child ages. Expressed affect also plays a significant role in the early cognitive development of toddlers, because expressed affect is an important part of sustaining fantasy play—a primary developmental task of young children (Sroufe, Schork, Motti, Lawroski, & Lafrenier, 1984). Children use fantasy to play out later relationships and begin the task of social problem solving (Erikson, 1950). Children who demonstrate avoidant attachment behavior have less skill at expressing affect, incorporate fewer themes about people in their fantasy play, and use more negative solutions to interpersonal conflict than do securely attached children (Sroufe, 1988; Weinfield, Ogawa, & Sroufe, 1997). The reality that attachment styles begin impacting cognitive development at such an early stage of development further emphasizes their importance (Sroufe,

2002). These patterns grow and adjust as the child ages. The child brings new attachment experiences to bear on old patterns, which are played out through fantasy. The ability of the child to explore, create themes, exert control, and adapt to new caregivers is essential for successful preschool negotiation (Spivak & Shure, 1974).

When attachment results in maladaptation and insecurity, the result could include difficulties with impulse control, aggression, and prolonged emotional dependency (Erickson et al., 1985). Children assessed as being insecurely attached at 12 and 18 months appear to have more behavioral problems, including noncompliance, bullying, fighting, and poor social skills when they enter preschool (Erickson et al., 1985). These behaviors are often seen in children in foster care and may be directly related to their attachment style. Secure attachment has been linked to positive school adjustment (Granot & Mayseless, 2001) and the ability to demonstrate more effective emotional regulation (Sroufe, 2002). Insecure attachment may also result in later childhood anxiety disorders, because the constant vigilance required to maintain the attachment system results in sustained levels of anxiety (Warren, Huston, Egeland, & Sroufe, 1997). Infant attachment assessments are also related to adolescent social competence (Englund, Levy, Hyson, & Sroufe, 2000), and the quality of attachment in infancy and early childhood (12–40 months) is a significant predictor of high school success or dropout rate (Jimerson, Egeland, Sroufe, & Carlson, 2000).

Attachment and Cognitive/Social Skill Development

Because the attachment process is the primary process of mother–child communication, logically, attachment is the primary cognitive process (Bowlby, 1969). A child with a secure base would theoretically have a caregiver who encourages exploration and therefore challenges the child (Bowlby, 1988). A child with a secure base, having learned to successfully adapt to the changing environment due to consistent caregiving, would also be better able to adapt to the cognitive challenges. Insecure children could develop cognitive difficulties because their anxiety about the attachment relationship prevents exploration, which in turn prevents cognitive growth (Jacobsen, Edelstein, & Hofmann, 1994). This process also relates to social competence. Secure attachment in infancy leads to positive social expectations because the child learns the basics of reciprocity:

If you give, you get in return (Elicker, Englund, & Sroufe, 1992). Similarly, a securely attached child develops a sense of self-worth and efficacy through the history of responsive care. A securely attached child believes that engaging with peers will be rewarding and that mastering the challenge of engaging with others is feasible. The secure child attains skills that promote successful interactive play from the initial relationship with the caregiver and, as a result, is capable of effective regulation of emotions (Sroufe et al., 1984). All these skills result in social competence (Sroufe et al., 1984).

A child with adequate social competence should be able to express a clear and appropriate range of affect, tolerate disappointments, and modulate affect in serving the goal of sustained positive interaction (Sroufe et al., 1984). Insecure attachment styles make achieving social competence more difficult. A child with a disorganized attachment system is at risk for developing poor relationships, viewing herself as powerless, and viewing peers as a potential threat (Jacobvitz & Haven, 1999). The importance of social competence for childhood development is profound. Children assessed as having poor social skills engage in more behavioral problems, demonstrate more learning difficulties, and have an overall more difficult time navigating developmental milestones (Sroufe, 1988).

Think of attachment as a child having a plug and the caregiver providing the outlet and energy. Children need to be plugged in to feel safe, and, in a secure attachment, they sequentially develop an extension cord and then eventually can tolerate being unplugged longer and longer; they are able to manage on their own, knowing they can plug back in when needed. Children with an insecure attachment cannot handle being unplugged and use the extension cord throughout their lives to ensure they feel safe.

ASSESSMENT

The first step to assessing the foster care child's attachment style should begin with observation. If possible, watch how the child interacts with her birth mother, foster parent, and other adults. Also watch how the child chooses to engage with you. There are several tools that help diagnose attachment styles, but most are for very young children or adults.

Children in foster care with attachment disorders may also receive a diagnosis of reactive attachment disorder according to code 313.89 in the

Diagnostic and Statistical Manual of Mental Disorders (5th ed.; *DSM–5*; American Psychiatric Association [APA], 2013). For this disorder, categorized under trauma- and stressor-related disorders, the *DSM–5* lists seven criteria a child must meet for the diagnosis. The *DSM–5* lists these criteria on page 265, but in general the criteria include behavior consistent with an avoidant or disorganized attachment style. These behaviors include avoiding the caregiver, not seeking adult support when stressed, a history of emotional neglect, and multiple inconsistent caregivers. According to the *DSM–5*, the disorder is rare (APA, 2013), but therapists working with this population will see that many children in foster care may receive this diagnosis. However, like any diagnosis, labeling comes with negative stigma, which might make adults less open to engaging with the child. Using the term *insecurely attached* might better serve the client. Children labeled as having a reactive attachment disorder might be viewed through a lens of pathology when improving an attachment system would alleviate their behavior.

Insecure Attachment Behaviors

Behaviors that indicate attachment problems vary according to the type of insecurity and the age of the child (see Table 7.1). Physically abused children may appear anxious-avoidant, whereas neglected children appear anxious-ambivalent (Finzi, Cohen, Sapir, & Weizman, 2000). In very young children, concerning behavior would include showing no preference for a particular adult and showing little distress when the adult leaves. Children may appear impulsive and hostile and may even verbally or physically attack the caregiver.

    Insecurely attached children might also be clingy and demand constant reassurance from adults. These children engage by refusing to let

Table 7.1 *Attachment Styles and Typical Behaviors*

Secure Attachment	Insecure Attachment	Reactive Attachment
• Tolerates separation • Links consequence to behavior • Expects consistency • Minimal anxiety when near caregiver	• Angry/rejecting • Clingy and demanding • Links consequence with rejection from caregiver • Impulsive and anxious	• Uninterested in adults • Artificially friendly • Rage/destructive behavior

CASE STUDY 7.2

The most obvious example of anxious-ambivalent attachment I have witnessed occurred during an observation I conducted of a 2-year-old child. I worked as a clinical supervisor in an agency that provided residential housing for adolescent mothers and their babies. In an attempt to keep families together, the mothers received therapy, support, and daycare. One 15-year-old mother had a history of verbal and physical abuse with her 2-year-old daughter. Staff witnessed her slapping the child in the face or yelling at her quite often. My boss asked me to conduct an observation of the child without her mother to determine her therapy needs. I came to see her during playtime. She sat on the floor playing with a large play vacuum cleaner. I asked to join her and she allowed me to play with her, which I did for an hour. I gave her a 10-minute, then 5-minute warning that I had to leave. She protested and told me I had to stay. I stood up to leave and she charged me with the vacuum cleaner, slamming the toy into my legs. She then had a temper tantrum as I left the room. This child clearly experienced rage at being left and handled the abandonment with anger and a violent outburst. Her attachment pattern with her mother had taught her that violence is a successful tool to get her needs met.

go of the caregiver or demanding attention often and expressing anger or rejection when rebuffed. For example, the child might follow adults around and ask for help with everything, and when the adult says, "You can do it yourself," the response is "I knew you thought I was stupid." This child attempts to engage the attachment system by demanding that the adult reassure her constantly, which usually leads to rejection.

In cases of disorganized or unattached children, a therapist might see a child who appears artificially friendly. This type of child portrays the emotion she thinks the adult wants to see, but the responses are not genuine and the child wants to be left alone.

Remember that attachment is related to anxiety. Children are fearful that their needs will not be met. The anxiety manifests itself in impulsivity, anger, rage, or avoidance.

CASE STUDY 7.3

Bobby was 10 when he entered foster care, and he displayed a classic anxious-ambivalent attachment. He would cling to his mother during visits, forcing her to pull him off her. He would ask at every therapy session "What are you getting me for my birthday?" even when his birthday was several months away. He engaged adults by screaming at them, and when scolded he responded, "I knew you didn't like me." Any adult who engaged with this child found his behavior off-putting and would push him away or scold him in order to decrease his behavior. The scolding never worked. Bobby had poor insight into the reasons for his anxiety-induced behaviors, and the adult attempts to change his behavior just further ingrained his belief that no one wanted him.

TREATING ATTACHMENT DISORDERS

Treating children in foster care with attachment disorders is challenging and emotional work because their behavior often triggers feelings of anger and disappointment in adults. Remember the reason children comply: because they want to please an adult they deem trustworthy and caring. Children with attachment disorders do not have this history and, as a result, struggle with building quality relationships (see Exhibit 7.1).

Consider what reaction a child refusing to follow directions will cause. Adults in general become angry when a child disobeys or refuses to follow a directive. This anger can lead the therapist to become parental, giving orders and threatening punishments. Remember that the therapist is not the parent. Although setting boundaries in the session is appropriate and necessary, therapy should not be a place for rules and orders.

EXHIBIT 7.1

The point of attachment treatment is to give the client a reparative therapeutic experience. Give the client the relational experiences she normally does not receive in order to reorganize the attachment system.

Table 7.2 *Effective Versus Ineffective Ways to Engage*

Effective	Ineffective
• Validate experience • Empathize • Focus on who the child is as a person • Respond to the meaning behind the behavior or action	• Ask questions about school and behavior • Respond with anger to behavior • Minimize anxiety ("You don't mean that" or "It'll be alright")

Parenting the child instead of conducting therapy causes problems for two reasons: First, it eliminates the necessary observational data the therapist needs in order to know the child's worldview, and second, it makes building rapport difficult and shuts the child down. Table 7.2 lists effective and ineffective engagement methods.

Therapists should know their own attachment styles and what types of behaviors cause them to become angry or respond in a nontherapeutic way. Identifying countertransference is a key aspect of providing quality treatment, because the child is usually entrenched in her attachment system and will be reluctant to let it go. Begin with the basics: building a quality relationship with your client.

CASE STUDY 7.4

Allen, an African American male, came to treatment at the age of 6 because of impulsive behavior in his foster home. He was the youngest of three children, all removed for neglect, and he displayed anxious-avoidant behavior. He ran from new adults and appeared impulsive and shut down. At the time, I worked in an old warehouse, with offices running along the outside of the building. The inner part of the building was a circle-like track with doors to close off sections. During Allen's first visit to therapy, he refused to talk to me. He began running around the office, refusing to obey his foster parent or any other adults with commands to stop. He laughed as he ran, but it was clear he did not want to come to therapy. I went into my office and pulled out a Slinky, then sat in the waiting room and played with it as he ran by. The foster parent took him home after 15 minutes of running, but when we tried again

(continued)

CASE STUDY 7.4   *(continued)*

at the next appointment, I sat in the waiting room again with my Slinky. He sat next to me and asked to play with it. I told him he could play with it in the room, but not if he ran around. He played for a few minutes, then put it down and began running again. On his third visit he came in asking to play with the Slinky. I told him we only play with the Slinky in the therapy room and that he had to come to the room to play with it. He could stay as long as he wanted and play and leave when he felt ready. He followed me to the therapy office, we kept the door open, and he played with the Slinky for 10 minutes and then left. By the fourth session he willingly came to the therapy room, allowed the door to be closed, and engaged in treatment. Sometimes we would take the Slinky to a staircase and watch it walk. This process took a lot of patience and ego strength. I worried what my peers and the foster parent thought about my inability to get him into the room. I worried if my intervention would ever work. Eventually the intervention worked, and Allen no longer needed to avoid adults because he witnessed an adult being consistent and caring.

Attend to Attachment Concerns

In the example in Case Study 7.4, the child feared being alone with a stranger, and although encouraged by his foster parent to attend treatment, he initially refused. Remember that insecurely attached children come to treatment fearful, full of anxiety, and displaying behaviors that do not immediately appear to be attachment related. A child who runs in and out of treatment might appear hyperactive rather than fearful that his caregiver will leave. An avoidant child might appear resistant or oppositional by sitting in a corner and refusing to talk, rather than afraid of trying to connect with another adult. Attend to the fear, notice it, and respect it. Validate the child's feelings and actively engage in action that helps calm the child. That might mean allowing a caregiver in session, shortening the session to what the child can tolerate, or encouraging the child to bring a toy or object into treatment.

CASE STUDY 7.5

Rhonda came to my agency to obtain psychological testing. She was 6 years old and had been in foster care for most of her life with different foster parents. Her mother had physically abused her, and her current foster parent planned to adopt her but remained concerned about her behavior. She appeared emotionless and cold but would also be destructive in the foster home. The testing room had a large window facing the parking lot of the agency. Halfway through testing, Rhonda heard a car drive out of the parking lot. She turned her head and calmly stated, "My mother just left me." I was struck by her lack of emotion. She made the statement again but did not cry or try to leave the room. She sat calmly looking at me with blank eyes. I stood up and told her to follow me. We walked to the waiting room to see her mother, and I stated, "Rhonda was concerned you left."

She stated, "Of course I didn't leave. I'm waiting for you."

Rhonda relaxed her body and returned to the testing room. Her lack of distress appeared to indicate that she didn't care about being left behind, but clearly she did.

Play Therapy

Children with attachment issues benefit from play therapy by being able to act out and work through the anger and fear of rejection. A therapist should choose toys that allow the child to represent her attachment patterns and work through them. Dolls are useful for attachment treatment. Ensure the dolls represent the child's ethnicity and that dolls appear to be of varying ages. For example, give the child access to a baby doll, toddler dolls, young children dolls, adolescent dolls, parent dolls, and grandparent dolls. Dolls should represent whomever the child wants them to, for example, a teacher or a clergy member. A dollhouse with separate rooms and furniture should also be in the room.

Other types of toys that help children work through attachment concerns include toys that represent nurturing. Play food, play baby bottles, play pots and pans, and a play stove or microwave oven allow the

CASE STUDY 7.6

Kevin, a 6-year-old Hispanic boy, had been cleared to go home to his mother, but the court wanted a treatment recommendation, so I was asked to meet with him for an attachment assessment. He came into the play therapy room and picked up a plastic dinosaur and proceeded to roar. As I watched him create a story about his worldview, he picked up another smaller dinosaur and told a story out loud about getting lost in a cave. The little dinosaur was scared but liked the adventure. Kevin then said, "Oh, it's time to go home." He moved the dinosaur to the dollhouse with the larger dinosaur and had the large dinosaur give the smaller one some dinner and milk, read him a story, and tuck him into bed. By using toys, Kevin was able to show me that he could go out and play, have an adventure, and trust that when he came home he would be safe. This information would never have come out had I questioned him about his home life, but the toys allowed him to show me how he saw his world. I didn't recommend further treatment.

child to represent nurturing through food play. Puppets or play animals that represent scary animals (a dragon or a wolf) or safe animals (a turtle or a kitten) also allow the child to process attachment issues through the puppets. A dragon, for example, allows the child to express anger safely, and the turtle allows the child to hide when needed. Any other tool that allows the child freedom of expression works as well, such as art supplies, a water tray, or a sand tray that allows children to bury items (which allows for the expression of anxiety).

Ego Strength Development

The following intervention involves helping the child view herself as strong and important. Allow the child to always take the lead in play and ask to follow. For example, when a child chooses to draw, ask to copy the child's art, stating, "I like what you are drawing; can I draw what you are drawing?" Ask the child for direction on what colors to choose, how large to draw an item, or how long to draw for (Pickover, 2010). This intervention takes the relationship back to the beginning of building attachment patterns. In normal secure attachment development, a primary caregiver claps or smiles when the infant smiles or coos, increasing the strength of the attachment. Sending a message to a child that how she draws or the decisions she makes is valuable mimics this process, creating the building blocks of a new attachment pattern.

CREATING NEW ATTACHMENT PATTERNS

Use a developmental approach to help a child create and maintain a secure attachment pattern. Keep in mind that attachment begins in infancy, so focusing on basic needs and object permanence will help the child begin to develop different working models. The goal of treatment should be to build new working models of attachment with the therapist, the foster or adoptive parent, and the birth parent. Going back to basics by focusing on nurturing, such as sharing a small meal with the child or reading a story, begins building new patterns. Insecurely attached children may feel as if their voice does not matter. Therapy should focus on giving the child a voice, an ability to express the voice, and consistent affirmations of strengths.

Restructuring the Attachment System

Once a safe, consistent relationship has been established, treating attachment issues needs to focus on restructuring the attachment system. Once a child has developed an insecure or disorganized pattern, the pattern becomes entrenched, and the child engages with all adults as if the adult is the original attachment object. The child engages in statements or behaviors designed to receive an attachment response that the child expects. A child expecting rejection will demand attention and expect the adult to administer a punishment. The child might cling to the leg of the adult or demand constant reassurance. When the adult becomes exhausted by the constant requests, the adult often pushes the child away, either literally or with words ("Stop bothering me!"). The child expects this response and uses the adult response as confirmation of the need to further engage in the insecure attachment behavior.

It will help to practice alternative responses to statements or behavior designed to elicit rejection or avoidance. The most effective responses do not display emotion when confronted with the behavior. Use a matter-of-fact tone and increase emotional responses to appropriate attachment behavior. One method is to respond to the meaning behind the statement rather than the statement itself. For example, if a child frequently states, "You hate me; I know you hate me," this statement is not literal but is fueled by the child's fear and anxiety of not being "plugged in." The insecurely attached child uses this statement as a way to engage the adult and eventually get needs met. The statement often results in an engagement of reassurance that does little to quell the child's anxiety. When the adult responds, "No I don't; you know I don't," the child often keeps stating, "Yes you do; you just say that you don't," and the cycle feeds into the destructive insecure attachment because that is the response the child expects and does not believe. Instead, try responding to the meaning behind the statement with empathy, such as by saying, "It makes you mad when you think I don't like you." This statement disrupts the entrenched attachment pattern in two ways: It gives the child an alternative response she has to adapt to, and it lets the child know her feelings are valid.

Similarly, if a child tries to destroy an item in the therapy room, state, "It seems like you are really mad at me. You have a right to be mad at me, but it hurts my feelings when someone destroys something I care

CASE STUDY 7.7

Tom, an 8-year-old biracial boy in care for physical abuse, often came into sessions angry and oppositional. He liked to throw items at me and make demands. I would state, "You can be angry and throw things, but you cannot throw things at me." A few weeks later in session, he wanted to play checkers and then stood up and ordered me to "clean it up!" I felt my inner parenting instinct rise, but I knew this behavior spoke to his anxious-ambivalent attachment style. He expected rejection and punishment.

I stayed calm and said, "In here, if you want something cleaned up you have to do it yourself."

He stared at me for a moment, confused that I didn't yell at him or comply, and said again, "Clean it up!"

I then stated, "In here, you have control. You can move the game or leave it there." He cleaned up the game.

about." We have discussed earlier the dangers to crossing the line from therapist to parent. However, insecurely attached children act out their attachment patterns in sessions, and the behavior can be difficult to tolerate. Avoid focusing on the child's behavior in the session. Remember that insecurely attached children do not view consequences as a normal part of adult interaction; instead, they view it as rejection. Set safe boundaries that focus on allowing the child freedom of expression while ensuring everyone's safety.

Another useful tool for reorganizing attachment patterns involves using a distraction to help the child disengage the attachment system. Once the child begins engaging in the insecure attachment behavior, begin another activity alone to see if the child will engage. In the case study of Allen presented earlier (Case Study 7.4), this technique was used to help an avoidant child disengage from insecure behavior. Other techniques include blowing up and popping balloons, drawing, building with Legos, and playing with a sand tray while not responding to the attachment behavior.

Transitional Objects

Transitional objects address the attachment process occurring during the development of object permanence. When an infant is 12 to 18 months old, the child can hold an image of the caregiver in her mind, which allows her to tolerate separation. Using transitional objects with older children with insecure or disorganized attachment builds on this process. The object represents the safe, consistent adult, and the child can view a visual representation of the attachment figure. A transitional object could be as simple as a photo of the therapist (or parent) that the child can carry. Giving a child an object that requires the parent to return it, such as an old credit card or keys, also sends a message of trust.

Transitional objects also help concretize the idea of self and other. By using a toy as a conduit between the attachment figure and the child, the child can begin to build a working model of attachment that focuses on safety rather than fear. For example, children in foster care often struggle with the transitions of going back and forth between foster home and birth home or foster home and visits. The attachment systems are disrupted on a regular basis, which results in fear and anxiety. Using a transitional object to help the child cope creates a link between the child and

CASE STUDY 7.8

Francine, a 4-year-old biracial (Hispanic and Asian) girl, came into foster care after experiencing neglect, physical abuse, and sexual abuse from her parents and her parents' peers. She would fade into the background during therapy, fearful to be noncompliant and never demanding attention. Her avoidant behavior included sitting in corners in the foster home or hiding in her room. Once, she stood up and said, "I want to leave!" but when I told her that she could, she sat back down, seemingly fearful that I would be angry with her.

To help Francine build her ego strength and develop a secure attachment style, I asked her to draw with me. She took scissors and cut strips out of paper then colored the strips. One day during therapy, she went over to my purse and put a strip of paper in my wallet. I knew she was making an attempt at establishing a new attachment pattern. I stated, "This way every time I open my wallet, I can think about Francine. I will wonder what she is doing all week and know when I see her she will tell me about her week!"

From that day forward, every time I came to her home to conduct therapy, she went straight to my wallet and opened it to view the strip of paper. I always reassured her that she mattered, that she was important, and that I thought about her all week. This intervention helped her build a new sense of self. She was someone who was important to me and was remembered throughout the week. She could tolerate separation and knew I would return with proof of her existence.

the attachment figure. For example, use a child's favorite stuffed toy as the object. When the child leaves the foster home, ask the foster parent to talk to the toy out loud. The foster parent may state, for example, "You watch Susie closely during her visit. I cannot wait for you to tell me how good the visit was." The child then attends the visit and the birth parent picks up the toy and makes a similar statement and gives a report: "Now you be sure to tell Susie's foster mom how good she was during this visit and watch over her until I can see her again. You report back to me next week how she did all week." The birth parent hands the toy back to the child to keep. This technique creates a bridge between the two attachment figures and lets the child know that each attachment figure thinks about her throughout the week. She only has to look at the toy to remember the exchange. The toy acts as the working model of secure attachment, allowing the child to hold in her head the idea that her care-givers think about her and she matters to them.

Building Quality Relationships With Unattached Children

Sometimes all the efforts to build a quality relationship fail and the child remains entrenched in the attachment pattern. Children with reactive at-tachment disorder are particularly challenging because they do not try to elicit rejection or cling to adults; they do not want to engage at all. Thera-pists working with these children need strategies aimed at increasing the child's desire to engage with adults. Choose an activity the child enjoys and needs adult interaction to engage in—for example, painting with acrylic paints or cooking a complicated meal that requires adult help.

A child might refuse to see adults as useful or resist engaging in a positive relationship for a variety of reasons. When a child does not want to engage with the therapist, the therapist must find some ways to demon-strate the benefits of developing a positive relationship. Case Studies 7.9 and 7.10 illustrate two different ways to engage particularly oppositional children, neither of whom wanted to be bothered with adults.

CASE STUDY 7.9

Adele, a 6-year-old African American child in care for physical and sexual abuse, displayed behaviors of anxious-avoidant and disorganized attachment styles. She never wanted to play with me and always demanded to play a game that allowed her to win. Week after week we played Candyland, and, using my theoretical orientation that she should have control over the game, she would take one token, move it to the end, and announce, "I win."

This play continued for weeks, and I became perplexed about how to move her forward. She wasn't playing with me and was not building a relationship. She used the game to distance herself from

(continued)

CASE STUDY 7.9 (*continued*)

me and maintain avoidance. I decided to try a simple experiment. When she won again I said, "It's no fun for me to play when I don't have a chance to win." My goal with this intervention was to help her see me as another person in the room with feelings. This intervention did not move her.

Then I decided to try an incentive. I told her we would play two games. For the first game she could make the rules as she always did, but for the second game I would make the rules, and if she followed them, she would earn a sticker.

We played her way first. She won. Then we played by the rules of the game. She won again, and when I gave her the sticker she said, "I win and I get sticker?"

"Yes," I replied. "You followed the rules."

This intervention allowed her to see a benefit in building a relationship with me. I was an adult who was consistent and followed through on my promises, and she did not need to beat me in order to win.

CASE STUDY 7.10

This case study continues the story of Susan, described at the start of this chapter in Case Study 7.1, who suffered from reactive attachment. She did not express a need for adults and did not want to engage in treatment. She found adults useless and would not seek any type of interaction unless she had a specific need, such as wanting money. All my interventions failed. She did not want to play games, she did not want to use a transitional object, and she did not want to engage in play. After struggling for several sessions, I remembered a training I had attended several years prior. The trainer recommended using origami as a way to build attachment. I began the intervention as a way to try to engage her in something

(*continued*)

CASE STUDY 7.10   (*continued*)

but later discovered the power of this type of play. Using a book of easy origami and some brightly colored paper, Susan and I would learn how to make a water bomb or a jumping frog. I had never tried origami and purposely made error after error, stating, "I cannot figure this out."

Susan would state, "I got it," and I would ask, "You did?" and watch her closely for help. I would then promise to go home and practice the steps.

Each week I would come back having learned a new step, and she would watch me and then teach me a new step. Together we created many paper animals but also created a relationship.

This intervention had several components. First was to engage the child in an activity that requires a step-by-step process. Susan learned that she couldn't jump ahead and get the desired result, and the consistency helped her begin to view the world as less chaotic and more structured. The second component was creating the need for a relationship with an adult. She wanted to know how to make the animals, and, because we worked together, she could tolerate asking me for my help. I allowed her to see an adult as vulnerable and imperfect. Finally, the origami also acted as a transitional object; it ensured her knowing that I thought about her during the week and requiring her to think about me.

CONCLUSION

Most of the children who enter foster care have developed some type of insecure attachment pattern. These patterns become further complicated by frequent foster home moves, transitioning back and forth to birth parents, and building relationships with a constant stream of caseworkers, therapists, and staff, all of which leave the child with few coping skills. Relationships are the foundation of human development. Without the ability to unplug long enough to learn and grow, the child may stay stuck. By helping the child create a positive working model of self and other, the therapist moves the child's kaleidoscope toward a new view of the world.

REFERENCES

Ainsworth, M. D. S. (1992). A consideration of social referencing in the context of attachment theory and research. In S. Feinman (Ed.), *Social referencing and social construction of reality in infancy* (pp. 349–367). New York, NY: Plenum Press.

American Psychiatric Association. (2013). *Diagnostic and statistical manual of mental disorders* (5th ed.). Washington, DC: Author.

Bowlby, J. (1969). *Attachment and loss: Volume I*. New York, NY: Basic Books.

Bowlby, J. (1973). *Attachment and loss: Volume II*. New York, NY: Basic Books.

Bowlby, J. (1980). *Attachment and loss: Volume III*. New York, NY: Basic Books.

Bowlby, J. (1988). *A secure base*. New York, NY: Basic Books.

Elicker, J., Englund, M., & Sroufe, L.A. (1992). Predicting peer competence and peer relationships in childhood from early parent-child relationships. In R. D. Parke & G. W. Ladd (Eds.), *Family-peer relationships: Modes of linkage* (pp. 77–106). Hillsdale, NJ: Lawrence Erlbaum Associates.

Englund, M. M., Levy, A. K., Hyson, D. M., & Sroufe, L. A. (2000). Adolescent social competence: Effectiveness in a group setting. *Child Development, 71,* 1049–1060.

Erikson, E. H. (1950). *Childhood in society*. New York, NY: W.W. Norton & Company.

Erickson, M. F., Sroufe, L. A., & Egeland, B. (1985). The relationship between quality of attachment and behavior problems in preschool in a high-risk sample. *Monographs of the Society for Research in Child Development, 50,* 147–166.

Finzi, R., Cohen, O., Sapir, Y., & Weizman, A. (2000). Attachment styles in maltreated children: A comparative study. *Child Psychiatry and Human Development, 31*(2), 113–128. doi:10.1023/A:1001944509409

Granot, D., & Mayseless, O. (2001). Attachment security and adjustment to school in middle childhood. *International Journal of Behavioral Development, 25,* 530–541.

Jacobsen, T., Edelstein, W., & Hofmann, V. (1994). A longitudinal study of the relation between representations of attachment in childhood and cognitive functioning in childhood and adolescence. *Developmental Psychology, 30,* 112–124.

Jacobvitz, D., & Hazen, N. (1999). Developmental pathways from infant disorganization to childhood peer relationships. In J. Solomon & C. George (Eds.), *Attachment disorganization* (pp. 127–159). New York, NY: Guilford Press.

Jimerson, S., Egeland, B., Sroufe, L. A., & Carlson, B. (2000). A prospective longitudinal study of high school dropouts examining multiple predictors across development. *Society for the Study of School Psychology, 38,* 525–549.

Main, M., & Cassidy, J. (1988). Categories of response to reunion with the parent at age 6: Predictable from infant attachment classifications and stable over 1 month period. *Developmental Psychology, 24,* 415–426.

Moriceau, S., & Sullivan, R. M. (2005). Neurobiology of infant attachment. *Developmental Psychobiology, 47,* 230–242.

Pickover, S. (2010). Multilevel timeline; racecar identification; client mirror. In S. Degges-White & N. Davis (Eds.), *Integrating the expressive arts into theory-based counseling practices* (pp. 39–40, 171–199). New York, NY: Springer Publisher Company.

Spivak, G., & Shure, M. B. (1974). *Social adjustment of young children.* San Francisco, CA: Jossey Bass.

Sroufe, L. A. (1988). The role of infant-caregiver attachment in development. In J. Belsy & T. Nezworski (Eds.), *Clinical implications of attachment* (pp. 18–38). Hillsdale, NJ: Lawrence Erlbaum Associates.

Sroufe, L. A. (2002). From infant attachment to promotion of adolescent autonomy: Prospective, longitudinal data on the role of parents in development. In J. G. Borkowski, S. Landesman, et al. (Eds.), *Parenting and the child's world: Influences on academic intellectual, and social-emotional development* (pp. 187–202). Mahwah, NJ: Lawrence Erlbaum Associates.

Sroufe, L. A., Schork, E., Motti, F., Lawroski, N., & Lafreniere, F. (1984). The role of affect in social competence. In C. E. Izard, J. Kagan, & R. B. Zajonc (Eds.), *Emotions, cognition, and behavior* (pp. 289–313). New York, NY: Cambridge University Press.

Warren, S. L., Huston, L., Egeland, B., & Sroufe, L. A. (1997). Child and adolescent anxiety disorders and early attachment. *Journal of the American Academy of Child & Adolescent Psychiatry, 36,* 637–644.

Waters, E., Hamilton, C. E., & Weinfield, N. S. (2000). The stability of attachment security from infancy to adolescence and early adulthood: General introduction. *Child Development, 71,* 678–683.

Waters, E., Merrick, S., Treboux, D., Crowell, J., & Albersheim, L. (2000). Attachment security in infancy and early adulthood: A twenty-year longitudinal study. *Child Development, 71,* 684–689.

Weinfield, N. S., Ogawa, J. R., & Sroufe, L. A. (1997). Early attachment as a pathway to adolescent peer competence. *Journal of Research on Adolescence, 7,* 241–265.

CHAPTER EIGHT

TREATMENT FOR LOSS AND TRANSITIONS

Transitions and loss are hallmarks of being in foster care. The more transitions and losses a child experiences, the more shapes there will be in the kaleidoscopic view. The more confusing and crisis-driven they are, the brighter the colors. For some children, there will not be any space between the figures because of the sheer volume of placements, replacements, predicaments, and losses. Shaking the kaleidoscope may hardly result in a sound.

Whether packed or loose, the kaleidoscopic view will include at least two transitions for every child: the initial removal and either reunification or adoption. Additional transitions include any replacements to foster homes, shelters, or residential treatment centers; separation from siblings; adoptions and disrupted adoptions; termination of parental rights; reunification; moving from foster care to independent living; and aging out of the system as a ward of the state. Some of these transitions will be planned and others will be abrupt. Crises such as self-harm or harm of others, additional exposure to neglect or abuse, and losses of loved ones often result in transitions as well, making the move more complex and often painful.

With every transition, children in care lose more and more. Although *family members* and *home* are their primary losses, additional losses may include contact with important *people*, such as relatives, neighbors, friends, and school staff; treasured *possessions*, such as bedding, toys, gifts, books, photos, and electronic devices; familiar *places*, such as their room, yard, neighborhood, and school; and family, spiritual, and community *traditions*, such as holiday and birthday celebrations, music, dancing, cooking, and even bathing and bedtime routines (Gregory & Phillips, 1997). Even with temporary removals, the jarring lack of familiar places, faces, routines, and things means that the children have not lost only their families, but also the environmental contexts of their lives and loved ones. This profound loss of control increases children's anxiety levels dramatically (Eagle, 1994; Goldman, 2004).

This chapter outlines therapeutic approaches aimed at understanding and empowering clients in their efforts to grieve losses and survive transitions in child welfare, as well as increasing the therapist's ability to offer specific treatment interventions in preparation of and during transitions and losses to minimize reactivity and need for crisis management.

TREATING CHILDHOOD GRIEF WITHIN FOSTER CARE

A majority of the losses that children in care go through are confusing and ambiguous, meaning that children know that their parents and homes still exist but have no control over their access to them. The separation is temporary but may feel and become permanent at any time. The sadness of grieving is shrouded in anxiety. Histories of maltreatment and current stressors may leave children without the ego strength, cognitive abilities, and emotional aptitude to be able to face even simple losses directly. "Normal" childhood grieving processes are typically not applicable to this population. Their grieving gets stuck and remains unresolved, similar to being "frozen" in trauma (Boss, 2006; Schoen, Burgoyne, & Schoen, 2004; Webb, 2003). Avoidance and denial of grief may account for many of the flat affects and lack of expressed "care" about seeing loved ones in children in care (Eagle, 1994).

Unfortunately, being in the child welfare system does not offer opportunities to grieve in healthy ways due to the lack of stability and empathic regard from, and nonexistence of, mourning rituals (e.g., funeral, going-away party) that offer permission and support for coping with a multitude of losses (Eagle, 1994). Instead, the system often focuses on expecting children to be grateful, quickly move on, and be unrealistically adaptable to having their lives turned upside down. Healthy grieving for these children may not occur until well after they have permanency, even into their adulthood. Nevertheless, despite these complications and barriers, there are many ways therapists can provide impactful grief-specific interventions to children in care.

Effective interventions to support healthy grieving in children in care include facilitating, witnessing, and validating the child's expression of grief; providing psychoeducation to normalize the experience of grief and child welfare; and fostering opportunities for children to connect with their losses. Although group therapy can be advantageous to help normalize feelings and relieve isolation, individual therapy is the ideal primary intervention for complicated grieving because it offers the client much-needed, in-depth, one-on-one attention that can follow the child's pace (Baggerly & Elkadi-Abugideiri, 2010; Webb, 2003). Caregiver involvement is necessary, and sibling therapy can be a major asset to treatment of grief, especially when addressing concerns around belonging, lost connections, and placement instability (Gnaulati, 2002; Goldman, 2004).

Facilitate the Expression of Grief: Witness and Validate

Make therapy a place where the child can safely express any emotion and feel understood without being judged. For example, foster children often have very ambivalent feelings about their birth parents and being separated from them. Research about children in care's long-term separations shows that effective grief interventions must respond directly to the child's "inner world" (Eagle, 1994). A strong, open therapeutic relationship with child-friendly interventions must exist in order for clients to share their inner worlds with the therapist.

Engage young children in nondirective, creative, and playful interactions to foster their sense of control and support their freedom to share on their terms (Kolos, 2009; Webb, 2006). Children often meaningfully play, draw, write, or sing thoughts and feelings that they cannot or will not talk directly about (Coholic, Lougheed, & Cadell, 2009; Goldman, 2004). Have toys such as dollhouses, puppets, figurines, and play food easily accessible in the office, and encourage clients to interact with what they like. While children play, follow their lead and name or reflect and normalize expressed feelings, strengths, and examples of resilience, such as courage, problem solving, and the will to survive (Baggerly & Elkadi-Abugideiri, 2010).

For example, a young boy removed from his mother after she abandoned him in a car while on drugs refuses to talk to the therapist and other adults but engages easily with the dollhouse and figurines. Despite the many behavior concerns that jeopardize his placement, the therapist makes time in each session to allow him to just play. He repeatedly engages in "hide and seek," in which every time the seeker finds who is hidden, the hiders "disappear" again. The therapist watches with interest and reflects only what is being shown by saying things like, "Oh where did he go again?" or "I keep trying and trying to find him! Ah, there he is!" The boy periodically "destroys" the whole house and then carefully replaces all the furniture to repeat the sequence again. The therapist responds with "Boom! Crash! It's all getting messed up now!" and then, "And now it gets put back together. You know where to put each thing." This boy did not have the language or emotional ability to explain his confusion, desperation, or rage about the abandonment and separation, but he worked through it very clearly with his play.

Giving children a safe and reflective space to release emotions, start to make sense of these complicated emotions, and practice "resolving" the story can help increase self-regulation and decrease many behavior concerns. Another example is a set of school-aged sisters who love performing their favorite songs in session but have trouble directly talking or even drawing about their many replacements, current instability, and troubling past. The therapist encourages their singing and reflects on the strength of their voices and ability to express a range of feelings in the songs they like. Gradually, they start making up their own songs that describe their own feelings of pain, confusion, anger, and hope about missing their father, being separated from their other siblings, and trying to make sense of their parent missing visits and not "getting them back" when Dad promised he would.

With older children and teens, simply listen to their stories, identify their losses, and validate their reactions (Boss, 2010). Allow the child to share without interjecting or correcting misinformation about what's happened. Avoid statements and gestures geared toward providing comfort, such as "It'll get better" or "It's going to be okay." These are incongruent with the child's experiences and derived from the therapist's need for the child to be okay as soon as possible. More relevant "comfort responses" involve active listening, reflection, and affirmation of the difficulties the child is facing. For example, make statements such as "It's horrible to wonder where you will wake up tomorrow," or "I wonder if you are tired of people expecting you to change and handle all of this so well." Also identify their resilience and personal strengths by making statements such as "It takes a lot of courage and strength to go through everything you've been through and still get up in the morning."

Find creative ways to encourage clients to let distressing feelings come out rather than burying them deep inside. For example, have them imagine being given a deli sandwich that they didn't really want so they

CASE STUDY 8.1

One 9-year-old girl I worked with was getting better and better at compartmentalizing her feelings of disappointment and heartache after week upon week of her mom not showing up for visits. She kept an upbeat attitude most of the time but started to "lose it" at school and home with explosive arguments and crying spells. In session, when I described some kids in care having "buried feelings" that they were afraid to pay attention to because they would be too hard to feel, she made a large paper collage showing a mound of "buried feelings" underneath the earth. She used the piece of art to identify and open up about the feelings. She sought and received comfort from others more easily, especially on visit days. Eventually she declared that she had "let all the buried feelings out" and had gotten the hang of how to "not bury them." Of course, she was right. There were no more aggressive or emotional outbursts, and when she did finally see her mom, she candidly told her how awful it felt to miss her and asked about the reasons for her absence.

decide to put it in their closet. The sandwich may be "out of sight, out of mind" at first, but with time the sandwich will become even more unwanted when it starts to smell up the whole house. Ask them to choose whether they would rather take care of it when they were first given the sandwich or after it becomes a moldy, rotten mess. Have them draw different parts of the sandwich and label them with the feelings that are the hardest for them to face.

Provide Psychoeducation About Grief and Child Welfare

Educating about what a loss is and how it affects children from a developmental perspective within their cultural contexts can normalize, provide comfort, and de-pathologize the strong, confusing feelings that grieving children and their caregivers struggle with (Boss, 2006). Start by helping clients to simply name their losses and identify which is hardest for them. One way to do this is to have a list available of the common

CASE STUDY 8.2

When providing a training for staff and foster parents on childhood grief and trauma, I used the comparison of an adult losing a loved one in death to a child's experience of being removed from her parent with no control over when she might see the parent again. I asked participants to remember how it felt to have others tell them, "It will be okay. You'll see them again one day," or "At least you still have your [insert name of other living loved one]."

One staff member, who was known for being especially calm and patient with children, responded with dismay, "I never thought about it this way. Those are the exact types of things I say to kids every week after their visits. I thought it would comfort them, but now I get why it doesn't. I hated it when people gave me that advice after my mom died. It made me feel worse."

losses that children in care face (noted at the beginning of this chapter), and ask clients to indicate which bother them the most.

It's important to know that children typically grieve in sporadic, unexpected bursts, often accompanied by somatic complaints (Boss, 2006; D'Antonio, 2011). Help caregivers understand how different grief is for children as compared with the more linear way adults grieve. With children, use metaphors such as a crashing wave or flash thunderstorm to normalize how powerful and overwhelming grief can feel at times and also how those out-of-control feelings will always come and go. Have clients draw pictures of their own grief "waves" or "storms."

Also give caregivers information about developmental differences in children's expression of grief to build empathy and support the use of effective coping skills (Goldman, 2004; Webb, 2003). Children under age 5 are still learning object permanence and will tend to repeatedly ask confusing, contradictory questions as well as latch on more quickly to the foster parent because they are more in need of a stable adult presence (D'Antonio, 2011). School-aged children tend to become more preoccupied with the reasons for the separation and what other bad things might happen to them and their loved ones (Goldman, 2004). Adolescents tend to be more focused on themselves and what will happen to them because of the loss. Their heightened insecurity will exacerbate their conflicting needs for personal control and support from adults. Depression, fighting, and risky behaviors are common in grieving teens (Baggerly & Elkadi-Abugideiri, 2010). Major losses experienced in early stages of development tend to reemerge as a child reaches a new developmental stage. Remind caregivers that their understanding and patience with the grieving child's behavior does have a positive impact on the client even if it does not seem so, especially for the younger child (D'Antonio, 2011; Eagle, 1994; Schoen et al., 2004).

Teach both children and caregivers Kübler-Ross's five stages of grief: despair, anger, denial, blaming, and acceptance (Kübler-Ross & Kessler, 2005). Add a sixth reaction of anxiety or fear because of the ambiguous and often traumatic nature of the losses experienced by children in care. Write these out on paper and invite clients to indicate which they experience and to what degree with lines, checks, or circles. Revisit this visual description of their grief and make changes as their feelings change with time. Updating this grief "tally" will help clients see how acknowledged and expressed grief feelings tend to decrease with time. Also share stories and read books about what it is like for children go through losses in and be in foster care, such as *Maybe Days* (Wilgocki & Wright, 2002), *Kids Need to Be Safe* (Nelson, 2006), and *Don't Despair on Thursdays* (Moser, 1996) (D'Antonio, 2011).

Perhaps surprisingly, many children in care do not have a clear understanding of how the child welfare system works. When helping clients to grieve losses and preparing clients for major transitions, it will help to give or review factual information about protective services, definitions of abuse and/or neglect, visitation progression, adoption, and termination of parental rights in order to help them make sense of the transition, reinforce the value of their safety, and correct misconceptions to alleviate shame or blame. For example, in preparation for termination and adoption, explain the basic sequence of being in foster care: (a) parents abuse/neglect their children, (b) the child goes to live with a temporary family while parents get help and follow the judge's orders, and (c) either the parents do what they were asked and the child goes back home to them or the parents do not change and the child lives with another family—either the one the child has been staying with or a new one. Remember that clients may or may not have a realistic understanding of what their parents did or did not do that resulted in their removal.

Engage in Mourning Rituals

Find ways to connect children to what they have lost rather than focusing only on dealing with the present. This may seem counterintuitive when adjustment to the foster home and misbehavior are primary treatment concerns. However, research indicates that children who feel respected and supported in their birth-parent relationship, through simply sharing memories and having concrete meaningful objects that represent that connection, are more likely to form positive relationships with foster parents as well as reconcile with the positive aspects of their past (Eagle, 1994; Goldman, 2004).

CASE STUDY 8.3

Max was 6 when his case was transferred to me. He did not act out or cause a lot of trouble in his adoptive home, but his parents believed he was troubled based on his restrictive affect and minimal engagement at home and with peers. Building rapport was like pulling teeth. His "inner world" was strongly protected; so strong, in fact, it appeared he did not even feel the need to lash out at others when they tried to get close. He just didn't respond. I gathered information about his past and found out he had grown up as the youngest of six brothers but had been separated from all of them after their relative placement had failed. I brought them up in session, and although he didn't say much, his face showed that they were important to him. Neither his workers nor adoptive parents had much information about his brothers and how he could get in contact with them. I spent some time looking through his old records and found photographs of him and several of his brothers that were over a year old. I showed them to him and offered to copy the images to create a family photo album. Max continued to be as serious and nonexpressive as ever, but I watched his rapt attention and care for every detail of this project. When he brought it out to show his adoptive parents, they started to tear up. Later the father explained that in over a year, he had never seen his son's face light up in the way it did when he shared the book with them. Beyond accessing Max's need to feel connected to his lost family members, the intervention also enhanced the bonding connection between him and his adoptive parents.

CASE STUDY 8.4

I was preparing 12-year-old Elise to be reunified with her birth mother outside of the country because her mother had been deported while Elise was in foster care. I engaged her in creating a quilt made of felt. She decorated each square to represent different parts of her life, including foster family members, memories of her birth family in this country, related mixed feelings, and favorite activities. She carried the quilt on the plane with her as both an expressive artwork of healing as well as a transitional object of comfort.

In session, encourage clients to identify the specific memories or features of their loved ones and places that they miss, such as their favorite bedtime song, family cookouts, or a prayer that their mom used to sing (Boss, 2006). Invite clients to decorate a container, make a memory album, or write poetry to honor their losses. Shoeboxes or stapled copy paper can be decorated with paint, cloth, writing, pictures, or magazine photos to represent anything that the child associates with the loss. Children may want to write down certain memories. Others may choose less concrete associations, such as a piece of blue cloth that "just reminds her of her mom." The pieces of artwork become transitional objects, and the practice of using art-making in meaningful and safe ways becomes a healthy coping skill to deal with transitions and grief (Betts, 2003).

Transitional objects can also be possessions and can be developed by caregivers as well. Blankets or stuffed animals are common transitional objects for infants and toddlers. Photos, storybooks, keepsakes, jewelry, clothing items, and household décor can have great meaning for older children (Kolos, 2009). Ask birth parents to come to sessions to share positive memories together and bring in photographs or meaningful items from the home, such as a piece of clothing or home décor (e.g., blanket, jewelry) for the client to keep. Be sure to ask the foster parents to acknowledge and support the child's connecting items. For example, a birth mom brought a young girl a dirty, used stuffed animal during a visit. The foster mom saw that the gift was meaningful to the child and offered to care for the toy in a loving, respectful way rather than discarding the toy, telling the child the gift was disgusting, or offering to buy the child a "better" toy. Therapists can also encourage foster parents to help children prepare for transitions and anticipate grieving the loss of the foster home. One foster mother who was preparing her foster daughter for transition into an adoptive home put together a keepsake box with photos of the child's time at her home and the foster mom's favorite mug, stating that every time the child drank out of it she would remember how much she was loved at their home. Children also tend to identify transitional objects on their own. For example, one young girl kept taking her foster father's socks from the laundry and stashing them in her possessions. When asked, the child explained that she wasn't sure if she'd have a dad at her next placement so she wanted to have daddy socks with her wherever she went. Therapists must notice and support such actions.

Children's expression of grief is also greatly impacted by family, community, cultural, religious, and spiritual contexts, each of which can

CASE STUDY 8.5

Stella was 11 when she started therapy but in social-emotional development she was closer to 6. She was very guarded, and I often observed her giving up when trying to explain herself to adults. I knew she had been removed due to neglect and that her mother did not visit regularly. I noticed her eyes light up when her foster mother mentioned trying to get her and her younger brothers together for a visit even if the mom didn't show. I invited her to tell me about her brothers, which led to her gradually sharing more memories of her life before foster care. She worked on a memory box decorated with dozens of small buttons and images that represented stories about her life before coming into care. Some memories were simple, such as the friendly dog her neighbors had, whereas others were painful, such as her mother's inebriation. I was surprised by her attention to detail and focus for multiple sessions because she was often described as careless and as having a poor attention span. Gradually, her foster mom described observing Stella's confidence growing, along with increased ability to open up instead of shut down. For Stella, revisiting the past allowed her to live more fully in her present during both her time in care and throughout her reunification in a new home with her sober parent.

offer cues for meaningful rituals, supports, and sources of strength and comfort for grieving children (Baggerly & Elkadi-Abugideiri, 2010; Gregory & Phillips, 1997). For example, a child may experience significant relief after his foster parent takes him to a church service or fishing spot similar to those he frequented before removal.

Part of grieving the losses related to the initial removal involves helping children make sense of who they are, where they came from, and how they belong (Eagle, 1994). Many children struggle with their lack of cultural and family belongingness when separated long term from their birth families or when the birth family was lacking in their sense of identity (Gregory & Phillips, 1997). For example, a child who never had a strong bond with her birth parents and frequently moved from home to home may struggle to make positive connections to her past. Through encouraging her to share positive memories of her past, the client recalls visiting a community center one summer where she reveled in learning sign language from a teacher who took an interest in her. Taking up sign language classes again or volunteering with the deaf may be deeply beneficial for her.

CASE STUDY 8.6

Frank came into care following the death of his mother. The youngest of a large sibling set, the family woke up one day to find their mother dead on the sofa from breast cancer. Their mother had refused treatment and had not informed her children of her illness. The family had no funeral or ritual after the death, and the family split apart, with three siblings placed in foster care and the older siblings left to fend for themselves. To help him process his grief I would state, "Your mother might want to know that you are sad, but you are going to be okay as well."

Frank imagined his mother in the sky, and, with direction, he drew a picture of his mother in the sky watching him cry, then eventually a picture of his mother watching him dribble a ball happily. Then, with the help of his older siblings, family members took the pictures to a park, tied them to balloons, and sent them to their mother.

COLLABORATION AND INTERVENTIONS
THROUGH TRANSITIONS

The following section describes ways to work collaboratively with families and professionals through transitions and interventions specific to major transitions. Throughout treatment, always proactively keep abreast of court and placement updates. When there is a change of permanency plans or the client is replaced, get as clear information as possible from adults before seeing the client. Do not place the responsibility of disclosing information on the child. Through all transitions, advocate to both caregivers and professionals for maintaining familiar social, educational, and community supports for the client (Gregory & Phillips, 1997). For example, if a child has problems at school, identify what types of support were helpful in past schools to drive the search for new supports, and advocate for the continuation of any individualized education plan (IEP).

Beyond the natural benefits of engaging relevant professionals, research shows that simply involving both birth and foster parents in mental health treatment will reduce the number of transitions for children in care (Collado & Levine, 2007). Also, by showing each family member respect and positive regard throughout treatment, the client will be more comfortable and receptive of grief interventions (Schoen et al., 2004).

Many clients going through transitions discontinue or change mental health service providers for a variety of reasons. Regardless, give clear mental health treatment recommendations to both parents and professionals for individual treatment, family therapy, and parent training. Participate in meetings in which the client's mental health diagnosis and treatment are reviewed with the next caregiver, whether birth, foster, or adoptive.

Initial Removal

Whether treatment begins immediately after removal or years into placement, therapists can help clients by giving them opportunities to tell the story of their initial removal using drawing, play, or writing to share what they remember (see Exhibit 8.1). Remember that the initial removal may have been experienced as more traumatic than the abuse or neglect that

EXHIBIT 8.1

I have seen countless drawings from children showing their initial removal by the police or protective services. The perspectives and details of these memories vary from child to child. What is consistent is their vivid recollection of the timing, images, and sounds, and profound feelings of alarm, fear, worry, blame, anger, and sadness. The most surprising part of this intervention for me is that more often than not, the children state that I was the first person to ask about this pivotal moment of their lives.

occurred beforehand. Children are taught to stay away from strangers for their safety, but placement in foster care expects them to immediately rely on strangers for their every need.

Replacement

The average child in foster care has three replacements (U.S. General Accounting Office, 2003). All replacements warrant therapeutic attention, regardless of the cause or how well the child appears to be coping. Changes in caregivers will affect the child's attachment patterns. Changes in home, school, and community will result in additional losses. Abrupt changes may lead to trauma reactions and developmental regressions. The client's reactions to each replacement impact case conceptualization and treatment focus moving forward.

Some clients may know in advance if they are being replaced. During these sessions of "waiting," help the client gain as much objective, concrete information as possible about the future placement—pictures, descriptions, rules, and so forth—to help decrease anxiety. Also help clients with making their good-byes. These normal, healthy rituals when moving are often overlooked for this population. For example, a boy had to abruptly leave his fifth-grade class due to a change in foster placement. He had thrived in that class and didn't get a chance to say good-bye. His therapist helped him write and mail a card in session saying good-bye and that he would miss and remember them always, an activity that provided him closure, feelings of relief, and increased readiness for the next school.

Many children in care are unclear about the details or reasons for the replacement, sometimes due to simply not being told or to being unable to accept or comprehend the information given. Regardless of the reason, children will tend to perceive the responsibility or blame for transition with themselves due to their egocentrism. Oftentimes, foster parents and workers alike also inappropriately blame the child, even if it was the parent who made an error. Helping children explore their sense of responsibility is pivotal in being able to help them move past it. When the transition occurs due to the child's behaviors, reframe the transition to focus on sharing the responsibility of safety between both children and adults. For example, say, "Adults are in charge of keeping children safe. Some adults have a hard time doing this. Some children have trouble making safe decisions. Children need adults who can be safe and help keep them safe no matter what." Provide constant reassurance both directly and indirectly that the client is not to blame for the separation and losses (D'Antonio, 2011).

Many of the clients' "behavior problems" during replacements are their ways of coping with an age-inappropriate level of distress and barrage of uncomfortable feelings while their primary support system is in flux. In treatment, target the behaviors that are causing the most problems, such as aggression or night wandering, and start modeling, teaching, and practicing alternative ways to deal with the underlying stressors or feelings. Reframe less harmful concerns to emphasize the child's strength and value. For example, recognize hardheadedness as tenacity and perseverance. When therapists help parents and clients see their strengths, it validates their intrinsic efforts to survive and frees them up to expand their potential and try new coping skills. In addition to engaging the client in coping skills development, direct caregivers to model coping skills, point out effective coping strategies in shows, or give personal examples of coping strategies. For example, a parent might say, "Did you see when [insert name of TV character] had to go to a new school? She was so nervous. But then she made a new friend and liked her teacher. The new school was different but not all bad" or "I sure miss my brother Andre—he moved out of state and I don't get to see him very often. I keep his picture right on my dresser and smile when I see it."

Reunification

Working with a client throughout reunification is a significant part of treatment. The therapist's role will chiefly focus on preparing the child and both birth and foster parents for the transition by providing psychoeducation about the process, grieving anticipated losses, reinforcing safety skills, and supporting readjustment based on family strengths and connectedness.

With the birth family, create a family portrait, collage, shield, or flag to represent their strengths, hopes, and sense of identity. Identify, normalize, and process lingering blame, guilt, or anger with clients and in family therapy if trained to do so. Encourage foster and birth families to create clear expectations and plans around future contact. In anticipation of losses, encourage foster families to create transitional objects based on meaningful items or activities in their homes rather than buying something new. For example, one foster father gave his foster son his own first baseball glove to take with him, as baseball was a primary way that the two bonded. Regardless of the changes the birth parent has made, engage the family in safety planning, specifically around the past maltreatment.

CASE STUDY 8.7

I worked with two middle-school-aged sisters for almost 2 years before they were reunited with their mom, who had a history of domestic violence and neglecting her children. The court had already reunified several of their younger siblings with their father whom the sisters did not share. They came into care as a family of eight and were leaving as a family of three. Regardless, both girls couldn't wait. Neither had adjusted well to multiple placements. Per my request, they came to two family sessions before they moved back in with their mom. I asked them to create a poster of a family shield by directing them to choose four characteristics of their family that would help keep them strong and safe together, which they worked on excitedly and seriously. The family returned to therapy once after reunification and proudly described hanging the poster in their new home. After that, Mom ended up not following through with my recommendation to continue counseling to help with the transition, but in many ways I understood that for her it was better

(continued)

CASE STUDY 8.7 *(continued)*

that way. The case had been full of tension, and my office was in the same building where the visits had been and where the child welfare staff worked. This family needed to move on from this very challenging chapter of their lives. I believe that the manner in which I supported this family in our final sessions—reinforcing their bond and power to care for themselves—did help them in the transition and also increased their likelihood of reaching out for more help in the future if needed, even though treatment did not end the way I wished.

Termination of Parental Rights

There are few treatment issues more challenging than working with a child through the termination of his parent's rights. Preparing a child for the termination of parental rights is not unlike the way one prepares a child for the death of a sick parent; it involves profound and lasting grief. Depending on the child's developmental age, this loss may be deeply internalized as the child's fault, or the child may be unable to understand or accept the loss and its terms. Other children may describe anticipating termination decisions because they long for finality to the separation, whether or not they wanted to go back. Work individually, with siblings, and with parents during interventions focused on termination (Gnaulati, 2002).

If termination appears imminent, begin preparation by explaining or reviewing the foster care process, including the potential outcomes. Provide caveats of children whose parents had their rights terminated. Next, support the child in personalizing the information and expressing related feelings. Never "correct" or minimize the child's responses. Some children will readily relate to their own foster care experience by making statements such as "Well, my momma's going to get me back," "It doesn't matter; when I'm 18 I'm going back with my mom," or "I never want to go back." Respond with reflective statements to both clarify and validate the client's feelings, such as, "It sounds like that's your wish—you just want to be back with your family." Engage children in making timelines of their own lives so far, with "alternate endings" for their future that show the possible outcomes of the court's decisions.

If the client is not able or willing to reflect on her own family's case, focus on exploration of feelings around the different outcomes in nonpersonal ways. For example, say, "I wonder what it's like for kids who can't go back to their parents?" or "Can you draw what kids would feel like if they were told they had to stay with their foster families or get new families instead of going back home?" If these invitations are still too threatening for a child, go ahead and name or draw emotional responses in the context of another child or even oneself. For example, say, "I knew a boy named Ethan who was told he couldn't go back to his mom. He was so mad—as mad as a giant volcano exploding this [gesture] big all over everyone and everything," or "I think my heart would feel like it was breaking into a hundred million pieces if I knew I couldn't see my mom again."

Although there is no one prescriptive best-practice way to give the child the news when parental rights have been terminated, delivery must be based on the individual child's worldview at that time, especially the child's knowledge and expectations about the parent's ability to "get the child back." Common features of delivery include (a) maximizing the child's sense of psychological safety; (b) communicating in a clear and developmentally appropriate manner; (c) validating and accepting all reactions; and (d) remaining calm, in control, and supportive.

Plan and rehearse what will be shared and by whom. One strategy is to have the foster care worker objectively deliver the court's decision and then have the therapist offer emotional support. Practice the delivery with each other. Even the most compassionate adult can get anxious and use wording that will be confusing or damaging to the client. Choose a time to meet that will not pull the client immediately back into responsibilities, such as before school, and block out a larger portion of time for the session. This extra time may not be needed, but its availability can prove beneficial. Choose a space that is familiar and comfortable to the child. Avoid having many breakable items around. Do have space, a place to sit, pillows and blankets, favorite snacks and drinks, along with familiar toys and art materials. If the child has other adults whom she feels close to, such as a foster parent, relative, or godparent, ask these adult supports to be available.

After the news is shared, simply validate and support the child's verbal and nonverbal reactions. Focus on being with the child rather than "intervening." Follow the child's lead and do not force the child to choose or engage in any activities. If the child seems stuck or does not say or do anything, wait with the child for a while, keeping yourself close

CASE STUDY 8.8

Tamia was my first client whose parents had lost their rights in court. When I started working with her, she was 13 years old, had recently been adopted after being in a few different foster homes, struggled with "anger issues," and didn't apply herself at school. Toward the beginning of treatment, I asked Tamia if we could create a timeline of her life so far to help me get to know her and all that she had been through. She described living through multiple traumas, losses, and replacements, but she identified the day she was told that her parents' rights were terminated as the most influential of her life. She vividly recounted details of the room and worker who delivered the news. She described reacting with a combination of complete dissociation and an uncontainable outburst of energy with which she completely destroyed everything around her that she could get her hands on, while the worker just stood by. When I first heard this, I instantly passed judgment on that worker for not comforting or keeping the child or space safe. Years later, after working with many other kids in foster care, I realized that what that worker did was one of the best things she could have done for that child at the time. By allowing Tamia to feel and express her rage, fear, and sorrow in that moment rather than suppressing it, Tamia was able to release so much that otherwise would have been stored in her mind and body for years and years to come.

and available but not intrusive. Remember that a child's lack of response may be related to the child's survival skills. Gently encourage the child to breathe. Offer suggestions to move around, use available art materials, write, or play with toys however the child chooses.

Once the judge orders termination, children may or may not be allowed a final visit with their parents. Unless there are current safety concerns, strongly advocate with the workers and court for a final visit in the form of a therapeutic visit. Carefully plan the final session with each member of the birth family. Help them identify specific hopes and goals for the visit. Focus on making this last point of contact one of both meaningful and positive connection. Similar to a memorial service or family reunion, plan on sharing food or music that is special to

CASE STUDY 8.9

I worked with 6-year-old Kaden for 2 years across three different foster placements after he and his sister came into care due to neglect stemming from their mother's mental health concerns and substance abuse. His mother's visits were inconsistent, and she was often under the influence when she came. I engaged their mom in family therapy during brief periods of sobriety, but her phone numbers and addresses kept changing. Eventually, the foster care worker let me know that the permanency plan had changed to adoption after 2 years without consistent progress. I started introducing the concept to Kaden in therapy, explaining the court process and the possibilities of what might happen next. We drew pictures of the judge, talked about child protection laws, and made a timeline of important events in his life. We talked about his life being like a book or a movie: full of both good and bad parts, with him still being in the middle of it and not knowing how it would end. He drew several different future timelines to show termination, reunification, and adoption.

When the judge terminated the parental rights, the worker and I agreed to tell Kaden together and practiced what we would say. In the next session, we gave Kaden the news as planned, and he responded by describing how his mom had a hard time doing a good job feeding, cleaning, and getting them to school, so he understood why the judge made that decision. We mostly listened and answered Kaden's few questions about what would happen next. Kaden vacillated between choking back tears, engaging in comforting self-talk, and expressing anxiety about his and their family's future. I responded with validation, normalization, and empathic regard.

We came up with a plan for their final visit, including favorite snacks and making pillows for one another so they would always have something to hold, because they were "a very huggy family." I called their mom to share Kaden's plan and encouraged her to acknowledge the court's decision and make their last contact a positive memory for her children. She was unsure and overwhelmed but also receptive. I contacted his sister's therapist to include them as well.

(continued)

CASE STUDY 8.9   *(continued)*

When the day arrived, the siblings eagerly shared their prepared snacks and cards. They hugged and cried together. I taped up a big poster on the wall and asked them to take turns writing down things they wanted each other to always remember. They filled up the whole page with memories, messages of love, and life advice. They decorated their pillows. I took pictures of the family and printed out copies for each of them; I also copied the poster's messages and gave a copy to each of them.

After about 90 minutes, all the plans for the session were completed and both the kids and their mom were ready to end the session. They hugged and kissed good-bye; clutched their dolls, messages, and photos; and went their three separate ways.

I worked with Kaden's foster mom closely in anticipation of emotional and behavioral reactions, but there were none. He continued to thrive in school, beg to get a new video game, and argue with his foster sister.

Within 6 months, Kaden smoothly transitioned to an adoptive home. He remained comfortable speaking of his mother and reflecting fondly on positive memories. He knew his mom had made mistakes, that he was not to blame for his family's separation, that his mother loved him no matter what, and that he was going to be adopted by another family that loved him and would do their best to take care of him, and that was enough for him.

the family. Encourage taking and sharing photos with one another and writing cards that express their love, hopes, and any apologies or regrets they might have. Especially with younger children, offer to create a transitional object in session together if the family members do not already have something in mind. For example, decorate pillows or blankets with fabric markers or make a handprint collage or family portrait with paint or drawing materials. Make sure each family member leaves with a copy of whatever is created jointly. Another idea is to make a family emblem or decorate a shield or flag to represent the family's identity. Remember that the family has experienced great pain, and although they are being pulled apart legally, they will always be connected to one another.

When preparing with the parents, encourage them to directly talk about the termination with their children. This will support children's grieving process by offering another level of finality. Empathically direct parents to explain the court's decision in a simple, straightforward manner, such as by saying, "The judge decided that I cannot take care of you anymore. This means that you are going to stay with another family. I want you to know that wherever you live, I love you and always will." Discourage parents from using this last point of contact to review their mistakes, blame others, or make their children feel guilty for being a part of a different family. Avoid allowing the parents' voices and emotions to overshadow the child's (Webb, 2003). It is never a bad thing for parents to cry in front of grieving children; however, parents must explain the reason for their tears and take the opportunity to remind the children that crying and sadness are okay to show when you can't be with the people you love (D'Antonio, 2011). Always stay in the session and interrupt or end it quickly if the parents' interactions become unsafe or inappropriate. If the parent is unavailable or unwilling to participate in a final visit, then proceed by engaging the child with the same interventions as described previously with only the child or with the child and any siblings.

Adoption

Start preparing clients for adoption and termination of parental rights at the same time. For example, when creating a past and future timeline, make "adoption" be one possible path their lives might take. Some children may identify multiple adoption paths with different potential parents. Have clients speculate what it will be like to have a new adoptive family and home. Common concerns for children may include whether or not they can take their possessions with them; go to the same school, church, or activities; and continue to see foster family members and birth siblings. They may also wonder about what will happen and what to do if they decide they don't want to live there anymore.

Just as with other transitions, tell stories or read books about other kids who have been adopted to give them concrete information and to help reframe unhealthy beliefs, such as the idea that adoptive parents completely replace birth parents. Reinforce that the memory and importance of their parents is something that is theirs to keep and cannot be "taken away." If the client is not being adopted by a current foster parent, anticipate grieving this loss as well as that of the other adult attachment figures in the client's life, such as child welfare staff and the therapist, if the plan is termination or transition services.

Children in foster care may visit with multiple prospective families before being replaced. Sometimes parents meet with a child several times before rescinding their interest. Remember that plans and people can change quickly and abruptly in child welfare. Avoid using absolutes with children regarding preparation for adoptive placements. The reality is that many adoptive placements fail both before and after the adoption has been finalized, resulting in the child returning to foster care (U.S. General Accounting Office, 2003). Children in foster care have already experienced the reality of broken trust and the pain of depending on adults. Whether they voice it or not, children experience a certain level of expectancy or preparedness for adoption plans to fail. Speak about adoptive placements in terms of possibilities, and increase clients' awareness and acceptance of what they can and cannot control. Honor the client's wishes, hopes, and dreams, and grieve these when they don't come true.

Especially when the therapist has a strong working rapport with a client, offer to host the first preadoptive family visit and recommend more frequent individual therapy sessions during early visitation. Help the child reflect on each visit by creating a visit journal with drawings and descriptions of who was at the visit, what they did, where they went, and how they felt about it.

Transition to Adulthood and Aging Out of the System

The population of youth aging out of the child welfare system is among our country's most vulnerable (Collins, Paris, & Ward, 2008). The lack of stability in people and places in their lives makes their search for identity and independence complicated and problematic. Therapeutic interventions with youth who are moving from foster care to independent living (IL) or supervised independent living (SIL) and who are aging out of the child welfare system should focus on maximizing the youth's internal and external strengths and resources to support them during this major transition time.

Although collaboration with the assigned worker is imperative, the therapist must prioritize maintaining a trusting therapeutic relationship with the individual client. Learned helplessness, blame, and pushing others away are, understandably, hallmarks of this population. Teach, model, and role-play healthy communication and advocacy skills with the client, both before and during contact with workers and judges, while also working to increase these professionals' empathy for the client. Be cautious of falling into parenting or enabling roles within the client's pseudo-family support system. Rather than focusing on what the client is doing wrong, the therapist's goals are to empathize with the client and refocus the client on utilizing personal strengths, identifying and using supports, and exploring different options for dealing with tough situations. SIL providers have different roles and expectations than those of foster parents. Some take on parenting roles, and others function more as landlords. Therapists must follow the client's lead as whether to involve providers in treatment or not.

CASE STUDY 8.10

I had seen Shayla for counseling on and off throughout her adolescence. Now I was sitting in my office with her, her SIL worker, and the placement supervisor. She had left or ran away from her third SIL provider in a year. The supervisor was chastising her for running away from her problems with care providers instead of working to resolve them. He threatened to remove her from the program if she couldn't comply with the rules. From our time in therapy, I knew she had lived in silence for years about being the victim of multiple forms of abuse and neglect and that she suffered from trauma reactions. Her decisions to run away were more of a protective impulse that she used when she felt disrespected or unwanted. After years of "freezing," she was working hard to avoid "fighting," and so went into "flight" mode and was on the move.

In the meeting, I watched her make a few attempts to defend her choices by naming the very inappropriate ways her providers had treated her, but the staff continued to talk over her. I watched her affect flatten and silent tears roll down her face. I got her permission to help her speak.

"She's not trying to fail at the program or ruin placements," I said. "Shayla's doing a lot of things right—on her way to graduating

(continued)

CASE STUDY 8.10 *(continued)*

high school with honors and carrying a part-time job. Families and homes have always been tough for her. Can we redirect this meeting to problem solving what might work for the next placement?"

The supervisor's tone changed and he instantly agreed that she had done really well in other areas and that he really wanted her to do well in a provider placement too. Shayla's face lifted, and I encouraged her to engage.

She said, "Can you find a placement that is close to my school? I just want to graduate and then move out on my own." She had a 2-hour commute to her school from her previous placement. The worker balked at the idea of this client being capable of living on her own, but I knew at this point making her own home was more realistic for her than taking the painful steps of making a home with others.

With continued advocacy and even role-playing and rehearsing ways to communicate her wants and needs to her workers without shutting down or becoming disrespectful, she did end up graduating high school and getting her own apartment. She met the requirements of the program and chose to stay in the program until she turned 21 by attending college and keeping a job, even through an unplanned pregnancy. She ended up living in that same apartment for longer than she had ever lived in any other home.

Age-appropriate behavior for teenagers involves forming close friendships, learning from their own mistakes, going through major cultural milestones such as prom and graduation, and exploring career and continuing education options. Many IL programs offer trainings, classes, and other opportunities for the youth to further develop independent living skills, such as budgeting, applications, financial assistance, and career planning. When therapists notice needs or barriers related to building these skill sets, they must advocate for and intervene with the client and the worker. For example, a worker expressed frustration to the therapist about a client struggling with monthly budgeting. The therapist reviewed the client's recent psychological testing results with the worker, which showed that the client had a significant learning disability in math.

The worker quickly changed the way he engaged the client in the budgeting process, with immediate success. The worker had assumed the client was being oppositional when, in reality, the client could not understand the directives being given.

Therapists might be surprised with the concerns that IL/SIL clients may bring to therapy, such as seeking explanations of tax withholding or how to fill out financial aid applications. Maintaining therapeutic boundaries can be a challenge. Therapists will find themselves in the projected parent role and face the choice to respond in an empowering or enabling manner. For example, one teen requested that her therapist keep a list of her login IDs and passcodes for her online college and job applications in her counseling file. The therapist responded by identifying how clever the request was and how helpful it must be to have an adult the client felt she could rely on. The therapist then asked the client to make two records of the list: one to put in her therapy file and one for her to keep track of on her own. This led to productive discussion about the difficulty of remembering so much information on her own (aka becoming an adult) and her need to both develop reliance on herself as well as use supports. It took a few months of her calling for passcode reminders, but then she figured out a system to remember them by on her own. Although seemingly unconventional for a therapeutic intervention, it was completely therapeutic for the client and ethically appropriate.

Also help IL/SIL clients navigate their existing support systems and create new ones. Have clients list the important relationships in their lives, both positive and negative, such as birth family members, foster family members, neighbors, friends, community or religious figures, coaches, teachers, mentors, and employers. Remember that for many teens aging out of care, their safest relationships have been with staff or professionals rather than family members. Have clients elaborate on these lists by indicating what they valued and didn't like about the person or relationship, whom they want and don't want to continue or resume contact with, and how they have impacted the relationship in positive and negative ways.

Many youth aging out of the system are interested in reuniting with their birth families, which is an important process for children in care to go through. Because the client was pulled from his family by someone else's choice, not his own, it will be natural for him to return to the family to reconnect and assert his autonomy on his terms. In therapy, empathically support this natural process and guide the client in making thoughtful choices about contact, especially when there are safety concerns or no-contact orders in place. If clients show no interest in reconnecting with their birth families, support reflection around their decision without jumping to conclusions or making judgments. Avoidance, anger, resentment, or fearfulness of further abuse or rejection often drive this lack of interest.

In session, balance reflecting on the past and surviving the present with building hopes and plans for the future. Work on creating or filling out life story books or journals, such as *For When I'm Famous: A Teen Foster/Adoption LifeBook* (O'Malley, 2006). Make an adaptable future-oriented timeline to identify their dreams, goals, and fears and how those may change with time to update periodically (Kolos, 2009).

Treatment with this population is a gradual discharge planning process. All interventions must contain an aspect of preparing clients to advocate and care for themselves. Continuing therapy past age 18 may not be an option. If continued treatment is recommended, the therapist must help the client plan for the transition far in advance by identifying adult referral sources. Be sure to include social support systems for the client when discharge planning, especially if mental health care is not readily accessible due to insurance or financial barriers.

CASE STUDY 8.11

Doing future timelines with teens in foster care has taught me a lot. Rather than making a linear timeline, one teen created a network flowchart of his future that included plans a, b, and c for his living arrangements, school, family, and career goals. I learned that he already anticipated life not going as planned and was planning accordingly. Another teen completed this activity by identifying very few goals but many "mysteries" in her future. For her, working through her present school and placement challenges was all that she was able to effectively handle. I learned that it was more comforting for her to reframe her unknowns as mysteries with positive, exciting connotations. With time, she gradually identified more specific goals and hopes for herself as she was ready.

CASE STUDY 8.12

Josh had virtually grown up in residential treatment placements from age 7 to 16 due to record-setting destructive behaviors, including the infamous story of "the boy who had broken 11 windows" once. He eventually successfully completed a program and moved into a semi-independent living home with a previous staff member with whom he had bonded. He was guarded, resistant, and uncooperative, but was able to remain physically safe at all times in our sessions.

When case conferencing with his psychiatrist, who had prescribed him multiple psychotropic medications, I expressed my frustration at our perceived "lack of progress" in addressing his traumatic past, as well as his often-voiced goal to kill himself one day without endorsing a current intent or plan. He looked at me with surprise and asked me if I could think of any reason why Josh would keep a plan like that. I was unsure because from my assessments and observations, he did not present as authentically suicidal.

"It's the only thing he feels he has complete control over," he said. "Don't see his suicidality as a failure on either of your parts; see it as his effort to assert control and autonomy in his life."

From then on, I changed my approach to focus on affirming his other efforts and options to control his life and influence its outcome. He continued to attend and participate in therapy even after the placement failed. Eventually he reconnected with his birth sibling who had been in residential treatment with him and was now in independent living as well. He asked to end counseling after being able to successfully get off of several of his medications, maintain his school and placement, and officially end his suicidal plans.

ENDING THE THERAPEUTIC RELATIONSHIP

Make efforts to keep client cases throughout transitions whenever possible. Continuity with a therapist during replacements can be a protective factor for the child. If services will be transferred elsewhere, advocate for a warm transfer by scheduling a case conference with the new provider to share case history, effective treatment approaches, and current status.

Many of the transitions addressed in this chapter may lead to the loss of the client–therapist relationship. All therapeutic relationships end eventually. Therapists must not underestimate the value and impact of their presence in the client's life. Giving the client an experience of healthy good-bye is a major treatment intervention for this population. Start by anticipating the termination and normalizing feelings of frustration, anger, sadness, and worry by naming and modeling them. For example, say, "I'm sad that we can't work together anymore." The intervention is not about taking care of the therapist's feelings; rather, the therapist's feelings serve as a powerful bridge for clients to cross in order to access and express their own emotions.

Take a session to review the "story" of the client's treatment. Go through artwork, pieces of writing or worksheets, and favorite toys or games. Remember the first meeting, memorable moments, struggles, and breakthroughs. Notice the changes in the client, no matter how small, from the start to end of treatment. Remind the client that those positive memories, lessons learned, and growth experiences are the client's to keep, regardless of the presence of the therapist in the client's life moving forward. Affirm the clients' ability to find other safe, helping adults in the future when they need to. For example, say, "Just like I helped you, others can help you too. Trust yourself and don't stop looking for people who understand you until you find them."

Identify or create a transitional object to represent both the growth the client has made and the meaning of the therapeutic relationship. For example, give the client a treasured toy or art supply from the office, a hand-written card, or a piece of art made especially for the client. Ask the client to give or make something similar of the client's choice for the therapist to keep as well. Show the client where you will keep the gift and what you will feel and think of whenever you see it. Plan some sort of celebration for the final session, with favorite snacks, a game, or music, to honor the positive connection that has been made with joy and gratitude.

Many times, it will be hard for the therapist to say good-bye too. Anticipate, reflect on, and attend to personal feelings of loss throughout termination in order to keep a healthy awareness and emotional boundary when treatment ends. Practice the type of self-care taught to clients. Facilitating a healthy termination is the therapist's final intervention with children in care.

REFERENCES

Baggerly, J., & Elkadi-Abugideiri, S. (2010). Grief counseling for Muslim pre-school and elementary school children. *Journal of Multicultural Counseling and Development, 38*(2), 112–124.

Betts, D. J. (Ed.). (2003). *Creative arts therapies approaches in adoption and foster care: Contemporary strategies for working with individuals and families.* Springfield, IL: Charles C Thomas.

Boss, P. (2006). *Loss, trauma and resilience: Therapeutic work with ambiguous loss.* New York: NY: Norton.

Boss, P. (2010). The trauma and complicated grief of ambiguous loss. *Pastoral Psychology, 59,* 137–145.

Coholic, D., Lougheed, S., & Cadell, S. (2009). Exploring the helpfulness of arts-based methods with children living in foster care. *Traumatology: An International Journal, 15*(3), 64–71.

Collado, C., & Levine, P. (2007). Reducing transfers of children in family foster care through onsite mental health interventions. *Child Welfare, 86*(5), 133–150.

Collins, M. E., Paris, R., & Ward, R. L. (2008). The permanence of family ties: Implications for youth transitioning from foster care. *American Journal of Orthopsychiatry, 78*(1), 54–62.

D'Antonio, J. (2011). Grief and loss of a caregiver in children: A developmental perspective. *Journal of Psychosocial Nursing, 49*(10), 17–20.

Eagle, R. S. (1994, July). The separation experience of children in long-term care: Theory, research, and implications for practice. *American Orthopsychiatric Association, 64*(3), 421–434.

Gnaulati, E. (2002). Extending the uses of sibling therapy with children and adolescents. *Psychotherapy: Theory, Research, Practice, Training, 39*(1), 76–87.

Goldman, L. (2004, April). Counseling with children in contemporary society. *Journal of Mental Health Counseling, 26*(2), 168–187.

Gregory, S. D. P., & Phillips, F. B. (1997). "Of mind, body, and spirit": Therapeutic foster care: An innovative approach to healing from an NTU perspective. *Child Welfare, 76*(1), 127–142.

Kolos, A. C. (2009). The role of play therapists in children's transitions: From residential care to foster care. *International Journal of Play Therapy, 18*(4), 229–239.

Kübler-Ross, E., & Kessler, D. (2005). *On grief and grieving: Finding the meaning of grief through the five stages of loss.* New York, NY: Scribner.

Moser, A. (1996). *Don't despair on Thursdays!: The children's grief management book.* Kansas City, MO: Landmark Editions, Inc.

Nelson, J. (2006). *Kids need to be safe: A book for children in foster care.* Minneapolis, MN: Free Spirit Publishing.

O'Malley, B. (2006). *For when I'm famous: A teen foster/adoption lifebook.* Winthrop, MA: Adoption-Works.

Schoen, A. A., Burgoyne, M., & Schoen, S. F. (2004). Are the developmental needs of children in America adequately addressed during the grief process? *Journal of Instructional Psychology, 31*(2), 143–148.

U.S. General Accounting Office. (2003). *Foster care: States focusing on finding permanent homes for children, but longstanding barriers remain* (GAO-03-626T). Retrieved from http://www.gao.gov/new.items/d03626t.pdf

Webb, N. B. (2003). Play and expressive therapies to help bereaved children: Individual, family, and group treatment. *Smith College Studies in Social Work, 73*(3), 405–422.

Webb, N. B. (Ed.). (2006). *Working with traumatized youth in child welfare.* New York: NY: Guilford Press.

Wilgocki, J., & Wright, M. K. (2002). *Maybe days: A book for children in foster care.* Washington, DC: Magination Press.

CHAPTER NINE

TREATING TRAUMA

It is impossible to look through the kaleidoscope's lens without seeing the impact of trauma. Removal from home and family, on top of being a victim of abuse or neglect, leaves many children in care reeling in survival mode and full of maladaptive behaviors that are poorly suited for adjusting to a new placement. Therapists working within child welfare must keep a constant awareness of the client's exposures, have a firm understanding of the fundamentals of how trauma works, and know how to effectively intervene.

Trauma treatment must be based on a thorough assessment of the child's individual exposures, types of reactions, and known triggers. Screen for trauma reactions to the substantiated abuse or neglect as well as the child's removal from the family and home, in addition to other pre- and post-removal trauma exposures. Not every exposure will result in trauma reactions, and the same incident may be traumatizing to one child but not to another. Therapists must take their time collaborating with others to gather information and link reactions to incidents in order to craft strategic and effective trauma treatment plans (Brown, McCauley, Navalta, & Saxe, 2013; Gil, 2006). Work together with a trauma-informed psychiatrist to incorporate medication management to effectively address severe symptoms (Perry & Szalavitz, 2006).

Many children in care will demonstrate trauma reactions without meeting the full criteria for posttraumatic stress disorder (PTSD) and will still benefit from trauma treatment (Cohen, Mannarino, & Deblinger, 2006; Coholic, Lougheed, & Cadel, 2009). Treatment must follow the child's trauma reactions in the context of the exposure, and not the other way around. Children may have trauma reactions when they are direct victims, witnesses, or even hear about a traumatic incident, whether or not they have a connection to the victim, and children too young to talk can still be traumatized. Additionally, once a child has been traumatized by a single event, the child is more likely to experience trauma reactions with subsequent exposures (van der Kolk, McFarlane, & Weisaeth, 1996). Therefore, if a child has already been traumatized prior to removal, the

CASE STUDY 9.1

Brandon had lived through multiple traumatic incidents since infancy: neglect; a car accident that killed his sibling; removal from his birth mother; and prolonged physical, verbal, and emotional abuse from his adoptive relatives. His foster parents and school were concerned about his tendency to hide small knives and hammers in his locker and backpack. Brandon was not aggressive toward others and did not make violent threats. In session, I inquired about a connection between his past traumas and keeping weapons now, knowing that his behavior is not uncommon for child victims of abuse. "Are you afraid that your foster parent or someone at school might hurt you?" I asked.

He laughed. "No, no, I know I could fight them off if they came at me." Brandon explained, "Didn't you hear about that boy who was attacked at a bus stop and got raped and beaten? After all I've been through, there is no way I am going to let that happen to me."

Brandon's fears and survival skills had fixated on having to ride the city bus.

child will be much more likely to experience trauma reactions to the removal and any subsequent incidents.

Trauma reactions are involuntary, meaning that a child never chooses to act traumatized. Trauma symptoms of reexperiencing, avoidance, hyperarousal, and negatively altered thoughts and feelings are direct results of neurobiological responses to perceived threat (van der Kolk et al., 1996). Hallmark concerns of traumatized children who may not meet the full criteria for PTSD include inattention, learning difficulties, sleep disturbance, inability to self-regulate, lack of trust and ability to securely bond to caregivers, low self-worth, lack of hope for the future, poor social skills, incongruent affective responses, trouble verbally expressing feelings, and lack of ability to stay in the present moment (Coholic et al., 2009; Webb, 2006). When left untreated, the debilitating features of trauma can last a lifetime, making those in this already vulnerable population at even greater risk for prolonged harm to themselves and others into adulthood (Perry & Szalavitz, 2006; van der Kolk et al., 1996).

Therapists do not need to know every exposure or detail in order to provide effective intervention. Trauma alters the brain in a similar manner regardless of the type of exposure (van der Kolk et al., 1996). However, the longer, more repeated, and complicated the trauma exposures, the more difficult the healing process will be (Blaustein & Kinniburgh, 2010). In child welfare, it is common to learn the full extent and nature of the child's exposures well into treatment rather than during the initial assessment. Regardless, therapists must still attempt to gather as much information as possible from both the child and involved adults about the child's exposure when beginning treatment (Jungbluth & Shirk, 2009).

Find out as much as possible about the type, timing, reoccurrence, and context of the exposures. Traumatic experiences can be categorized as acute, chronic, or complex cumulative (Malchiodi, 2008). Acute traumas are single incidents that occur once. Chronic traumas are single experiences that are repeated over a period of time. Complex cumulative traumas involve experiencing multiple traumatic events over a period of time in the context of a caring relationship or place (e.g., by a parent at home). A majority of traumatized children in foster care have experienced complex cumulative traumas. The story in Exhibit 9.1 illustrates the profound impact of complex cumulative trauma.

Now read the same story with additional details in Exhibit 9.2.

EXHIBIT 9.1

Justin had a terrible week. His car was stolen, he got fired, and he and his girlfriend broke up. On top of that, he broke his leg after falling down the stairs.

EXHIBIT 9.2

Justin happily lived with his girlfriend of over 10 years. He was closer to her family than he was to his own. However, she had recently developed a drug problem. He knew it was bad when, one morning, he discovered she had sold his car to buy drugs. Ensuing transportation issues resulted in him losing his job. After verbally confronting her, she overdosed, ended up in the hospital, and reported to police that he had physically assaulted her, which was untrue. Her brother, who was one of Justin's best friends, then came to his house to defend his sister and pushed Justin down the stairs, breaking his leg.

By adding the context, the traumatic potential of Justin's experiences greatly increased. Knowing the details also makes it much easier to understand why Justin has trouble getting close to others, gets anxious around police and hospitals, and never takes the stairs. This set of stories illustrates the importance of gathering as much information as possible about trauma exposures.

The instability of a lack of loving adults and home, as well as the absence of the familiar, are major complicating factors for treating traumatized children in care (Gil, 2006; Tarren-Sweeney, 2013; Webb, 2006). The adults now responsible for the child's care did not know the child in her pre-trauma state. Some children's lives have been in perpetual trauma exposure since infancy, making internal and external stability something to be newly discovered rather than returned to. Child victims may view "glimpses" of healing and peace as trauma triggers—the calm before the storm of more hurt and terror. The following messages must be repeatedly given, both verbally and nonverbally, by multiple sources to help reverse the impact of complex cumulative trauma in children:

Hurting others is never okay.
Kids are not responsible for adults' behavior.
I see you, and you matter.

Many birth parents and even grandparents of children in care have their own trauma histories. Their communities may also witness frequent traumas. Many of the professionals and agencies operating in the child welfare system struggle with trauma reactions as well, whether direct or vicarious. Although the task is challenging, building an understanding of intergenerational, systemic, and helping professionals' experiences of trauma to help mitigate trauma's effects on both themselves and others through self-care, education, advocacy, and collaboration is well worth striving for (Brown et al., 2013; Conradi et al., 2011; Webb, 2006).

NEUROBIOLOGICAL IMPLICATIONS

An influx of neurobiological research has greatly increased therapists' understanding of trauma and how to intervene. Following is a brief summary of key points based on the works of van der Kolk et al. (1996), Steele and Raider (2009), and Perry and Szalavitz (2006) that every therapist should grasp when offering trauma interventions. Additional reading and training in an evidence-based model are strongly recommended (National Childhood Traumatic Stress Network, 2008; Racusin, Maerlender, Sengupta, Isquith, & Straus, 2005).

Wired to Survive

When humans perceive severe threat to themselves or loved ones, the lower or more primitive parts of the brain that are shared with mammals and reptiles are responsible for sensing danger and instinctually activating fear responses to promote survival. From the amygdala to the vagus nerve, people are biologically hardwired to survive (Geller & Porges, 2014). "Fight, flight, or freeze" is a fairly accurate portrayal of the ways that the brain and body react when terrified. The same parts of the brain regulate all emotions, as well as basic physical functions such as body temperature, heart rate, balance, and coordination. Thinking, reasoning, and logical problem solving are all done in the upper, more advanced parts of the brain. When fear responses are activated, the brain automatically decreases access to the upper layers' functions in order to conserve energy for the survival functions. Thinking delays instant action. Human survival instincts can cause our bodies to take action before reasoning out the situation.

When children perceive danger, their brains start pumping increased levels of hormones, such as adrenaline and cortisol, through their bodies to give them extra energy to run away or fight. Once the child has run away to safety or fought off the danger, the giant "dose" of energy will be used up and the child can return to pre-danger biological functioning. Unfortunately, this cycle is not completely played out by many traumatized children in care because their attempts to run or fight (i.e., discharge the energy) are interrupted by debilitating injury; being told or forced to stop fighting, stay still, and be quiet; or by the irreconcilable urge to seek comfort and safety in the same person who is scaring them. The end result is that the child's brain becomes "frozen" in defense mode, perpetually activated and pumping out extra energy in anticipation of danger. The same neurological discharge made to protect the child ends up harming the child's normal brain development. This frozen state of readiness is the basic root of arousal, avoidance, and re-experiencing symptoms of trauma. The traumatized brain continues to restrict use of upper-layer brain functions in order to conserve energy and focus on survival tactics. This process leads to physical and mental exhaustion, dissociation from reality, detachment from others, and emotional numbing. When some traumatized children do start to feel safe, a trigger or reminder of the original trauma can throw their brains right back into survival mode.

The prolonged state of activation makes learning new information very challenging or impossible. Hearing and making sense of directions and using logic or problem solving are all upper-layer brain functions. In other words, when in an activated, aroused state, the traumatized child literally cannot focus and attend to learning new information or skills that parents, teachers, and even therapists are trying to teach them. Instead of listening to what is being said, they are looking for signs of danger, especially in others' nonverbal communication (body language, tone, volume, facial expression, etc.). This is quite a conundrum because interpersonal connections and closeness are some of the best ways to neurobiologically help children relax and rest after being upset. If the adult trying to help the traumatized kid is talking or moving his hands in a way that is triggering the child, the adult inadvertently can make himself an additional source of threat. This example illustrates the importance of observing children's reactions and understanding their triggers in order to identify what is comforting and what is exacerbating.

It also increases understanding of how children functioning under traumatic stress often seem to feel more relief than regret about physically fighting others or running away from parents, classrooms, and other situations. Those actions, seen by adults as oppositional and disrespectful, are actually fulfilling their overriding biological drive to use up energy given to protect themselves. They may *know* their behavior is wrong, but they are more likely to *feel* better or confused rather than apologetic or "bad." Many foster parents misunderstand traumatized children appearing to "not care" about their misbehavior and related consequences.

If a child in care's traumatized brain could speak, here's what it might say: "I am so scared all the time and will do anything I can to feel ready, powerful, and in control. If I let someone else call the shots or tell me what to do, that person might hurt me, and I can't risk that. I don't have time or energy to think through what the person is saying and why. I just need to do what makes me feel better right now. All I know is that more bad things are coming."

The impact of trauma on brain development is particularly significant for young children due to the nature of the brain's use-dependent formation and the sequential nature of growth. Neurological capabilities exist and expand only when they are actively being engaged on a consistent basis for a prolonged period (Perry & Szalavitz, 2006). In addition, a majority of the brain's active growth is completed by the time a child turns 5 years old (Webb, 2006). The last "layers" of brain function to develop are those that allow children to concentrate, link cause and effect, anticipate consequences to their actions, and think before they act. When infants, toddlers, or preschoolers experience trauma, they stay in whatever base layers of functioning they have already developed up to that point. Upper-layer brain development can become permanently delayed. Intervention involves returning to where development was interrupted and starting growth there. Traumatic stress, not unlike traumatic brain injuries, has the potential to cause varying degrees of temporary or permanent cognitive dysfunction, emotional dysregulation, and sleep- and eating-cycle disturbance. If children's brain functioning has been compromised due to trauma, they may need to literally relearn basic adaptive functioning and emotional regulation.

Implications for treatment include creating opportunities for the client to safely "discharge" the stored, activated energy in a way that does not perpetuate the cycle of threat and traumatize the child further. Treatment must find ways to increase the child's sense of psychological safety in order turn off the fear response and allow increased access to upper-layer brain functions. Child welfare works hard to keep children physically safe; however, achieving psychological safety once their bodies are no longer in danger is a different, arduous task.

When children are in survival mode, they are constantly relying on strong gut feelings to tell them what is okay and not okay rather than more advanced thinking skills. This gut feeling tells them whether they need to get away or get "it" before "it" gets them. Trauma is about perceptions, not necessarily reality. Learning about how the brain stores traumatic memories will increase therapists' understanding of how this happens and what they can do about it.

Senses Versus Sense

Each side of the brain handles environmental input differently. The left side deals with information primarily with language-based reasoning, linking cause–effect relationships, and solving problems. The right side focuses on nonverbal sensory input through the eyes, ears, nose, mouth, and skin; body position; and movement; as well as iconic symbolization. Every experience is received and processed with both sides of the brain working together. For example, when I put my hand in running water, my right brain feels the ice-cold chill and makes me want to pull my hand away. My left brain then thinks, "This is too cold for me to wash my hands in. If I turn the faucet, I can warm up the water." The two sides of the brain work beautifully together to help make sense of things, reach goals, and learn through experience to get my hands cleaned comfortably and effectively.

Just as the two sides of the brain receive information differently, they also store memories differently. The left brain stores explicit memories—verbalized and analyzed facts and lessons learned with descriptive words. People give meaning and solve problems using explicit memories. The right brain generates implicit memories unconsciously in a purely sensory way, making them hard to describe but easy to feel. The implicit memories are where "gut" feelings come from. Normally functioning memory processing includes input from both sides of the brain. However, when the brain is exposed to a trauma, the memory of the incident often gets "locked" or imprinted on the right side without moving to the left.

This is why traumatized children are often literally unable to talk about traumas clearly. If they offer any information, it is disjointed and confusing. It also explains how trauma reminders work. They are sensory based, meaning that colors, sounds, movements, scents, and tastes in one context can activate the traumatized brain to respond to a completely different context from the past. For example, when a therapist raises her arm quickly to offer a high five, the traumatized child may react like he is about to get hit. Trauma triggers act as a warning indicator based on the imprinted traumatic memory, leading to immediate increased avoidance, hyperarousal, or reexperiencing of symptoms. A major part of trauma treatment involves identifying the triggers, which may be obvious or subtle. Therapists, foster parents, and workers must be "investigators" and put together clues about triggers, because the traumatized child may be unable to verbalize what it is the child is afraid of and why.

CASE STUDY 9.2

Cheryl loved Winnie the Pooh even as a 14-year-old. Coloring Pooh pages or watching the show was one of her favorite ways to relax herself. One day she noticed a Mickey Mouse puzzle in my office. I anticipated her showing interest in it because of the similarities to the Pooh character, but her reaction was startling. Her face visibly fell and she literally backed away from the puzzle, unable to stop staring at it but not saying anything. I gently spoke to her, "Cheryl, what's going on?"

She looked away quickly, saying, "Miss Heather, please put that puzzle away. I can't see it here. Please." I immediately moved it out of view. It wasn't until several sessions later of trauma interventions that Cheryl described the first time her father raped her. She was 10 and watching Mickey Mouse on TV. His bouncy, smiling figure and the sound of his chipper voice were engrained with the horrific memory.

Anticipating and reacting to triggers provides context for many traumatized children's rapidly shifting behaviors and moods. The reasons behind the changes are often misunderstood. Traumatized children have trouble explaining why they did what they did or learning from mistakes. Instead, they remain stuck in victim thinking, expecting and perceiving danger where there is none and reacting to triggers in confusing and sometimes dangerous ways. These repeated patterns generate and reinforce the negatively altered thoughts and feelings about themselves, others, and the world around them that must be addressed in treatment both individually and collaboratively.

TRAUMATIC ABUSE, NEGLECT, AND LOSS

The following sections review specific treatment indications for traumatic grief, sexual abuse, physical abuse, domestic violence, and neglect to be used *in addition to* the subsequently described trauma treatment approaches.

Traumatic Losses

There is much crossover between the presentation of grief and trauma reactions, but treatment indications differ. The emotional seed of trauma is fear, and the resulting behaviors are neurologically based efforts for survival. The emotional seed of grief is sadness, and the resulting behaviors are relationally based expressions of deep pain and loss. When individuals are grieving, they usually want and are able to talk about the loss and what happened. When individuals are traumatized, they often do not want to or cannot talk about it. Trauma-related anger tends to become destructive and dangerous, whereas grief-related anger does not. Dreams and nightmares in traumatized children usually involve the child being hurt or dying, whereas those of grieving children tend to be about the person who is no longer with them (Steele & Raider, 2009). Children in care who experience traumatic losses will show symptoms of both trauma and grief. Depending on the nature and sequence of the traumatic loss, grief and trauma interventions may be given one after the other or in conjunction. For example, a child who lost a sibling in a traumatic accident may require trauma intervention to reduce arousal before he is able to consciously grieve the loss. Another child's trauma treatment may benefit from being interrupted to grieve the loss of a loved foster family or staff member to mitigate compounding the complicated nature of the child's trauma exposure. Therapists should follow the child's lead and attend to whichever experience the client feels safest addressing first.

Sexual Abuse

Sexual abuse (SA) thrives on secrecy and shame, and most SA reports come out after a child is already in foster care (Hoyle, 2000). Therapists treating victims of SA must be knowledgeable about normal childhood sexual development, common childhood reactions to SA, and a range of perpetrating behaviors. They must feel comfortable talking to both children and caregivers about each of these topics in order to educate, normalize, and empower their clients.

Treatment will involve teaching basic, clear facts about private parts and identifying common reactions to SA based on the child's developmental age and ability to tolerate potentially triggering information and imagery safely. Use dolls, books, drawings, stories, or handouts to make this

CASE STUDY 9.3

Carrie was 16 and a fighter. She had been expelled from six different high schools by her sophomore year. Her supervised independent living (SIL) worker recommended counseling for some time, but Carrie was resistant. Finally, attendance was made mandatory by her judge in order for her to stay in the program.

When she came into my office she was not disrespectful or defiant, but rather very aware that she was struggling with a profound sense of despair and fear that was complicated by her present circumstances. She did not have a stable home environment or social supports. From her perspective, the current fighting was progress compared to her past and showed impressive self-control as compared with a majority of her family members and friends who struggled with drug use, homelessness, and criminal activity.

The loss of the most reliable caregiver she'd ever had and a childhood full of neglect and domestic violence were clearly driving forces of her explosive anger, feeling the "need" to fight, along with self-medicating marijuana use and superficial cutting to cope with her deep emotional pain.

After effectively engaging her in safety assessment and planning for the cutting and referring her to substance abuse intervention, I supported her focusing on the death of her uncle, whom she identified as the most significant person in her life. She and her other siblings had relied on him for care and safety before entering the system. His death from cancer almost 2 years prior had resulted in protective services involvement and her wardship. Even though he was never her legal guardian, she clearly had the most secure attachment with him, and his availability had balanced out her parent's lack of care for her.

She participated in multiple sessions focused on grieving his loss in a trauma-informed approach. Carrie almost immediately felt relief. The self-harm and fighting decreased rapidly. She was not in an emotionally or physically safe or stable enough place in life to take on some of the other traumas and hurt from her past and present but greatly benefited from the grief work.

information more accessible and reinforce that it's okay to talk about it. Because many SA victims in care keep their abuse secret, psychoeducation around SA can also be an important intervention for children when SA is strongly suspected but not confirmed. For example, teach children that both men and women of all ages may abuse both boys and girls and that most of the time the abuser is very familiar to the child, such as a neighbor, family member, or friend. Continuously weave in messages that SA is never the child's fault, that sexually abusing a child is never okay, and that how the client feels and what happened to the client really matters.

Review normal and atypical sexual development as well as common signs and reactions to sexual abuse with caregivers and even workers if they do not know. Explain that addressing the abuse in treatment can increase symptoms before relieving them and that full disclosure of abuse is not necessary for treatment to be effective. Emphasize the importance of parents examining their own attitudes and beliefs about sex, the need to take care of themselves, and the need to protect themselves against false allegations by keeping communication open and clear about all sexual concerns and their reactions. There are numerous online resources, books, and workbooks available to assist both parents and children on each of these topics.

Child victims of sexual abuse may or may not engage in reenactment of their SA with themselves or others. The need for stress relief, to feel powerful, or to be in control of others can also lead to sexual acting out. Identify the driving forces behind any inappropriate sexual behavior to steer interventions. The caregiver must be supported and feel comfortable in directly addressing concerns related to sexual acting out in the home in a respectful, clear, and empathic manner. Model and role play how to talk about sexual issues with children. If caregivers struggle with this, alert the foster care worker and collaboratively address the issue by increasing support and training or considering replacement. *The Sexualized Child in Foster Care* (Hoyle, 2000) and *Helping Children With Sexual Behavior Problems: A Guidebook for Professions and Caregivers* (Johnson, 2011) are recommended for therapists and caregivers alike.

Physical Abuse and Domestic Violence

Violent homes teach dysfunctional problem solving and inappropriate expression of feelings, as well as strongly devalue a child's self-worth, sense of personal power, and accountability. A child exposed to physical abuse or domestic violence learns that hurting others is okay, people deserve to get hurt, hurting people needs to happen to get what you want, and the victim causes the perpetrator's actions ("Look what you made me do"). Educate children about what physical abuse and/or domestic violence is, and be prepared to answer questions about why parents hurt each other and their children. Use psychoeducational books and tools such as *Something Happened and I'm Scared to Tell* (Kehoe, 1987), and teach the cycles of abuse and violence. Name and work to alter children's beliefs that they are to blame for their parents' behavior or that they have the responsibility to stop it (Webb, 2006). Children's reactions to these interventions may include relief ("I knew something wasn't right"), confusion ("but I love them"/"they are good—how could they do something bad?"), or avoidance/denial (directly of the abuse and any acknowledgement of it and its affects).

Neglect

Neglect can wreak havoc on a child's sense of self-worth, self-regulation, and development of empathy (Perry & Szalavitz, 2006). Children of neglect often close in on themselves, truly believing that what they do, think, and feel doesn't matter. They tend to fundamentally distrust adults and engage them manipulatively and not reciprocally. Remember that repeated behaviors such as hoarding, stealing, and lying were very adaptive for their neglectful environment and will take time, effort, and coordinated interventions to understand and change (Forbes & Post, 2010). Most neglect has been lifelong for children in care, and eliminating these behaviors completely may be unrealistic. Focus on utilizing behavior modification strategies as well as psychoeducation and empathy building with caregivers.

Many children of neglect take on parentified roles with their younger siblings. This can be difficult for foster parents. Help parents understand that taking on this role helped the child and the child's siblings survive for a long time before the foster parent ever came into their lives. Do not disparage or punish the child's parentified behaviors, rather allow older siblings to "show" parents how to care for their younger siblings. Focus efforts on building trust with current caregiving adults. Bring such children's attention to times when others responsibly care for their siblings and increase their exposure to age-appropriate activities such as being on a sports team or joining a choir.

TREATING TRAUMA REACTIONS

Trauma interventions for children in care that engage clients' senses are necessary in order to decrease their arousal, increase their psychological safety, access and make sense of their trauma memories, increase their ability to self-regulate, and learn how to identify and cope with trauma triggers. Expressive art making, drawing, using metaphors with imagery or props, playing with toys, writing stories and poetry, making and using music, and engaging in body awareness and movement activities are all examples of appropriate trauma intervention methods (Coholic et al., 2009; Klorer, 2000; Malchiodi, 2008; Webb, 2006). Psychoeducation, cognitive reframing, and creating a trauma narrative to tell and make sense of their stories will also be effective when clients are not in an aroused state (Blaustein & Kinniburgh, 2010; Gil, 2006; Levy & Orlans, 1998).

Start With the Therapeutic Relationship and Space

Build, maintain, and repair the therapeutic relationship and safety of the therapeutic session and space in order to provide effective trauma interventions (Grasso, Joselow, Marquez, & Webb, 2011; Levy & Orlans, 1998). Even the smartest, most trauma-informed therapists will fail in treatment if they do not prioritize tending to a strong therapeutic alliance (Allen, Oseni, & Allen, 2012). This text gives multiple examples of how to build therapeutic rapport. This section provides some additional recommendations for the traumatized client.

Make sessions as predictable as possible. Schedule sessions on the same day of the week and at the same time of day. Meet in the same room. Keep toys or art materials in the same places so that the child knows where to find them. Designate a specific folder or spot on a shelf for the client to store artwork or favorite toys. Start and end each session with a similar greeting, facial expression, and some kind of ritual. For example, eat a snack, water a plant, draw a picture, notice the weather outside, make a wish with a magic wand, or set an intention for the session while holding a special object. Giving clients control in sessions will help them feel psychologically safe. Share session plans at the beginning of the appointment, identify plans for the next session at the end, and ask for clients' consent to the plans. Give clients permission to interrupt and end interventions at any time. Role play with them how to do so by saying, "I don't want to do this right now. Can we move on?" This teaches clients to trust themselves and ask for what they want, both of which increase self-regulation. Anticipate changes or potential triggers inside the session and the immediate surroundings. Therapists are responsible for actively observing clients throughout interventions and must interrupt themselves when a client's trauma symptoms are being activated beyond what the client is able to manage safely without further dissociating (Malchiodi, 2008). Pay attention to clients' physical reactions (fidgeting, avoiding eye contact, tightened posture or muscles), ask them to stop, breathe, and notice what's happening with them, while giving them permission to reflect or change session focus (Prather & Golden, 2009). Traumatized children will benefit from therapists who strive to empathically witness their inner worlds. Invite rather than direct. Be authentic and adaptable. Use body language, tone, cadence, and volume that are consistent, inviting, and calming (Geller & Porges, 2014).

CASE STUDY 9.4

One of my offices had particularly thin walls. The staff member next door had a loud voice and often hosted meetings. I watched clients of all ages visibly react to the sounds coming through the walls, whether it was laughter or more serious talking. Whenever I heard a sound, I immediately stopped the session to curiously notice the noise by saying something like, "I just heard a voice coming from over there. Did you hear that?" After allowing and observing the child's response, I shared, "There is another office next to mine with my coworker in there. Would you like to go see?" Time after time, clients visibly felt better after watching me go through this process and then peeking in to see for themselves that friendly adults were making the sounds and not some unseen danger. Soon I started incorporating an introduction of my noisy neighbors whenever a new client came up to my office, saying (and showing), "Here's my office where we will meet, and next door is so-and-so's office. Sometimes we might hear him talking or laughing through our wall. Would you like to meet him now?" and "We can always go check things out for ourselves just to make sure everything's all right."

Family and Systemic Engagement

Having a stable, nurturing relationship with a caregiving adult will have the greatest positive impact on reducing trauma symptoms, more so than any other factor, even excellent therapy (Blaustein & Kinniburgh, 2010; Klorer, 2000; Levy & Orlans, 1998; Oetzel & Scherer, 2003; Perry & Szalavitz, 2006; Seita, Mitchell & Tobin, 1997). The absence of this relationship is a major barrier for trauma treatment of many children in care. If their connection with their birth parents is strong, the restricted access and history of maltreatment undermines the stability and security of the relationship. It takes a lot of time and energy for foster parents and traumatized children to really get to know each other and develop a trusting relationship. For many children in care, home and any type of parent figure in itself is too threatening because of their past experiences. These children may build the stable relationships they need with group home staff, foster care workers, or even the therapist. Therapists must recognize that if a child in care does not have a stable, accessible adult relationship in which the child feels understood and unconditionally accepted, the potential effects of trauma treatment will be limited. Traumatized children will benefit from caregivers who respectfully interact with them; use healthy communication; effectively regulate their own emotions; maintain structure; and keep consistent expectations, rules, rewards, and consequences (Allen et al., 2012; Brown et al., 2013; Forbes & Post, 2010). Referring caregivers for parenting support or behavior management training can greatly assist in improving the psychological safety of a placement for a traumatized child.

Do not assume that all foster or birth parents are familiar with their child's trauma exposures. Caregivers will be able to offer more support and understanding, especially with traumatized children, if they know the child's trauma history (Dorsey et al., 2011). Therapists must teach caregivers what trauma is and how it works. Normalize and empathize with the out-of-control and confusing experiences they are going through. Help them directly apply the information about trauma to better understand the child's specific reactions and to identify potential triggers. Help them "major on the majors" rather than try to address every strange or inappropriate behavior (Brown et al., 2013).

Tell parents clearly that traumatized children do not act out for attention; *they act out because they need attention.* Draw their attention to the simple things they can do to make a huge difference, such as lowering and softening their tone of voice, making a calendar showing where the child will go and whom the child will be with, sing and dance together, stand eye to eye rather than over the child, and mirror the child's actions playfully when the child is calm. Research shows that repeated attuned sensory input is clinically proven to reduce and eliminate the continuation of trauma responses in children (Perry & Szalavitz, 2006; Steele & Raider, 2009). Help parents try different interactions with their children and remain persistently optimistic and adaptive when something doesn't seem to help (Forbes & Post, 2010). Not every interaction will help every child, and in order to take effect, help must be done "on repeat."

Bring parents' attention to traumatized children's heightened state of vulnerability at meals, bedtimes, and daily transition times. Teach parents that they can anticipate traumatized children to struggle more at these times, making them prime opportunities to thoughtfully create or alter routines and rituals to help reduce arousal and connect safely with the child (Blaustein & Kinniburgh, 2010; Grasso et al., 2011). For example, a parent might make up a song before every mealtime that tells what's for dinner and who will be there. Offer the child a choice of being a special helper or engaging in a known relaxing activity close by while the caregiver prepares the meal. These few minutes of extra time, patience, and effort on the parent's part will be worth it.

Last, many children in care who have experienced complex trauma exposures will attempt to engage their foster parents in reenacting the hurtful dynamics of their past (Levy & Orlans, 1998). Because reenactment is a mostly unconscious way of coping with hurt, fears, and the expectation of danger, teach them about the concept and its purpose. Reenactment's functions include re-creating the familiar ("it may have been bad but at least I knew what to expect"), speeding up and fulfilling the expectation of abuse or rejection ("I know you don't want me/ are going to hurt me, so go ahead and get it over with"), and gaining a sense of mastery or control over a confusing and threatening dynamic ("I will keep doing this until I understand and/or control it instead of others"). When parents understand what reenactment is and how their children may be using it, they will feel more empowered to tolerate and safely shift the dynamics by repeatedly choosing not to reinforce it while creating opportunities to counter the child's negative belief system and strengthening a healthier parent–child dynamic (Prather & Golden, 2009).

Because children in care are operating within a larger system, trauma-informed interactions must occur with professionals at multiple levels to maximize impact. In addition to individual interventions, build systemic supports for both child welfare professionals and parents (birth, foster, and adoptive) that include trauma training, parenting supports, and referral sources for individual adult trauma treatment (Brown et al., 2013; Conradi et al., 2011; Grasso et al., 2011; Prather & Golden, 2009; Webb, 2006).

Individual, family, and group trauma interventions may be targeted toward specific trauma symptoms or trauma's impact overall through a combination of psychoeducation, arousal reduction, self-regulation strategies, coping skill development, trauma narrative reflection, and cognitive reframing (Gil, 2006; Webb, 2006). Always prioritize the child's sense of psychological safety when deciding how to intervene (Perry & Szalavitz, 2006). Because the source of trauma is fear, it is counterproductive to induce more fear than the child is able to safely handle during sessions. Pace interventions based on where the client is at the time of the session, especially when the child is being currently exposed to ongoing traumatic stressors such as weekly contact with a former abuser or difficulty adjusting to a placement. Follow children's lead, be present, and see their actions through the lens of trauma.

Groups can be powerful interventions for traumatized children in care but must be carefully implemented (Steele & Raider, 2009). Members must be screened thoroughly for appropriateness. Co-lead with another trauma-informed therapist and keep membership small and within the same developmental age range and history of similar exposures and reactions. For example, a child who is having active flashbacks and dissociative episodes that compromise his and others' safety would not be an appropriate candidate for joining a group until these symptoms have markedly decreased.

Psychoeducation

Use imagery and metaphors to explain how trauma works, normalize children's reactions, and teach what will help them feel better based on what thousands of other traumatized children have learned. Share this information in a developmentally appropriate manner, and plan on returning to it throughout treatment. Engage the caregiver and child together if they have a mutually close relationship or separately if they do not. There are several excellent psychoeducational handouts, booklets, and storybooks geared to teach different age groups about trauma, such as *Brave Bart: A Story for Traumatized and Grieving Children* (Sheppard, 1998), *A Terrible Thing Happened* (Holmes & Mudlaff, 2000), and *A Trauma Is Like No Other Experience* (Steele, 1999). Following are examples of a few metaphors that can be adapted to the client's individual experiences. Using pictures or props to illustrate the metaphor will help the traumatized child connect with the material.

Bad Storms

Traumas are like bad storms. When they come, we can't go outside and play like we want to. Instead, we feel so scared! The loud thunder, pouring rain, dark clouds, and flashing lightning make us want to run and hide or do something to stop it! Can we stop a storm? No, we can't. We have to wait for it to pass and find something else to do in the meantime. Sometimes, on top of being in a horrible storm, we get stuck waiting somewhere we don't want to be. Do storms last forever? No. Even really bad scary ones? No. All storms end and the sun comes out again. There will always be more storms and more sunny days. It helps to find ways to pass the time while we wait for storms to end, especially when we're waiting someplace we don't want to be (Steele & Raider, 2009).

Scary Movies

Talking about trauma memories is kind of like seeing a scary movie for the first time. You can hardly sit still and watch the whole thing. You can't stop thinking about it, especially at night. Parts of it pop into your head out of nowhere. But the next time you see the same scary movie, it's still scary but not quite as much. The third time you see it, you already know what's going to happen, and after you're done watching it, it doesn't bother you nearly as much. But if you go somewhere new or something bad happens to you, the scary thoughts might come back. By the fourth, fifth, or even sixth time watching the same movie, you still may not like it, but it doesn't make you feel scared and out of control anymore, no matter where you go. Drawing and talking about trauma will be hard at first, but the more you do it, the less those memories and feelings will bother you (Steele, 1999; Steele & Raider, 2009).

Upstairs and Downstairs Brain

Our brains have an upstairs and downstairs (Siegel & Bryson, 2012). The upstairs is the best place to play, read books, play games, and enjoy the view outside from up high. This is the part of our brains that we use when we learn new things, relax, and have fun. The downstairs is the best place to go when something dangerous is happening outside, like a tornado, a wild animal running loose, or a robber trying to break in. This is the part of our brains that keeps us safe and hidden away from danger and stores the weapons we need to protect ourselves. When a trauma happens to kids, they rush downstairs and stay there until they feel certain that the danger has passed. Once they go back upstairs, some kids hear, see, or even smell things that remind them of the danger, and they hurry back downstairs without taking the time to figure out what it was. Sometimes they look out the upstairs window and the view has completely changed. This might make them rush back down too. Some kids stay downstairs for a really long time because they don't trust upstairs being safe anymore. Other kids go up and down all day long. It can take a while before kids feel comfortable going and staying back upstairs to have fun, play, and learn new things again. Other people who understand what trauma is like can really help them.

Creating a Trauma Narrative

Traumatized children in care will benefit from telling, retelling, and making sense of their traumatic exposures (Cohen et al., 2006; Grasso et al., 2011). However, not all children in care will be capable of safely revisiting these memories. A strong therapeutic alliance, use of psychoeducation and normalization, and engagement of the child's adult supports will positively impact the child's ability to directly reflect on traumas. Even with all of these in place, the child may still be too aroused, avoidant, and easily triggered. Following are key approaches to effectively engaging children in care in creating their trauma narratives when clients can effectively manage their arousal.

Because therapists will already have information about the child's exposures and related symptoms from the assessment, this intervention must focus solely on witnessing the client's perceptions and perspectives (Steele & Raider, 2009). Start by asking clients to pick one traumatic memory to draw, write, play, or animate with a computer program (Grasso et al., 2011). If the client appears willing to share but is unsure which trauma to choose, suggest that the client should pick the most recent one or the one that still bothers the client the most. Leave the choice up to the client. Some children will be forthcoming, whereas others will be unable or unwilling to share. Their response to the invitation will reveal the extensiveness of their trauma reactions (Grasso et al., 2011). For example, a hyperaroused or highly avoidant client may refuse directly, shut down, or engage with other toys or materials in the office. Follow the client's lead. For avoidant clients, share examples of other children's trauma pictures or poems and revisit the psychoeducational metaphors to empathize and normalize their resistance. For aroused clients, engage in anxiety-reducing activities to help them regulate themselves, such as free play or drawing (Crenshaw & Hardy, 2007; Malchiodi, 2008). The initial trauma narrative is not an investigation of what happened, but rather the clients' platform to show how able they are to safely revisit and make sense of the memory by sharing what it was like for them *on their terms*. It takes many children in care months or even years of therapy before they describe or even disclose the extent of their victimization.

CASE STUDY 9.5

Working with 13-year-old Luke seemed smooth compared with treating other teens in care. I started working with him just after his abrupt removal from his father, who had been arrested and incarcerated for battering his girlfriend. Luke shared in detail about his traumatic removal and openly struggled with his grief and mixed emotions toward his dad. He was well matched with his foster placement and appeared open and invested in both the assessment and treatment process.

After almost 2 years of excellent rapport, consistent participation by both Luke and his foster mother, and steady progress on each of his treatment goals, Luke started engaging in high-risk behaviors with his peers.

Just before his father was scheduled to be released from prison, Luke disclosed being sexually abused by his father for most of his childhood and was terrified to go back to him. He had never told another adult until then, which spoke to both the vastness and desperation of his shame and fear as well as the superior quality of the relationship he had built with his foster mother and me. No one blamed him for not disclosing at the beginning of treatment or for repeatedly denying what happened during his numerous interviews and assessments by protection services, doctors, workers, and myself.

For young, developmentally delayed, and hyperaroused clients, use projective play with relevant toys and props, such as stuffed animals, villains, superheroes, weapons, police, a house with furniture and dolls, anatomically correct dolls with removable clothes, toy food, music and noise-making toys, and bedding (Klorer, 2000; Malchiodi, 2008). Allow the child to lead the play and start out by reflecting and narrating the child's actions. Watch for repetitive themes and dynamics to naturally occur. Allow the child to direct the therapist's involvement. If the child plays out abusive interactions, name the feelings and actions of the characters, such as "He doesn't like that; he is scared and wants that guy to stop hitting him! He's running away!"

When the client does share a trauma memory, the way the therapist reacts really matters. Show, not just tell, that the therapist can tolerate hearing the client's living nightmares and not judge the client's feelings and reactions (Steele & Raider, 2009). Ask about the sounds, smells, images, tastes, and textures that stand out to the client or remind the client of the memory, no matter how simple or unrelated they may be. Reflect back what the client describes without interpretation. For example, if the child fills most of the picture of being raped with the image of a floor lamp, simply notice the features of the floor lamp and ask the client to tell more about it. Also ask sequential questions, such as "What happened next?" and "When did he stop?" Ask questions about trauma-related emotions, such as "What was the scariest part?" "What made you the angriest?" "What did you worry about the most?" and " What do you wish you had done differently?" (Steele & Raider, 2009). Avoid "why" questions because they increase defensiveness and implicate fault. If the client is able to respond to these types of questions, continue by asking about the client's current experience of trauma-related feelings to identify possible triggers (Steele & Raider, 2009). For example, ask, "What makes you the angriest now? How can you tell when you feel worried now?" Conclude the session with a relaxing or fun activity, such as sand play, eating snacks, or playing a game.

The client's trauma narrative can be revisited strategically during treatment following clients' increased ability to tolerate the exposure by utilizing effective coping skills in order to make sense of what happened to them and feel empowered and hopeful about their future (Cohen et al., 2006). As arousal and avoidance reactions decrease, interest in revisiting their stories to add details will increase. Heightened avoidance or arousal expressed through resistance, missed appointments, and sabotaging the

CASE STUDY 9.6

I knew Janine's parents were under investigation for multiple accounts of domestic violence, physical abuse, and incest. After spending multiple sessions building rapport by enjoying the 15-year-old's talent for drawing and reflecting on life in her busy foster home, I invited her to draw a picture of one of the traumatic incidents from her past. She quietly huddled over the paper, working intensely and hiding the page from my view. I sat quietly and relaxed. Then she started erasing, redrawing, and then scribbling over the page. When she sat back to show me, it was hard to see what the image was. "Can you tell me about this part?" I asked, pointing to some swirly, blurred lines.

"That's me when I was little underwater. My dad held me down when I told my mother what he did—"

She broke off and hurried out of my office, into the bathroom down the hall. I calmly followed her in, let her know I was there, and told her that whatever she was feeling was okay. She had locked herself in the stall. I expressed genuine concern for her safety and asked if she was safe with herself. After a few minutes, she opened the stall door. We ended up sitting side by side on the bathroom floor. She was teary and overwhelmed. She kept questioning what would make someone do "that" to his own children. I didn't ask what "that" was. I didn't try to answer her questions. I realized that processing with her further might be more than she could handle in that moment, so instead I just listened and stayed with her until she finally made a joke about having therapy in the bathroom and was ready to go back to my office.

Treatment continued for 2 more years, through reunification, additional abuse, and return to care. We both ended up testifying in a juried termination trial that ended her parents' rights. After all the work I did on that case, those moments on the bathroom floor were some of the most powerful and pivotal in her treatment.

therapeutic relationship will occur when the therapist focuses on the narrative too much before the client is ready. When this happens, treatment must shift to rebuilding trust and arousal reduction, with the goal of the client being able to return to the narrative safely (Allen et al., 2012).

Therapists must take care not to expose a child to more trauma input than the child is able to safely handle, or the child may dissociate further. When the clients are able to reflect on their trauma comfortably without trauma reactions, they will express feeling like they have learned from their experiences in a way that has helped them grow as individuals, will feel optimistic about their futures, and will show interest in helping others in similar circumstances.

When the client has completed the trauma narrative, encourage the client to share it with one or more trusted adults (Grasso et al., 2011). For children in care, this may be a birth parent, foster parent, case worker, or staff member at their placement. This process can greatly strengthen the client's capacity to ask for and receive support from trusted adults. It will also be a celebrated milestone in treatment. Let clients choose whom they want to share it with and rehearse what exactly they want to say and show. Focus on arousal reduction and building secure adult relationships if the client cannot identify someone or feels too scared to engage in this intervention. After these sharing sessions, debrief and reflect with both the child and the adult separately (Steele & Raider, 2009).

Lowering Arousal

Just as they benefit from other anxiety-reducing interventions, hyper-aroused children in care will greatly benefit from simple daily routines, predictability at home and school, clear and consistent communication with authority figures, and familiar environments to increase their sense of control and psychological safety (Perry & Szalavitz, 2006). Because caregiving adults are primarily responsible for implementing these strategies in their households, lowering arousal with individual therapy but without parent understanding and investment will prove challenging. Therapists must not underestimate the importance of engaging resistant caregivers patiently and respectfully in order to work collaboratively to lower the child's arousal (Forbes & Post, 2010).

Individually, giving children the experience of being able to relax themselves with their own bodies in session is paramount to reducing arousal and increasing self-regulation (Coholic et al, 2009; Grasso et al., 2011; Levy & Orlans, 1998). Learning to use and trust one's own body is an invaluable and powerful resource for traumatized children who lack external stability. Do this by teaching clients deep breathing through imagining inflating and deflating a giant balloon in their bellies while keeping their chests still. Use a count of 3 to 5 seconds for both the in and out breaths. Once they get the hang of it, encourage them to slow down their out breath by a second or two. Blow bubbles with young children or draw figure eights in sync with their breathing. Once the client has mastered deep controlled breathing, introduce progressive muscle relaxation by teaching them to tighten one part of the body, hold it, and then let it relax (Malchiodi, 2008). Incorporate imagery and imagination in muscle relaxation exercises, such as pretending they are turtles hiding in their shells when they squeeze their neck and shoulder muscles together, or cats tightening the arms, legs, or back when taking a giant stretch.

Help clients to notice their bodily sensations in conjunction with their scary memories or feelings (Steele & Raider, 2009). For example, a child is aware that her stomach feels like it is tied in knots when she imagines having to get replaced again or remembers her sibling getting hit. The client is told to direct her attention to her stomach by breathing into it and using tension reduction to ease the tight feeling in order to relieve the emotional tension related to the memory and gain a sense of control over her body and mind. Conversely, by picturing positive, safe, and calming memories, clients can learn the power they have over changing the sensations in their bodies by choosing to think about different things. This experience is incredibly empowering for traumatized children. This coping skill will decrease their overall arousal as well as increase their ability to safely tolerate revisiting trauma memories and exposure to triggers (Malchiodi, 2008). Little by little, the stored-up frozen energy in their bodies can get discharged safely. Caregivers may also benefit from learning these body-based relaxation skills to cope with their own trauma reactions and be more present and able to support the child (Grasso et al., 2011; Racusin et al., 2005).

Many hyperaroused children may also benefit from intentionally "discharging" energy through movement and exercise (Blaustein & Kinniburgh, 2010). Find out what physical activities the child enjoys or wants to try, and come up with structured, supported times and places for them to engage in the activities. For example, a girl might benefit from doing cartwheels down the hall every morning before school and when she gets home in the afternoon. Teens may find relief from running track and cross-country. Young children need large amounts of time set aside each day for free play on a playground and open space to run around.

Another arousal-reducing intervention involves drawing clients' attention to the sensory aspects of feelings or memories they consider "opposite" to their trauma. Do this by inviting clients to name the first thing that comes to their minds when asked about a smell or scent that makes them feel calm, safe, and strong. Follow the same directive for each of the five senses, including body position (e.g., curled up) and movement (e.g., jumping). Write down or draw each response. Clients who engage in this intervention will feel differently in the moment. Identifying comforting and safe sensory triggers gives both the client and the therapist a powerful set of tools to use with arousal or reexperiencing of symptoms.

Addressing Reexperiencing

Clients who experience active flashbacks, nightmares, or other intrusive images, sounds, and thoughts will benefit from the arousal-reducing strategies described earlier. In addition, work collaboratively to identify trauma reminders because these lead to reexperiencing. Through the trauma narrative and body awareness interventions, clients can become more consciously attuned to recognizing sensory cues that may be triggering them as well as body-based trauma reactions even when the particular cue isn't clear. For example, a teen who realized through developing her trauma narrative that shouting the words "idiot" and "stupid" is strongly associated with her trauma exposure will have greater understanding, and therefore control, over her responses when walking down a crowded school hall where teens may holler these words.

Bringing specific trauma triggers into a client's conscious verbal awareness may in itself decrease their negative influence on the brain's trauma reactions. If not, avoidance of the trigger may be feasible while the client continues to work on developing other coping skills. For example, a foster mother noticed that her child got a better night's sleep on the floor than when in her bed. The foster mom continued to allow the child the option to sleep this way, resulting in improved sleep patterns, instead of insisting that the child choose the more comfortable or appropriate arrangement. The parent and child did not need to understand why the bunk bed had such a negative impact on the child in order to be flexible in creating sleep routines that worked better for the child. Another foster parent realized that taking a certain route home from school seemed to heighten the child's state of arousal. The child pointed out that it looked

CASE STUDY 9.7

I had been working with Belinda for almost a year, and we had developed a strong rapport and treatment focuses including a combination of trauma, grief, and behavior modification interventions. My vision is quite poor and I typically wear contact lenses, but one day I had on my glasses. From the moment we sat down in session, I could tell something was wrong. Belinda could hardly look at me. She was fidgeting and restless. She reminded me of a cornered animal desperate to find a way out of a trap. This was strange because usually I had a hard time getting her out the door. Finally she blurted out, "Ms. Heather I'm sorry but you've just got to take off those glasses—I can't stand it. Please just take them off." She was begging me and her face showed a level of distress I hadn't seen before.

"Okay, Belinda," I responded evenly and calmly removed them from my face. She watched carefully as I put them in my drawer and then instantly relaxed and was ready to move on with our typical session routine.

It felt astonishing to watch. I followed her lead and moved on with our session. She was never able to explain why my glasses had bothered her so much, but knowing what I did about her history and how trauma works, I had no doubt that something about those glasses was deeply linked to a terrifying memory for her. By responding empathically to her expressed need even without fully understanding it, I reinforced her ability to trust herself, use words to ask for help, and increase the feeling of safety in our relationship.

like a place where his substance-abusing mom used to leave him. The foster mom started anticipating the sight of the building before he became aroused and planned to play a certain song he liked while clasping their hands together when passing it by. When repeated, these interactions gave the child the experience of safety and connection when facing a trigger, which in time reduced its negative impact and even the need for the intervention.

Using mindfulness in sessions with clients who struggle with re-experiencing and arousal is also a powerful way to help them both

CASE STUDY 9.8

After working with a traumatized and insecurely attached 7-year-old, Samuel, through multiple placements, he was finally matched with a committed adoptive parent, to whom I gave basic psychoeducation about trauma and how it applied to his son. He struggled with making sense of Samuel's 24-hour hyperarousal and efforts to reenact abusive and neglectful dynamics that he has experienced repeatedly in his past.

As time went on, Samuel's dad shared that he noticed Samuel's affect and body language changed abruptly at seemingly random times. He knew when he saw "the look" to anticipate Samuel engaging in often oppositional and unsafe behaviors but couldn't figure out what caused it. Then one day, his dad came to session with tears in his eyes.

"Ms. Brown, the other day, I took Samuel to get a snack at the store. As he started to eat, I saw that 'look' come over his face. I braced myself, but instead of acting up, Samuel turned to me and said, 'Dad, I don't know why but eating this makes me remember when I had to go to the hospital with my brother. Can I get something else?'"

Samuel had been hospitalized at age 5 for failure to thrive. It was a simple, but significant turning point in treatment.

anticipate reminders more safely and self-soothe when triggered (Webb, 2006). Mindfulness describes being aware of what is going on inside and around oneself in the present time and place, apart from the past or future and without judgment. Although children naturally tend to be more mindful than adults, traumatized children are so frozen in their fears from the past and anxious about what might happen in the future that they struggle with being able to rest in the "here and now." There are countless ways to engage children and teens in practicing mindfulness. For example, the body relaxation and awareness exercises described earlier each involve mindfulness. Movements such as active role play or dancing are also child-friendly ways to give clients the relieving experience of mindfulness. Art invites mindfulness while it is being created and once it is finished. For example, have clients create collages of calming images to hang on their walls or in their lockers, and have them make textured, comforting pillows, blankets, or dolls to have at home. The more sensory components an activity involves, the more mindfully engaging it will be. For example, have the client use aromatherapy during body exercises, listen to music while creating the collage, or sew a cinnamon stick into the soft pillow.

Replacing Avoidance

Traumatized children use avoidance to protect themselves from feeling the terror, pain, and anxiety that come with reexperiencing and arousal. Dissociation and numbing are common in children in care. Unfortunately, children cannot numb selective feelings only. If they are avoiding fear then they are also avoiding joy and pleasure. Engaging avoidant clients with arousal-reducing interventions that decrease their perceived need for avoidance and psychoeducation that normalizes and validates their avoidance are effective approaches (Gil, 2006). Following are several strategies to engage avoidant traumatized clients.

Interventions that increase clients' comfort level with their feelings overall, and specifically positive feelings, will help empower their internal strengths and thaw the frozen barrier to accessing all feelings. Start by engaging clients in making photo collages about their hopes and dreams and things they like and dislike about themselves, their families, and foster care (Malchiodi, 2008). When they choose images of things or places, ask them to identify how they feel about the images and notice how they feel in their bodies when they look at the images. When they choose images of people, ask them to imagine what the characters are thinking about, feeling, or saying. Intervene in a similar way when children are engaged in projective play by noticing when they express preferences, wants, thoughts, or actions, and connect these to having emotions. Validating whatever feelings clients express can empower them to push the limits of discomfort that are safely tolerable to themselves and others (Grasso et al., 2011; Prather & Golden, 2009).

Another way to increase clients' awareness of and comfort with their feelings is to list the major emotional themes related to trauma, and give basic psychoeducation about how feelings work and why they are helpful (Blaustein & Kinniburgh, 2010). For example, teach children how feelings, thoughts, and actions all affect one another and that changing thought patterns and actions to influence their feelings is much easier than trying to directly change how they feel. Teach that having feelings is okay and actually very helpful. Describe how feeling fear helps us know when we need protection. Worry and anxiety help us anticipate and prepare for problems. Hurt and sadness show us that something important to us has been lost or wronged. Anger gives us energy to do something about it. Teach that it is the way people choose to deal with their feelings that can be harmful to themselves and others. Give the same attention to the client's perceptions of accountability, such as feelings of guilt, shame, and revenge. These normal reactions to trauma must be validated nonjudgmentally in order to be relieved and restructured (Grasso et al., 2011). Help clients concretely differentiate appropriate and inappropriate responses to each feeling through writing or drawing (Prather & Golden, 2009). Further their awareness and ownership of feelings by practicing I statements and filling in the outline of a body to show where different feelings show up in their bodies (Gil, 2006). Ask clients to create their own visual representation of what different feelings are like to them. Say, "If your anger was a picture, what would it look like?" and then follow the same directive with an opposite feeling, such as peace or calm. These interventions will increase their ability to emotionally regulate themselves (Prather & Golden, 2009).

Avoidant clients will engage more easily in indirectly expressing their need for safety and protection in ways that do not involve revisiting their trauma memories (Malchiodi, 2008). For example, ask clients to choose a small animal figurine and invite them to draw or create a safe place for the figurine with craft supplies. Direct the child to give the creature everything it needs to feel safe and comfortable in its space. An extension of this intervention is to have the child, a sibling set, or group design an entire map of a city that provides everything its residents need and is ready and able to deal safely with any threat. Engaging clients in a basic, brief guided imagery focused on imagining their own safe places of peace and calm can also help clients to access internal feelings of safety and rest. Have them draw their imagined places. Similarly, invite them to picture revisiting one of their most safe, calm, and connected memories with secure people or places. Again, clients can use art materials to express the memory. For example, a child may draw himself sitting alone in a quiet library surrounded by books, splashing down a water slide at an amusement park, or sitting at Thanksgiving dinner at Grandma's with the smells of the food and view of his family members' smiling faces.

Making or decorating masks is another powerful way to validate the child's avoidance in terms of the child's need for protection

(Malchiodi, 2008). Therapists can do this by using paper plates or cardboard cut-outs to model different types of feelings. Therapists can also have the client decorate both the inside and outside of a mask to represent what the client shows to others and the feelings the client keeps hidden. For older children, engage in a discussion about the purpose of a mask (to hide or conceal something for protection), and share poetry that speaks to the masks people wear to cover their feelings. Allow the client to express or interpret the directive in the way the client chooses, whether personalizing it meaningfully or staying quiet and focused on the art making.

Changing the Victim Mindset

Once traumatized clients feel psychologically safe with the therapist, have stable and trusted homes and caregivers, and are effectively using coping skills to manage arousal, decrease reexperiencing, and lower their avoidance, they will be more able and ready to confront and change their negatively altered thinking patterns, belief systems, and feelings about themselves, others, and the world around them (Gil, 2006; Grasso et al., 2011; Webb, 2006). This is a key time in treatment to expound upon the trauma narrative in efforts to make sense of what happened and their reactions in terms of a survivor rather than a victim. Remember that each of these interventions involves upper-level brain functions and may not be accessible to children who are in constant arousal, who lack the stability and the support of a safe adult, or who are being actively triggered (Perry & Szalavitz, 2006).

When projective play has been the primary treatment intervention, the therapist will be familiar with repeated dynamics or themes. Cognitive reframing for these clients involves the therapist taking a more assertive role in the play by initiating changes to the child's patterns that essentially model alternative coping skills or "endings." For example, if a child repeatedly makes a small cat hide all over the house while a dragon comes in, tracks it down, and destroys the house, intervene by making the cat say, "I can't have any fun when I spend all my time hiding away from that good-for-nothing dragon. I don't like this anymore! Stop dragon! Get out of here!" With repetition, the child will either adopt a new pattern of similar scenarios or will lose interest in that play pattern altogether because the child has mastered this fear.

With the client who is school aged and older, have the client pretend to revisit a trauma memory as a "fly on the wall" and see it as though it was happening to another kid, not the client. Afterward, ask the client to describe what he saw, including anything that surprised him. Then ask him what advice he would offer to the child in that scenario. An alternate approach is to give the client some concrete information about how many other children go through traumatic experiences similar to those of the client. Engage the client in reflecting on what other children might find helpful to hear or know, and have the client describe it in a letter, sign, or piece of art.

With older children and teens, show them contrasting thoughts, feelings, and belief systems of victims versus survivors (Steele & Raider, 2009)—for example, not expecting good things to happen in life versus knowing that good things, along with bad, will be a part of their futures, or feeling like getting close to others will only cause more problems versus knowing that there are people out there that they can trust and get close to who will not hurt or leave them. Have clients identify which mindsets most describe where they are right now. Then ask them to reflect on any changes they notice. For example, a boy might describe feeling like he used to believe that he caused the abuse, but that he now knows that it was not his fault or responsibility to stop his parent from being violent toward him and his siblings. Continue to validate any existing victim thoughts and feelings in the context of what the client has been through. Then empathically confront and reframe the thoughts and feelings to reinforce the client's survival mentality. For example, when a girl shares that she still believes she will never trust another adult woman in her life, respond with, "Of course you never want to risk putting your faith in another adult, especially a woman who says she wants to help you, after all that your mother has put you through!" followed by, "Clearly not every adult will be trustworthy, and you are the one who gets to decide whether to trust them or not. I know that there is a part of you that must know that there are some adults you can trust. I know this because you wouldn't have opened up with me as much as you have unless you thought you could trust me." Exception finding, thought stopping, modeling, normalizing, and reflecting on trauma psychoeducation, the successfully employed coping skills, and paradoxical interventions are other examples of interventions to use in cognitive reframing of trauma-related thoughts (Gil, 2006; Webb, 2006).

Last, many victims of abuse, neglect, and loss expect these experiences to continue in their futures. Building safety skills is a key part of trauma intervention with children in care (Grasso et al., 2011). Give clients concrete tools to (a) avoid unsafe situations by learning to trust their bodies and assess risky situations, (b) verbally and physically respond to unsafe people, and (c) identify who and how to tell if an incident of abuse or neglect occurs. Use sensory-based, developmentally appropriate interventions to increase clients' awareness of their choices. For example, have young clients trace their hands and write or draw five different people and places they can go to when they need help (Malchiodi, 2008). With school-aged children, create a map of key places in their lives: home, school, babysitter's house, and so forth. Have them write or draw what they can say and do in each setting if they feel scared or are victimized. This is an especially important and timely intervention for children who are being replaced or reunified.

When therapists observe the traumatized client connect with others more easily, enjoy fun activities, look forward to future plans, and show a stronger sense of positive self-worth, they will know that the bulk of individual trauma treatment has been done (Grasso et al., 2011). The next stage of treatment, better for group interventions, focuses on enhancing posttraumatic growth, which naturally connects children to others who can relate to being in child welfare (Coholic et al., 2009; Webb, 2006).

CONCLUSION

All children in care are exposed to trauma, and many struggle deeply with its devastating influence. However, there are many ways to help these children heal and feel better. Providing therapeutic interventions for traumatized children in care is intense and rewarding work. The more trauma-informed collaboration that is done with families and professionals, the quicker and greater the impact will be on the child. Even the most trauma-filled kaleidoscope holds beauty and wonder. Keep turning to see it.

RESOURCES

National Childhood Traumatic Stress Network: www.nctsn.com
The National Institute for Trauma and Loss in Children: www.starr.org/training/tlc
Child Trauma Academy: www.childtrauma.org

REFERENCES

Allen, B., Oseni, A., & Allen, K. (2012). The evidence-based treatment of chronic posttraumatic stress disorder and traumatic grief in an adolescent: A case study. *Psychological Trauma: Theory, Research, Practice, and Policy, 4*(6), 631–639.

Blaustein, M. E., & Kinniburgh, K. M. (2010). *Treating traumatic stress in children and adolescents: How to foster resilience through attachment, self-regulation, and competency.* New York, NY: Guilford Press.

Brown, A., McCauley, K., Navalta, C., & Saxe, G. (2013). Trauma systems therapy in residential settings: Improving emotion regulation and the social environment of traumatized children and youth in congregate care. *Journal of Family Violence, 28,* 693–703.

Cohen, J., Mannarino, A., & Deblinger, E. (2006). *Treating trauma and traumatic grief in children and adolescents.* New York, NY: Guilford Press.

Coholic, D., Lougheed, S., & Cadel, S. (2009). Exploring the helpfulness of arts-based methods with children living in foster care. *Traumatology, 15*(3), 64–71.

Conradi, L., Agosti, J., Tullberg, E., Richardson, L., Langan, H., Ko, S., & Wilson, C. (2011). Promising practices and strategies for using trauma-informed child welfare practice to improve foster care placement stability: A breakthrough series collaborative. *Child Welfare, 90*(6), 207–225.

Crenshaw, D. A., & Hardy, K. V. (2007). The crucial role of empathy in breaking the silence of traumatized children in play therapy. *International Journal of Play Therapy, 16,* 160–175.

Dorsey, S., Burns, B., Southerland, D., Revillion Cox, J., Wagner, H., & Farmer, E. (2011). Prior trauma exposure for youth in treatment. *Journal of Child and Family Studies, 21,* 816–824.

Forbes, H. T., & Post, B. B. (2010). *Beyond consequences, logic, and control: A love-based approach to helping children with severe behaviors.* Boulder, CO: BCI.

Geller, S. M., & Porges, S. W. (2014). Therapeutic presence: Neurophysiological mechanisms mediating feeling safe in therapeutic relationships. *Journal of Psychotherapy Integration, 24*(3), 178–192.

Gil, E. (2006). *Helping abused and traumatized children.* New York: NY: Guilford Press.

Grasso, D., Joselow, B., Marquez, Y., & Webb, C. (2011). Trauma-focused cognitive behavioral therapy of a child with posttraumatic stress disorder. *Journal of Psychotherapy, 48*(2), 188–197.

Holmes, M. M., & Mudlaff, S. J. (2000). *A terrible thing happened.* Washington, DC: Magination Press.

Hoyle, S. (2000). *The sexualized child in foster care: A guide for foster parents and other professionals.* Washington, DC: Child Welfare League of America, Inc.

Johnson, T. C. (2011). *Helping children with sexual behavior problems: A guidebook for professions and caregivers.* San Diego, CA: Institute of Violence, Abuse and Trauma.

Jungbluth, N. J., & Shirk, S. R. (2009). Therapist strategies for building involvement in cognitive–behavioral therapy for adolescent depression. *Journal of Consulting and Clinical Psychology, 77*(6), 1179–1184. doi:http://dx.doi.org/10.1037/a0017325

Kehoe, P. (1987). *Something happened and I'm scared to tell.* Seattle, WA: Parenting Press.

Klorer, P. G. (2000). *Expressive therapy with troubled children.* Lanham, MD: Rowman & Littlefield.

Levy, T. M., & Orlans, M. (1998). *Attachment, trauma, and healing: Understanding and treating attachment disorder in children and families.* Arlington, VA: CWLA Press.

Malchiodi, C. A. (Ed.). (2008). *Creative interventions with traumatized children.* New York, NY: Guilford Press.

National Childhood Traumatic Stress Network. (2008). *Trauma-informed interventions: Clinical research evidence and culture-specific information project.* Retrieved from http://www.nctsn.org/resources/topics/trauma-informed-interventions

Oetzel, K. B., & Scherer, D. G. (2003). Therapeutic engagement with adolescents in psychotherapy. *Psychotherapy: Theory, Research, Practice, Training, 40*(3), 215–225. doi:10.1037/0033-3204.40.3.215

Perry, B. D., & Szalavitz, M. (2006). *The boy who was raised as a dog and other stories from a child psychiatrist's notebook: What traumatized children can teach us about loss, love, and healing.* Philadelphia, PA: Basic Books.

Prather, W., & Golden, J. (2009). A behavioral perspective of childhood trauma and attachment issues: Toward alternative treatment approaches for children with a history of abuse. *International Journal of Behavioral and Consultation Theory, 5*(1), 56–74.

Racusin, R., Maerlender, Jr., A., Sengupta, A., Isquith, P., & Straus, M. (2005). Psychosocial treatment of children in foster care: A review. *Community Mental Health Journal, 41*(2), 199–221.

Seita, J. R., Mitchell, M., & Tobin, C. (1997). Connections, continuity, dignity and opportunity: Essential ingredients for creating our village: Reclaiming children and youth. *Journal of Emotional and Behavioral Problems, 6*(1), 45–47.

Shepard, C. H. (1998). *Brave Bart: A story for traumatized and grieving children.* Clinton Township, MI: TLC.

Siegel, D. J., & Bryson, T. P. (2012). *The whole-brain child: 12 revolutionary strategies to nurture your child's developing mind.* New York, NY: Bantam Books.

Steele, W. (1999). *A trauma is like no other experience.* Clinton Township, MI: TLC.

Steele, W., & Raider, M. (2009). *Structured Sensory Intervention for Traumatized Children, Adolescents and Parents (SITCAP): Evidence based interventions to alleviate trauma.* Lewiston, NY: The Edwin Mellen Press.

Tarren-Sweeney, M. (2013). An investigation of complex attachment- and trauma-related symptomatology among children in foster and kinship care. *Child Psychiatry Human Development, 44,* 727–741.

van der Kolk, B. A., McFarlane, A. C., & Weisaeth, L. (Eds.). (1996). *Traumatic stress: The effects of overwhelming experience on mind, body, and society.* New York: NY: Guilford Press.

Webb, N. B. (Ed.). (2006). *Working with traumatized youth in child welfare.* New York: NY: Guilford Press.

CHAPTER TEN

BEHAVIOR MODIFICATION
AND SOCIAL SKILLS

Oftentimes adults working in the child welfare system view everything through the lens of behavior. The kaleidoscope becomes stuck on one shape and color and fails to turn or move. Remember to always turn the kaleidoscope and view the reasons behind a behavior before embarking on a behavior modification plan (see Exhibit 10.1). Many behavior modification plans fail because the therapist and other adults do not have a solid understanding of the reasons behind the behavior. A therapist may not properly draft a plan that realistically allows the child and parent to succeed. The result of a poorly executed behavior plan is usually failure for both the child and the family. The foster parents or birth parents return to complain that the plan did not work, and they blame the therapist. Creating an effective, workable behavior modification plan takes skill, time, and planning.

NEGATIVE ATTENTION-SEEKING BEHAVIOR

Often therapists hear statements from foster parents, colleagues, caseworkers, judges, and peers that describe a child's behavior as "negative attention seeking." This term reduces the gravity of the child's current experience. The term *negative attention seeking* also reduces the child's purposeful actions to "just wanting attention." All human behavior exists to seek attention from others. Of course foster care children seek out attention due to their unique emotional and mental health needs. Reducing the child's actions to "negative attention seeking" eliminates the need to properly and adequately assess the reasons for the behavior. Behavior modification should not begin until the child's motivation for her actions are clear, and attention seeking is not a clear or useful motivation to describe behavior. Children in foster care learn behavior that helps them

EXHIBIT 10.1

Ideally, only use a behavior modification plan when you have support from all stakeholders involved. These parties include foster parents, birth parents, case managers, supervisors, school personnel, and any other therapist involved with the child. Realistically, ensure that at least the adult responsible for implementing the plan supports the plan. Creating a plan that fails can be as detrimental as not creating a plan at all.

adapt to their situation. Like most people, they are reluctant to change or develop new patterns that might cause them to risk their survival. Children in foster care might "negative attention seek" in order to ensure the proximity of a caregiver. Likewise, a foster care child might "negative attention seek" after experiencing neglect out of fear of being left alone again. Effective behavior modification comes from a place of empathy and theoretical understanding of the meaning behind the behavior.

Behavior modification plans begin by considering all the shapes and colors in the kaleidoscope, such as trauma, attachment, the child's developmental level, the child's history of grief and loss, the concerns of the foster parent and birth family, and cultural considerations. For example, let's examine the behavior of a child who refuses to go to sleep. Seen through the lens of trauma, the behavior could be motivated by a desire to avoid dark, scary places. Seen through the lens of attachment, the behavior could be motivated by a desire to maintain proximity to a caregiver or fear of losing an attachment figure. Seen through the lens of grief, the child could feel despair and be unable to sleep due to depression and anxiety. Remember that behavior could be motivated by multiple reasons, and understanding the reason(s) will better ensure success. Understanding the motivation also allows the therapist to better determine how to change the behavior. A child experiencing a trauma reaction to going to sleep should not receive punishment for failing to sleep. A child with attachment issues would benefit from a behavior modification plan that focuses on having a concrete reminder of the parent with him during the night.

Finally, devise the plan around the child's developmental needs and abilities. Children under 7 years of age need to develop autonomy but do not have the ability to manage a plan on their own. Older children need to have a sense of control in changing their behavior and will be more resistant to change.

This chapter reviews the steps needed to craft a workable plan and provides several examples for therapists to use.

BRIEF BEHAVIOR THEORY REVIEW

This review is based on the work of Wolpe (1990) and offers general principles of behavior therapy; it then provides examples and step-by-step techniques for carrying out successful plans.

Classical Conditioning

Classical conditioning occurs when someone encounters an event (unconditioned stimulus) and has some type of reaction (unconditioned response) to the event. If the event occurs several times or the event is traumatic, the thought or site of the event will become a conditioned stimulus and will result in an anxious response (conditioned response) without the actual event occurring.

For example, many kinds of events make individuals feel nervous or anxious (unconditioned stimulus). When we feel nervous our hands sweat, our stomachs hurt, and we might feel our hearts beating loudly. This process of the central nervous system is an unconditioned response, something that happens naturally in our bodies in response to fear. It is the fight-or-flight response, and our bodies are preparing to either fight or run to survive. Imagine someone has never been afraid of elevators, and one day the elevator she is riding on becomes stuck and then begins to sway (unconditioned stimulus). She would experience a fight-or-flight response (unconditioned response). Now imagine that this swaying happens over and over for at least 2 hours before she is rescued. Each time the elevator lurches, her body responds with panic and anxiety. When she is finally free, she is able to calm down and does not have to use an elevator again for several weeks. When she approaches an elevator for the first time in several weeks (conditioned stimulus), she experiences the panicked response and refuses to go near it (conditioned response), so instead she takes the stairs. In this example, the fear associated with the danger of being stuck in the elevator became paired with the elevator itself. The body no longer needs to be inside an elevator and in danger to have the fear response; it just needs to see the elevator to panic.

This process happens without thought and is often beyond our control. It is the primary process believed to occur during a traumatic situation and the reason why classical conditioning treatments are often applied to victims of trauma. Classically conditioned responses do not respond to rewards or punishment, and instead the focus of treatment should be on increasing relaxation techniques and teaching coping skills to alleviate the panic. These techniques include systematic desensitization, implosion, and flooding. Systematic desensitization is the process of creating a scale of progressively fearful situations involving the stimulus, with 1 being the least fearful and 10 being the most fearful; for example, for the scenario with the elevator described earlier, a 1 could be seeing a picture of an elevator, a 6 could be standing outside an elevator, and a 10 could be riding the elevator. The client is taught relaxation techniques and is then exposed to each stimulus, starting with 1. Each exposure requires the client to relax

---

CASE STUDY 10.1

Adrienne was a foster parent who had received a placement for twin toddlers, both with an inability to sleep through the night. The boys would refuse to sleep alone in their room and scream and complain of nightmares, keeping her up all night. I theorized that the boys had paired bedtime (conditioned stimulus) with a negative fearful event (conditioned response). In order to eliminate the conditioned response, I asked the foster parent to alter the bedtime routine. Realizing the process would take time, I provided emotional support to the foster parent. She added two nightlights to the room that each child could control. She added a new nighttime ritual that included two bedtime stories, first away from the room, then eventually in the room. The stories focused on safety. She also taught the children a song about being calm and would sing it each night. If the children experienced anxiety, she would sing it with them again. All of these techniques were designed to pair bedtime with a new conditioned stimulus—stories and singing—rather than fear. The new conditioned response would be the ability to be calm and sleep. The process took 2 weeks, but the toddlers were eventually able to sleep in their room.

and reduce anxiety. The client then continues this process until she has reached the highest level. Another type of exposure therapy that relies on teaching the client relaxation techniques is called implosion. In implosion, the client is taught relaxation techniques but is then exposed to the most frightening stimulus. Flooding exposes the client to the stimulus without benefit of relaxation techniques. The goal of flooding is to treat anxiety/panic like a broken thermostat. Flooding causes wave after wave of anxiety until the body reaches the point where no more adrenaline can pump out, and then it drops off completely. All of these tools are designed to break the conditioned response from the conditioned stimulus.

Classical Conditioning Treatment Steps

   Step 1: Determine the conditioned stimulus. This process takes time, and the use of a daily journal is helpful. Ask the caregiver to document what happens before, during, and after a conditioned response. If the child is old enough, ask the child to keep a journal and, each time an incident happens, to write down what caused the event. Document how the child responds to attempts to calm the child.

   Step 2: Determine what already works. Therapists often like to come up with their own advice for calming down, but unless it resonates with the child it will not work. Find out how the child currently tries to self-soothe or what other adults have done to help. Also find out how the child distracts herself when bored or upset. Again, having someone observe the child helps in figuring this out.

   Step 3: Create a relaxation plan pertinent to the child. If the child has tools she already uses, ensure that the child uses them more frequently or in a more structured way. If nothing has worked, teach controlled breathing. Help the child create a list of possible distractions such as reading a book, playing a video game, coloring, working on math problems, or doing origami. The point of a distraction is to block the anxiety or angry responses by forcing the brain to focus on a structured task. Avoid open ended or unstructured activities, such as freehand drawing, because these activities could increase anxiety. Rhythmic drawing synced with breathing (figure eights) can be helpful. Ensure you have the caregiver's cooperation with this plan. For example, if a child uses a video game to prevent a rage outburst and the foster parent takes the game away due to bad behavior, the plan will not work.

Step 4: Create a scale of 1 to 10 items that describe a mild conditioned stimulus to a severe conditioned stimulus. This step might not be needed for all issues but does work to help the client practice the distraction and relaxation techniques in the therapist's office. This step also illustrates that the problem cannot be eradicated all at once but will take small steps of progress.

Step 5: Continue keeping a journal and document success. If the process is not working, remember to evaluate every 4 to 6 weeks and adjust the plan as needed.

CASE STUDY 10.2

Seven-year-old Jonas had frequent nightmares and would wake up screaming every night. He did not want to go to bed; he would get out of bed, leave the room, and wander the halls. The foster parent would find him asleep on the stairs, but if she tried to move Jonas, he would wake up and scream. After careful journaling, we discovered that Jonas would force himself to stay awake and sneak out of the room after he was put to bed. The bedtime ritual included a 10-minute bedtime story and then lights out. After more observation, the foster parent noticed that when upset during the day, Jonas would find crayons and draw monsters. When asked about the drawings, he stated that the monsters came to him in his dreams. He would rarely seek out the comfort of his caregiver due to his history of neglect.

First, I worked with Jonas to develop a list of items that caused increased anxiety. Number 1 was going into his room during the day for a nap and number 10 was going to bed at night with the lights out. I worked with the foster parent to create several distractions for Jonas to have available at night, including coloring books, crayons, and a nightlight he could turn on and off. I also instructed the foster parent to begin spending the night with Jonas in his room because he needed comfort and security and could not ask for it. Using an attachment technique, I also instructed the foster parent to share a transitional object with Jonas: a teddy bear. In this case, I was creating a new conditioned stimulus and conditioned response.

(continued)

CASE STUDY 10.2 (*continued*)

I wanted to link the foster parent with the teddy bear, so the stimulus of being comforted by his foster parent could become a conditioned stimulus of receiving comfort from his teddy bear. We also created a magic wand that could transform the monsters into a cookie or a hot-fudge sundae.

Jonas said, "I can eat them up!"

Because the thought of going to bed with the lights out proved terrifying for him, we began with asking Jonas to go into his room with the foster parent and color after story time. The foster parent left the lights on and would leave after incrementally shorter time frames. First she might stay the whole night, then she would stay less and less, each time knowing Jonas had the teddy bear and a distraction available to handle stress. The process took about 3 weeks until Jonas could tolerate going to bed with the nightlight. His nightmares decreased as well.

As with all treatment modalities, classical conditioning requires supporting adults who understand that the process is slow and may require fine tuning. In the case of trauma exposure, extreme care should be taken because exposure can result in an increased traumatic response.

Operant Conditioning

First, a brief review of operant conditioning is in order. The premise is fairly simple: A behavior plus a reinforcer equals more behavior. However, a reinforcer does not mean a reward. Although most rewards are reinforcers, not all reinforcers are rewards. A reinforcer is any stimulus that increases behavior. For example, money acts as a reinforcer to ensure people keep going to work, but other factors also reinforce work behavior, such as pride in doing a good job, a sense of accomplishment, or wanting to avoid losing your home. Two types of reinforcers exist: positive reinforcement and negative reinforcement. Most individuals equate negative reinforcement with punishment. It is not punishment; the term *reinforcement* means that negative reinforcers are designed to increase behavior. In the previous example, money and pride are positive reinforcers, whereas the fear of losing your job or home is a negative reinforcer. Negative reinforcers are best conceived of as logical or natural consequences when behavior stops. If you don't pay your mortgage, you lose your house. The threat of losing your house is a negative reinforcer because it increases the behavior of going to work. Here is another example: If a parent wants a child to clean his room, the parent could provide a reward at the end of each day when the room is clean, such as an allowance or a favorite treat. This is an example of a positive reinforcement. However, if the parent instead chooses to not do the child's laundry and continues putting dirty clothes into the room so that the child cannot even sleep on the bed, making the child clean up to avoid going to school dirty, this is an example of negative reinforcement. The only person who can determine what will reinforce behavior is the person engaging in the behavior. In other words, we determine what reinforces us. For example, a therapist might decide to use a sticker as a reinforcement to clean the therapy room, but the client hates stickers so she refuses to clean the room. Adults who yell or punish children assume that the children hate being yelled at, so the children will stop the behavior. Actually, for maltreated children, yelling might be viewed as a reinforcer. Yelling might increase the behavior because the child has been noticed by the adult.

Reinforcers work by increasing behavior, but how much they work depends on the frequency and amount of behavior. There are four types of reinforcers: fixed ratio, variable ratio, fixed interval, and variable interval. In the ratio model, a child must perform the behavior a specific number of times to receive the reinforcement. In the interval model, the child receives a reinforcer based on a specific time frame. Table 10.1 illustrates the different types of positive reinforcement schedules for a child who needs to do math homework.

Table 10.1 *Positive Reinforcement Schedules*

Type	Description
Fixed ratio	A sticker for every three math problems
Fixed interval	A sticker for sitting in math class for half an hour
Variable ratio	A sticker for completing math problems—the number of problems changes each time
Variable interval	A sticker for sitting through math class—the amount of time to reward changes each day

The most effective models for increasing behavior are either variable interval or variable ratio, or both. When an individual does not know when the reinforcer is coming, the behavior will increase at a greater rate than when the individual knows when to expect the reward.

Behavior Elimination

There are two ways to eliminate behavior: punishment and extinction. Punishment is the introduction of an aversive stimuli that will stop behavior. Extinction is the removal of all reinforcement. Extinction is much more effective than punishment to eliminate behavior but is often difficult for adults to tolerate. When extinction occurs, the adult removes all reinforcement from the behavior, and, as a result, the child dramatically increases the behavior to get the reinforcement back. For example, if every time a 5-year-old boy threw a temper tantrum before bed the adults allowed him to stay up and watch television, the adult attention and the ability to watch television would both act as positive reinforcers of the behavior. Assuming the parents choose to use operant conditioning to eliminate the behavior, they have two choices: punishment or extinction. If they choose punishment, here is a likely scenario: Every time the child starts a tantrum he loses a toy. The child keeps throwing tantrums until he has no toys, and the parents continue to engage with him as he loses toy after toy. The parents continue to escalate the punishment. In this case, the parents view losing the toy as aversive to the child, but the attention and control the child receives is in fact a stronger positive reinforcer than losing the toy, so the behavior continues. If the parents choose extinction, they remove all reinforcers from the child by not responding in any way to the tantrum while ensuring that the television stays off. The child will continue to scream and yell, but if the parents stay firm and do not respond, the child will eventually realize that the reinforcer is gone and will stop the behavior.

Addressing Behavior Problems

Foster parents or other caregivers often struggle with the notion of not being able to "punish" the child and will often look to the therapist for advice. Some foster and birth parents struggle with the inability to use physical discipline of any kind with children in foster care and create draconian punishments that often fail or exacerbate the problem. When working with foster parents, differentiate between punishment and discipline. Punishment is the process of reducing behavior; discipline, however, is how humans learn order and structure. Discuss the origin of the word *discipline* by reminding adults that it comes from the word *disciple* and means "follower" or "to have order." It does not mean to hit someone. When we use the term a "disciplined athlete," we don't suggest that the coach hit the athlete to improve the performance. Behavior management should focus on helping the child create an internal locus of control—in other words, self-discipline.

Try to encourage the caregiver to avoid using harsh punishments or removing privileges (see Exhibit 10.2). Remember that children in foster care have already suffered the loss of their parents, homes, siblings, toys, communities, and so forth. Threats to remove a toy often fail because the child does not respond to something that has already happened and believes will happen again. Children with a history of neglect do not typically respond to losing a toy because they are used to not having items and do not expect to keep items. Punishments such as making the child go hungry or standing in a corner are also ineffective for children who have experienced abuse and neglect. If you are used to being hungry, not having access to food merely increases your anger; it does not eliminate unwanted behavior.

Behavior modification plans should focus on shaping desired behavior and avoid focusing on punishment or withdrawing privileges. Finally, therapists must remember to manage expectations for the child, the adult, and themselves. Changing behavior takes time for both adults and children. The seriousness of the behavioral problems often puts pressure on everyone involved to make change happen immediately, but reminding everyone to manage expectations and that humans take time to adjust to change will allow the process to work.

EXHIBIT 10.2

Punishments that appear to be "common sense," such as removing a privilege or grounding a child to his room, only work because of the quality of the relationship the child has with the caregiver and the child's desire to please the adult. If this relationship does not exist, the child most likely will not respond.

BEHAVIOR MODIFICATION CHARTS

This section presents step-by-step instructions for creating an effective behavior modification chart, followed by examples that demonstrate successful behavior modification plans.

Step 1: Observation. This step is often missed because charts are created based on caregiver or teacher feedback. As in classical conditioning, treatment should start with journaling and specific observation of behavior, including what happens before, during, and after the behavior. How does the child react to the adult, and what makes the behavior increase or decrease? Determine what adults do to reinforce the child before beginning behavior modification. This part is challenging. A neglected child might seek out punishment as a way to get noticed, so this child becomes reinforced by parental admonishments; an abused child who received physical contact from hitting will view being hit as reinforcing.

Step 2: Determine what is reinforcing to the child. This step is vitally important in order to determine what would make the child increase behavior. Observation helps, as does talking to the child and finding out what type of reward she wants. Do not forget to include verbal praise as a reinforcer, assuming the child responds well to adults praising her behavior.

Step 3: Choose only one or two behaviors to increase. The focus on behavior modification must be on increasing or shaping the behavior you want. The plan should be measurable and easy for everyone to follow, and the desired behavior should either be small, specific, and easily observable, or very broad. A specific behavior plan focuses on increasing one or two behaviors, such as brushing teeth each day or making the bed. A broad behavior plan focuses on overall positive behavior throughout the day, such as "caught being good." The child receives a reinforcer for any behavior the adult views as desired.

Step 4: Choose a goal the child can meet. Create the chart with easy-to-meet goals, initially using either a fixed-ratio or fixed-interval system. As the child meets the goals, move to a variable-ratio or variable-interval system.

Step 5: Set the child up for success. Ensure the adults work together to ensure the child meets the goals. This is a step not often addressed in behavior modification plans but is a technique that is very useful with this population. When a child comes to treatment, no one is used to success. The child often receives messages of failure, and the foster parent or birth parent may also feel ineffective in changing the behavior. Behavior modification plans often fail because the expectation for change is too high or because they focus on eliminating behavior. When the plan fails, hopelessness takes over, and both adults and children view the failure as more evidence that change cannot occur. Therefore, create a chart, at least initially, that allows the adult to see that he or she effects change and that allows the child to see that she can earn the reward.

Step 6: Work with the child and parents to create the chart, and ask them to work together. The chart should be colorful and include pictures as well as words. The system for earning the rewards should be clear and the rewards should be easy to obtain. The chart should not include removal of already-earned points and should not require the child to achieve 100% to receive the reward. The best charts have small rewards and large rewards. The ratio or interval should be based on the developmental needs and abilities of the child. For example, a 5-year-old child probably cannot tolerate waiting all day to receive a reinforcement and will not strive to meet the goal unless the reinforcement occurs more frequently. A 10-year-old child might be able to wait a day or two to receive the reinforcement, but, again, it depends on the developmental needs of the child. Some 10-year-olds might initially need reinforcement every hour.

Step 7: Implement the chart and evaluate progress every week in treatment. If the child has not met the goal, then step 5 was not implemented correctly; go back and try again. If the child has met the goal, remember to move to a variable-reinforcement system. With success, you can begin adding new behaviors to shape.

Table 10.2 provides a checklist for use in creating behavior modification plans.

Table 10.2 *Behavior Modification Checklist*

✓ Avoid punishment
✓ Find what reinforces the child
✓ Shape the behavior you want
✓ Use positive wording
✓ Manage expectations
✓ Set the child up to succeed

BEHAVIOR MODIFICATION EXAMPLES

Example 1: Daily Chart (Ratio)

This type of chart is designed to help remind the child of daily activities. Use pictures along with words, and build in behaviors that the child can meet without much effort. Because children in foster care often come from homes with little structure and may not know how to behave in a structured way, this chart provides them with a visual tool. Have the child or parent mark on the chart after each task, and imbed the reward.

Tables 10.3 and 10.4 show two daily task charts—one for tasks to be completed before school and one for tasks to be completed after school, respectively.

As you can see from this fixed-ratio chart, the child can easily earn 2 points by waking up and eating; if the child completes one more task, the

Table 10.3 *Task Chart Before School*

Daily Task Chart: Complete 3 out of 5 for one sticker, complete 5 out of 5 for two stickers. Complete 10 by end of the week to be allowed to watch one show.

Before School	Each Day
Wake up	
Brush teeth	
Fold sheets on bed	
Eat breakfast	
Put dishes in dishwasher	

Table 10.4 *Task Chart After School*

Daily Task Chart: Complete 3 out of 5 for one sticker, complete 5 out of 5 for two stickers. Complete 10 by end of the week to be allowed to watch one show.

After School	Each Day
Come in house	
Hang up coat	
Eat snack	
Ask for help with homework	
Pick a story for bed	

child achieves the reward. This chart gives both the parent and child initial success and begins the process of shaping behavior. The chart should get more complicated over time as the child ages and/or masters the tasks. The ratio can change to variable by telling the child that at the start of each week the parent will randomly draw a number from 2 to 5 that will determine how many items the child needs to complete in order to get the stickers or video. Create the chart with the parent and child, and remember to use pictures or ask the child to draw himself waking up, brushing teeth, and so forth. The parent should use verbal praise and encouragement throughout the process if appropriate to the child.

Tables 10.5 and 10.6 show similar charts for an older child.

Example 2: Broad Behavior Chart

This is a behavior modification plan devised to work with a child who has multiple behavioral problems. Rather than craft a strategy to attack them one by one, create a very simple plan to address them all at once. "Caught being good" (Pickover, 2002) is a strategy that addresses broad behavioral issues. Use a large notebook or a large glass jar. Each time the child is "caught being good," the adult or child puts a marble or penny in the jar or places a star in the notebook. The child also receives lots of

Table 10.5 *Task Chart Before School for Older Child*

Before School	Each Day
Wake up on your own	
Brush teeth	
Straighten the bedroom	
Clean breakfast dishes	
Check backpack for homework	

Table 10.6 *Task Chart After School for Older Child*

After School	Each Day
Hang up coat	
Talk to parent about day at school	
Spend 1 hour on homework	
Go to bathroom before bed	
Set alarm clock	

verbal praise. To address the problems associated with the adult needing to address the unwanted behavior, use a check system. The child gets a check each time she acts out and then receives a consequence. If the child changes the behavior, the child receives the marble or star. In order to receive the reward, the child needs to have more stars (or marbles) than checks. In other words, it does not matter how "bad" the child is throughout the week; she just needs to be "good" one time more. Initially, ensure that the adult knows to set the child up to succeed. As the child improves behavior, move to a variable-interval plan, with the child not knowing when she will receive the reward during the week.

Table 10.7 provides an example of a partially completed broad behavior chart.

Example 3: Shaping Behavior Chart (Interval)

Desired behavior: Staying in seat at school

If the child currently cannot stay in her seat at all, the intervals should be small and easy to achieve at first and then increase. Manage expectations; the child cannot go from never sitting still to always sitting still. In this example, the child has been observed to be able to sit still for 15 minutes at a time. Begin the goal with what the child already achieves to ensure success (Table 10.8).

In order to shape the behavior, the child should earn a larger reward at the end of the day. For week 1, give a reward for earning 10 stars (lower if the child cannot meet this goal). Also, if the child cannot meet the goal

Table 10.7 *Broad Behavior Chart*

Sunday	Monday		Tuesday	Wednesday	Thursday	Friday	Saturday
****/////	*******////////	*****	**				

Table 10.8 *Sample Shaping Behavior Chart*

Week 1	Week 2	Week 3	Week 4
Star every 15 minutes (24 stars possible)	Star every half an hour (18 stars possible)	Star every hour (6 stars possible)	Star on variable interval (10 stars possible)

of 15 minutes, drop the interval down until the child can meet the goal and then slowly build back up.

Example 4: Creative/Paradoxical Interventions

Creative/paradoxical interventions work best when traditional methods prove unsuccessful. Oftentimes, behavior modification plans fail because they are too straightforward or the adult and child do not buy into the plan. The adult does not want the child to get a reward for any behavioral change, or the child seems unmoved by a promise of reward. Here are some ways to change behavior using paradoxical methods.

First, consider prescribing the symptom. With the adult and child in the room, give the parent some coping tools for handling the behavior in a more effective way, and ask the child to demonstrate the behavior in front of you. For example, encourage the child to throw a tantrum so the parent can practice how to respond. The child may refuse or the child may throw the tantrum, but either way the child has confirmed that he has behavioral control over the tantrum. Ask the parent to have these "practice sessions" at least one time per day. The goal of this intervention is to change the relationship between the parent and child and to shift the symptom to another, less toxic behavior. The parent and child team up to work together, and the child sees the tantrum as no longer useful. This intervention is best used in conjunction with shaping behavior modification.

GROUP THERAPY FOR SOCIAL SKILLS
AND ANGER MANAGEMENT

Another effective intervention to modify behavior is with the use of group work, specifically for social or coping skills. Group therapy allows children to interact with each other, role-play scenarios, obtain support from each other, and practice social skills in a natural setting. Specific major benefits of group therapy for youth in child welfare include decreased sense of isolation, shame, and despair; improved social and coping skills; and increased positive sense of identity and empowerment (Cone, Golden, & Hall, 2009).

Often therapists struggle with logistical issues when trying to create therapy groups. Foster parents might not arrive on time, visits interfere, and court hearings and different school schedules may inter-fere as well. If a therapist can manage to bypass these roadblocks and schedule a treatment group, focus the group on the needs of the children by age and issue.

Social Skills

Social skills are best taught in a group setting, and many models exist that provide instructions and techniques on how to build social skills with children in foster care. A therapist should remember to manage the size of the group and not run a large group (i.e., six or more children) alone. Here we provide examples of social skill groups, as well as refer-ences for several others.

Ensure the group members are matched by age and developmen-tal level. Be careful when creating topic-specific groups, such as anger management or social skills development. Although these groups can be helpful, groups should also allow for processing and free expression rather than workbooks and lesson plans. Children who have been abused and neglected will have "anger" issues, but really these are issues of emo-tional regulation related to trauma, abuse, and neglect. Remember to con-sider the child's worldview when conducting group treatment focused on social skills and anger management training. Otherwise, the topics can appear dismissive to the child's experience.

For example, consider the child who experiences physical abuse, is removed from his parents and siblings, and is forced to change to a new school, all within a 5-day period. The child goes to the new school and has several physical altercations with his peers; he then receives a sus-pension with a requirement to attend an anger management group. The school officials are responding solely to the behavior of the child and not the child's situation. Foster parents might do the same, but remember that any human would be unable to cope with that much transition in such a short time without struggling.

The following social skills group models provide the therapist with several options. Play therapy groups involve using the techniques of play therapy in a group setting, such as sand play or drawing. Small groups of children (no more than six) work together to play games, draw, or engage in some type of play expression. This type of group therapy is effective for increasing social skills in preadolescent children (Siu, 2014).

Group therapy might also include the utilization of computer technology to provide automatic feedback on facial or social interactions (Fenstermacher, Olympia, & Sheridan, 2006). Owens, Granader, Humphry, and Baron-Cohen (2008) developed a social group treatment modality using Legos. They assigned children to a task of either giving instructions, seeking pieces, or building the structure and found that this treatment modality improved social competence. Overall, social skills groups work by allowing children to interact with one another, practicing social skills in a safe environment.

Anger Management Groups

Anger management groups developed over the last 20 years due to an increase of violent incidents in schools and community settings (Herrmann & McWhirter, 2003). These groups are primarily based on cognitive behavioral principles and focus on the identification of triggers that cause anger arousal, teaching coping skills to decrease arousal, and maintenance of the newly learned coping skills. Several thousand models exist, and options should be researched for efficacy before choosing a specific modality. Remember that for children in foster care, anger is a symptom of a larger issue related to abuse and trauma rather than the issue itself. Here we review just a few of the many programs available.

The Emotional Skills Building Curriculum (Pickover, 2010) focuses on increasing emotional regulation by building skills to identify emotion, increasing perspective taking and empathy, and understanding how to manage the range of emotions. The 13-week program was designed for children ages 10 and up and begins with validation, helping children identify their own feelings, link feelings with physical arousal, learn to adjust the range of emotions, identify another person's perspective, and build support.

Markus and Mattiko (2007) described a seven-stage cognitive behavioral program designed to help children identify angry responses and coping mechanisms. Their model follows traditional cognitive behavioral therapy (CBT) tenets that include brainstorming angry responses and practicing coping skills during the group sessions.

The Student Created Aggression Replacement Education (SCARE) program was developed to work with preadolescent children (ages 8–10) and consists of 15 sessions broken into three sections. The first section focuses on identifying anger and violence in the community, the second section focuses on decreasing angry responses, and the third section focuses on identifying ways to help others curb angry responses (Herrmann & McWhirter, 2003).

Although these modalities are often effective, always remember to keep the child's emotional issues at the forefront of the kaleidoscope.

REFERENCES

Cone, J. C., Golden, J. A., & Hall, C. W. (2009). The effect of short-term cognitive-behavioral group therapy on adolescents with attachment difficulties. *Behavioral Development Bulletin, 15*(1), 29–35. doi:10.1037/h0100511

Fenstermacher, K., Olympia, D., & Sheridan, S. M. (2006). Effectiveness of a computer-facilitated, interactive social skills training program for boys with attention deficit hyperactivity disorder. *School Psychology Quarterly, 21*(2), 197–224.

Herrmann, D. S., & McWhirter, J. J. M. (2003). Anger and aggression management in young adolescents: An experimental validation of the SCARE program. *Education & Treatment of Children, 26*(3), 273.

Marcus, D., & Mattiko, M. (2007). An anger management program for children with attention deficit, hyperactivity disorder. *Therapeutic Recreation Journal, 41*(1), 16–28.

Owens, G., Granader, Y., Humphrey, A., & Baron-Cohen, S. (2008). Lego® therapy and the social use of language programme: An evaluation of two social skills interventions for children with high functioning autism and Asperger syndrome. *Journal of Autism and Developmental Disorders, 38*(10), 1944–1957. doi:10.1007/s10803-008-0590-6

Pickover, S. (2002). Breaking the cycle: A clinical example of disrupting an insecure attachment system. *Journal of Mental Health Counseling, 24*, 358–366.

Pickover, S. (2010). The emotional skills building curriculum. *Journal of Offender & Addiction Counseling, 31*, 52–58.

Siu, A. F. Y. (2014). Effectiveness of group Theraplay® on enhancing social skills among children with developmental disabilities. *International Journal of Play Therapy, 23*(4), 187–203. doi:10.1037/a0038158

Wolpe, J. (1990). *The practice of behavior therapy* (4th ed.). Elmsford, NY: Pergamon Press.

PART FOUR

WORKING WITH ADULTS IN CHILD WELFARE

CHAPTER ELEVEN

ENGAGING FAMILIES IN TREATMENT

We now turn the kaleidoscope toward working with families. Whether working with foster families, birth families, or adoptive families, as a therapist working in child welfare, perhaps the most difficult challenge is remaining family focused rather than child focused. Treating abused and neglected children stirs up many emotions, and the desire to protect the children and vilify the adults is normal but unproductive. Therapists might view either a birth or foster family as resistant to change or hostile to treatment. Remember the pain people feel when they lose their children or are challenged on their parenting. Then think about engagement as an ethical function of treatment. Therapists who work with children often expect parents to want to engage and take immediate responsibility for their actions. However, like their children, family members come to treatment with their own list of personal foibles and pain that prevent their ability to trust in the therapeutic process. When beginning treatment with an adult mired in the child welfare system, it is best to avoid the mindset that family members should want treatment. The examples and recommendations in this chapter come from clinical experience, trial and error, and training in systemic family therapy approaches.

CASE STUDY 11.1

In my first job, I remember a sign on the desk of our executive director that stated "To accept the child's family is to accept the child." Years later I attended a training with family therapist Harry Aponte, who stated, "Families do the best they can with what they have." An ongoing struggle remains, reminding me that not everyone has access to the same resources or the same optimal development. I have to meet my clients where they are, not just where I expect them to be. *Family members are not responsible for working with therapists; we are responsible for engaging and working with them.*

BIRTH PARENTS

As reviewed in Chapter 3, birth parents come to treatment with a host of mental health, social, and personal concerns. Birth parents are mandated clients, meaning they are not choosing to come to treatment but rather are forced into treatment under the threat of losing their children. Birth parents may obtain treatment in a family setting or on an individual basis. Remember to remain focused on cultural competency throughout treatment. Culture refers not only to ethnicity, but also to socioeconomic status, religion, gender, sexual orientation, or any other issue the family members identify as their culture. Understand that not all of the interventions outlined in this chapter will work with every culture. A therapist unfamiliar with a particular culture must learn about the culture both through conducting research and asking the family for understanding. The simplest way to find out is to say to the family, "Tell me about your family."

A Family-Focused Approach

The first key to engaging birth families in treatment is allowing the families to identify their own members and determine their own support systems. Each individual should determine what the word *family* means. Although the child welfare system often draws boundaries around who is allowed in treatment, families should still be given the autonomy to determine who they define as family (Lewis, 2011). Beginning treatment by identifying all the players allows the therapist to craft a clear picture both for the child and the parent. Genograms are a very useful tool to clarify family members, but a simple family tree works as well. Having each member draft the tree separately, then together, also gives the therapist a clearer picture of how each member views the family connections. View the entire family system as the client rather than just the child. By doing so, the therapist always remembers to focus on using counseling techniques when interacting with each family member.

ENGAGEMENT TECHNIQUES

Figuring out how to convince someone to enter treatment requires some skill and understanding of the individual's worldview. Similar to understanding the worldview of the child in foster care, the therapist must consider the worldview of the birth parents. The kaleidoscope's turn often becomes stuck on the reasons for removal and the parent's behavior. Remember to view the parent from multiple perspectives, including the parent's own history of trauma, grief, mental illness, developmental concerns, educational concerns, and fears.

Here are some recommendations of ways to handle the initial engagement. First, call the family member, briefly introduce yourself, and explain your function as the child's therapist. Allow the family member to vent or ask questions. Invite the family member to meet with you. Be accommodating of family members' schedules and respectful when speaking to them. Use words like "Sir" and "Ma'am." Answer in a nondefensive tone even if they refuse to come in, and focus on how much their help would be appreciated. Allow the families to determine who they consider family members and whom they want to bring for support.

Assessment

Begin with determining each family member's stage of change. Prochaska and DiClemente (1984) theorized a transtheoretical model of change. These stages help the therapist determine how ready the client is to engage in the therapeutic process. The stages—precontemplation, contemplation, preparation, action, and maintenance—are often used in substance abuse treatment, but are helpful parameters when treating birth parents in the child welfare system.

Individuals in precontemplation do not acknowledge a problem. Parents in this stage may blame their children or the child welfare system for the loss of their children and deny making bad parenting decisions. These parents are often angry, appear defensive, and might make a statement like, "No one has the right to tell me how to parent my child." Parents in contemplation begin to acknowledge that problems exist but are reluctant to admit them. These parents might admit some bad parenting choices but are often still defensive and shift blame onto others. For example, a contemplative parent might admit that the home has no heat or water but would also claim that the situation would have been rectified in a few days. Parents in preparation acknowledge the problem but feel judged and unwilling to examine the reasons that led to the removal of the child. A parent in preparation will admit to poor decision making and will want to get out of the court system as soon as possible, but might not

CASE STUDY 11.2

Susan had several children living in her home with her new, younger husband. They ranged in age from 4 to 24, and each child exhibited some type of mental health issue. The older children had all been exposed to sexual abuse, two by the 24-year-old sibling. When I started treatment, Susan denied any responsibility for the sexual abuse and blamed her son for committing the abuse (*precontemplation*). I conducted in-home family therapy every week for 6 months. Within 2 months she began to discuss her own history of sexual abuse and foster care and wondered if her son's behavior was connected to it (*contemplation*). A month later Susan discussed wanting her mother to apologize to her for not protecting her from past abuse. She wondered why her own adult son had so much anger toward her (*preparation*). Four months into treatment, I challenged Susan on the lack of boundaries in her home and encouraged her to allow only her biological children and husband to live in the house. She agreed (*action*). She also apologized to her son for allowing him to be sexually abused (*action*), and by the time we closed treatment she had maintained the boundaries in her home (*maintenance*).

be open to examining other factors that led to the neglect. Parents in action are ready to change. These parents make statements indicating that they understand the reasons for removal and want to take steps to avoid reoccurrence of the problem. Parents in maintenance have made changes and work toward developing coping skills and support systems in order to sustain the change.

Most mandated clients enter treatment in the precontemplation or contemplation stage of change, whereas most therapists, judges, case managers, and other child welfare workers expect the parents to be in the action stage. Unlike the angry child who garners sympathy and empathy, parents often fail to receive the same level of emotional support from the system. Remember that parents are in crisis when they enter treatment. They have lost their children, been flung into a system they do not understand, and feel angry and hurt. Sometimes the most effective treatment will mean moving the parent from one stage to another, not all the way

CASE STUDY 11.3

An older, single, Caucasian mother struggling to support herself and her 8-year-old son came into treatment after losing custody of her child for physical abuse. The child acted out at private school, and his mother disciplined him with a tree branch, leaving marks. During the first session, the client expressed anger at losing her child and at the child welfare system for interfering in her faith-based belief in corporal punishment. She entered treatment in precontemplation, defensive and angry. I provided empathy and validation. I also focused on the reality of the situation. She had the right to her beliefs, but because the beliefs conflicted with state law, she had to face the reality that the state would win. Although she never admitted being wrong, she could eventually identify the amount of pressure she felt to appear competent and how she felt she did not have the ability to make mistakes.

This case reminded me that humans need to feel safe and have enough ego strength to examine their mistakes. *Challenge without unconditional positive regard is just judgment.*

to action. However, therapists feel terrible pressure to "fix" the situation and as a result may move too quickly or try to force change before the client is ready.

Next, determine the parents' strengths and triage the areas for change. The point of treatment with birth parents in the child welfare system is to prepare for either reunification or termination. The myriad of issues present cannot be treated all at once, so keep the focus on ensuring the child can be safe at home. Finally, determine the parenting style of each parent. Baumrind (1971) identified three types of parenting styles: authoritarian, authoritative, and permissive. Authoritarian parents do not negotiate with children over rules and do not display as much warmth. Authoritative parents talk to their children about rules but still enforce rules while demonstrating warmth. Permissive parents allow the child to make the rules, and although they demonstrate warmth, the lack of consistency and control may cause distress for the child.

Building Empathy

From the onset of the first interaction with the family, empathy and validation should be at the forefront. Parents come to treatment with fear and anger, not out of choice. Society judges parents harshly, and this judgment causes emotional wounds to self-worth and ego strength. Imagine being judged by a myriad of people without the ability to defend yourself. The child welfare system expects parents to be humble and repentant, which is hard to do when feeling attacked and condemned. Parents are judged by case managers, judges, lawyers, their families, and their children. Focus on making the therapist's office a no-judgment zone.

Empathy and validation should focus on parents' feelings rather than their behavior. Finding empathy for clients who enter treatment with anger, resentment, and resistance requires the counselor to identify the meaning behind the resistance and hostility, which is often feelings of helplessness and hopelessness. Many clients feel as if they have failed at the one task every human should be able to accomplish. Validate feelings of helplessness and anger at the system and the sense that the client is being treated unfairly. This intervention focuses on utilizing the foundation of unconditional positive regard and the person-centered belief in establishing trust and safety within the therapeutic relationship (Raskin & Rogers, 2005). Some therapists fail to validate feelings for fear that they are giving clients permission to act out. For example, stating "You

CASE STUDY 11.4

While working for a faith-based organization, approximately 5 years into my career, I attended a panel discussion of parents who had lost custody of their children. The members of the focus group spoke on issues of multiculturalism, discussing their feelings about working with counselors from different ethnic backgrounds. During this process, one parent succinctly stated the obvious: "I don't care who you are or what you look like—you are coming into my home and telling me I'm a bad parent." This statement still resonates with me every time I meet a family or train new counselors and is the basis for the simplest of family engagement techniques: Validate the clients' experience.

just want to be able to raise your children your own way" validates the client's feelings of anger and frustration, but does not give the client permission to abuse her children. Table 11.1 offers more examples of effective empathy and validation statements.

Table 11.1 *Effective Empathy and Validation Statements*

- It sounds like you feel judged and belittled by the system.
- You just want to be able to raise your child in peace.
- I wonder if you feel helpless, like every decision you make is wrong.
- You were going about your life and the system threw a bomb into it and expects you to pick up the pieces on your own.
- You just want everyone, including me, out of your life. I want to help you get me out of your life.

CASE STUDY 11.5

Sandy was a 35-year-old mother of three children (one boy, two girls) who had lost custody temporarily due to her substance abuse and homelessness. When protective services removed her children, the family had been living in an abandoned house without heat or water. She claimed a history of domestic violence with the father of her children and viewed her decision to live in the house as a reasonable solution to keeping her family together. When I began treatment with Sandy, her children had been in care for almost 2 years and a permanent custody petition had already been filed. Her decision to attend therapy appeared to be based on her fear of losing her children and not on a belief that she had made any errors in parenting judgment or committed neglect. When she entered treatment, she presented as angry and defensive, often stating she did nothing wrong. I spent at least five sessions providing empathy and validation, making statements such as, "You don't think you did anything wrong and now the court is taking your children. Of course you are furious!" and "You have been through so much in your life and feel like the system is trying to destroy you again." Although building trust with this client took time, after a month of validation she could tolerate a discussion of her decision making and address the reasons her children entered care. Although this case proceeded to a termination trial, Sandy did eventually regain custody of her children.

Denouncing Self as Expert

The next intervention involves an awareness of the helplessness and powerlessness felt by parents who have lost custody of their children or who have been identified as "bad" parents. Parents who may already feel disenfranchised from mainstream society expect to be infantilized by the child welfare system, and the system rarely disappoints their expectations. The more members of the system treat them as children, the more they respond with resistance, hostility, or hopelessness. In order to combat this systemic issue, take the stance of parent as expert rather than therapist as expert. Engage parents by asking for their help with their children. First, ask them to meet with you, but in a way that suggests you need their help rather than that they need your help. For example, state, "Could you please come in and give me some help working with Jane? I know you know her better than anyone."

Although the parent may not suggest a workable idea, the therapist can morph the idea into something workable and continue to engage the parent in the therapeutic process. Giving the parent some measure of control over parenting decisions also helps increase engagement in treatment. Asking the parent's permission to give the child a treat in therapy or asking the parent's opinion on a behavioral issue sends the message that the therapist still sees the parent as relevant and important in decision making.

CASE STUDY 11.6

I conducted family therapy with a young mother with two teenage sons. Her youngest son had been hospitalized for depression, and the mother had a history of hospitalizations for a substance abuse disorder. Although she was a caring and committed parent, her interactions with the mental health system and the child welfare system had left her questioning every decision she made, and she often made statements like, "I'm an addict, so I don't know what I am doing." She asked for approval on every parenting decision, and her sons looked to the caseworker or therapist for direction. With my insistence that she knew her sons better than anyone, the therapy focused on validating her decisions, and her children responded by viewing their mother as their parent and no longer needing direction from the therapist.

Building on Child and Parent Strengths

Identifying strengths in parents and children remains a challenge for even the most seasoned therapist. Families and children in the child welfare system are often viewed through the lens of pathology, with a focus on their deficits by all parties involved. Do not allow this negativity to define treatment. For example, make statements like, "You have all these people in your business, telling you what to do, and you still came in to talk to me. You have so much courage and strength for handling all of this." Statements like these send a message of respect and dignity to the parent, which helps the parent drop defensiveness and anger.

Once in treatment, continue to focus on the strengths of both the child and the parent. Attribute positive aspects of the child to the parent. For

CASE STUDY 11.7

I began working with a 12-year-old biracial male, Bobby, in individual therapy. Bobby demonstrated several troubling behaviors, including pulling fire alarms at school, fighting with peers and teachers, making verbal threats, and refusing to follow directions. However, Bobby also displayed some positive personality characteristics as well: He appeared mischievous, had a great laugh and sense of humor, and demonstrated caring for his younger brother. During my first family therapy session, I introduced myself to his mother and father. His mother presented herself as an engaging woman who was desperate to help her son. I began the session by stating, "Bobby is a really kind boy with a great sense of humor; I can see that he's a lot like you."

His mother began to sob uncontrollably, and I remember becoming panicked, not sure of what I had done.

When she could finally speak she stated, "You don't know what it's like when everyone you meet tells you what a little shit your kid is." She referred to her prior experience with other professionals at her son's school, and I realized that I was the first person who had said anything positive to her about her child. This incident occurred over 20 years ago and remains a cornerstone of my strategies to engage families.

CASE STUDY 11.8

I conducted family therapy with a dad and his four children. He had not been in their lives much and knew little about them. During the first session I created a game called "How much do we know about one another?" Each member wrote down his or her favorite food, television show, movie, comic book, and dessert and his or her shoe size, dress size, and eye color. I collected the papers and asked the questions. If a member guessed the answer correctly, the member received a ticket or prize. The game allowed the family to laugh with one another and learn what they knew and did not know about one another and demonstrated that what the members did know illustrated love and concern. We could then build on these strengths throughout treatment.

example, commenting on the child's sense of humor or artistic talent to the parent and noting how the parent contributed to the child's strengths allows the parents to view themselves as worthwhile. The point of this intervention is to find a strength, no matter how inconsequential, and move the kaleidoscope toward a different image of the parent, not just for the parent, but for the therapist and other child welfare professionals. Avoid focusing on pathology and negative behavior in each session. Use the positive-negative-positive intervention approach. Begin each session with a statement that identifies the strength of the parent and end each session with the same. When conducting family therapy, the first few sessions often succumb to adults and children lodging complaints about one another rather than identifying one another's strengths. Use a cohesion-building intervention that gives children and parents an opportunity to talk about their relationship outside of the child welfare system.

Maintaining Dignity

The final intervention involves remembering to treat parents with dignity and respect despite their parental shortcomings, even during confrontations. Based on structural family systems theory (Minuchin, 1974), this intervention focuses on building and maintaining a strong parent subsystem. This technique allows the adults to hear feedback without sending the message to their children that they are incompetent. This intervention involves making statements to the parents that imply that the parents already have the knowledge they need to make sound parenting decisions. For example, state, "I know you already know that your daughter needs a regular bedtime each night. How can we work together to achieve it?" This intervention provides the counselor with a method for confrontation while giving the parent the ability to "save face." Remember to avoid confronting parents in front of their children unless there is a specific therapeutic reason. Families in the child welfare system already suffer from power imbalances, with foster parents, therapists, caseworkers, and judges making decisions for them without their input. When confronted about their behavior in front of their children, parents lose even more credibility and power. This power imbalance might end up *parentifying* the child or sending the message to the child that the parent cannot take care of the child.

CASE STUDY 11.9

I had been assigned the case of a 30-year-old mother with six children. Her youngest child was 1 month old, and she had three older children ranging in age from 4 to 12. Desperate to regain custody of her 7-year-old son and maintain custody of the rest of her children, she rented a home but had no money for furniture. She believed that she had been ordered to obtain housing and that housing alone would meet the court mandate. When I entered the house, I witnessed milk crates in the living room serving as chairs and the 1-month-old infant propped against the corner wall in the kitchen with a bottle in his mouth. I knew I had to address the lack of furniture and the infant's precarious state but also worried about confronting this client in front of her children. I also knew that no matter what I said she would be embarrassed. I also feared destroying our rapport. I chose to pull her aside from the children and stated, "I know you know that the baby needs to be off the floor. I bet you are just really stressed right now with the move and lack of furniture." She blushed, picked up her infant, and stated that his father had placed him in the corner. I continued to talk to her about her lack of furniture and offered to locate a crib and high chair for the baby, which she accepted. Although this was not an ideal situation, I believe that this approach prevented a rapport breach because I suggested the problem was stress and not a lapse or absence of parenting knowledge.

FAMILY THERAPY

There are many texts and courses available to explain and demonstrate family systems treatment and methods for providing treatment for adults. At the end of this section, there is a list of resources and texts to explore. However, if working in the child welfare system, therapists are strongly recommended to obtain training in family therapy before attempting to conduct family therapy. Otherwise, please be sure to seek supervision from a qualified family therapist when providing family treatment. Family therapy is not a linear therapeutic approach and should only occur with specific intentions. For example, a therapist should not bring a parent into a session to be confronted by a child, and a parent should not enter a session in order to confront the child and the child's behavior. These types of interventions are often destructive, and their therapeutic intention is questionable. How does alienating a child from her parent help the child? How does watching a child be berated by a parent help the family functioning? Plan to speak with parents at the end of the session to share their concerns. If a family session occurs, ensure that the treatment goals for the session are well defined and benefit both the child and the parent. Following are some recommended resources, but again, the authors recommend seeking training and supervision.

FAMILY THERAPY RESOURCES

Goldenberg, I., & Goldenberg, H. (1991). *Family therapy: An overview* (3rd ed.). Belmont, CA: Thomson Brooks/Cole.

Henggeler, S. W., & Borduin, C. M. (1990). *Family therapy and beyond: A multisystemic approach to treating the behavior problems of children and adolescents.* Pacific Grove, CA: Brooks/Cole.

Lewis, C. (2011). Providing therapy to children and families in foster care: A systemic-relational approach. *Family Process, 50*(4), 436–452.

Timmer, S. G., Urquiza, A. J., Herschell, A. D., McGrath, J. M., Zebell, N. M., Porter, A. L., & Vargas, E. C. (2006). Parent-child interaction therapy: Application of an empirically supported treatment to maltreated children in foster care. *Child Welfare, 85*(6), 919–939.

Wachtel, E. F. (1994). *Treating troubled children and their families.* New York, NY: Guilford Press.

FOSTER AND ADOPTIVE PARENTS

Many of the recommendations described earlier work well for foster and adoptive parents. Throughout this section, the term *parent* will refer to both foster and adoptive parents. Engaging foster parents in treatment may be challenging because of the power differential present in the relationship. Parents may view their parenting skills as superior and do not want assistance, or they want to be treated as a collaborator rather than a client. We recommend engaging with foster parents from a therapeutic stance while respecting and maintaining their power in the relationship. Simple behaviors such as asking the parent for permission before giving a child a treat or asking permission before walking around the parent's home decrease defensiveness.

Assessment

First, assess the parent's parenting style. This assessment will help the therapist determine the best course of action to engage in. To assess parenting style, observe the parent and consult other therapists and the caseworker, as well as ask the foster parent about her parenting style. Determine the parenting style based on the styles listed in the previous section. Determine the social support available to the parent, and if the parent appears overwhelmed, recommend further support from a support group, the parent's own therapist, or other family members.

Assess the level of empathy the foster parent demonstrates toward the child and parent as well as the level of investment in the therapeutic process. Oftentimes the biggest barrier to engaging the parent in treatment is the parent's perceived lack of empathy for the child and/or the birth parent. This lack of empathy occurs often when working with a behaviorally challenged child. The lack of perceived empathy might cause the therapist to become angry with the parent, resulting in unproductive consultations. Many factors combine to decrease empathy: the amount and type of previous fostering experience, the type and quality of training, the parent's own trauma and attachment concerns, conflict and stress in the home, the parent's communication style, and a lack of knowledge or understanding of the child's development needs.

Overcoming Barriers

Once the therapist has assessed the parent's level of engagement, begin with empathy and validation. Spend time understanding the parent's worldview and begin with a focus on strengths. For example, "It's annoying having to listen to everyone else tell you what to do in your own home," or "You have so much experience with kids; tell me what you think I should do." Unlike birth parents, foster parents are part of your treatment team. However, foster parents come to treatment with varied agendas and life histories. The parent may not demonstrate an understanding of the needs of the child or birth parent or may want a quick fix. Psychoeducation is always helpful, but other techniques should also be used to help the foster parent see the child's worldview. Use of metaphors that mimic the child's experience in an adult context helps the foster parent feel what the child feels. For example, out of frustration, foster parents often resort to threatening the foster child with removal from the foster home. Of course the parent considers this threat motivating because she thinks the child wants to stay in the home. As demonstrated throughout this text, children suffering grief, loss, and trauma are unmoved by such threats as they expect this result to happen anyway and will increase their acting out in order to make the removal happen. Saying to the foster parent, "Don't do that—it won't work" is often too direct of an approach and doesn't achieve the desired result. Instead, validate the reason the foster parent makes the threat by saying, "You are so frustrated that everything you are doing to help the child isn't working."

Engaging the foster parents' spiritual beliefs might help as well. Respect their faith and learn about their culture and beliefs the same way that a therapist would learn about a birth parent or foster care child. Advocate for the foster parent with the agency when possible, provide resources, and agree to provide support. The simple act of listening and providing emotional support often carries the day.

A primary task of conducting quality treatment for children is ensuring that the families they live with feel as though they are part of the treatment process. Always keep the focus on engagement strategies. If the birth or foster parents do not engage, try something different, but avoid blaming them or writing them off as resistant. Ultimately, a quality working relationship with the adults always benefits the child.

CASE STUDY 11.10

I spent many years trying to figure out how to combat the threat of "I am going to throw you out of my house." I tried to educate the foster parent on the reason for the child's behavior; I tried offering materials and books, and nothing worked. Then, I developed two metaphorical stories that helped illustrate how the child felt.

Tell this story to the foster parent: Imagine you own your home. You love your home, you worked hard to pay for it, and value everything in it. One day your mortgage company calls and states, "Maybe we're going to foreclose today; maybe we're not," and then hangs up. You don't know what you did. You think you made all the payments and you go back and check. The calls keep coming. Sometimes every day, sometimes only once a month. How long would it be before you told the mortgage company to take the house?

This story illustrates the inability of the child to live in a constant state of fear, and how anger, frustration, and anxiety would cause anyone to give up in order to make it stop. Most foster parents stated they wouldn't be able to tolerate the stress for more than 2 weeks. Once I related this story back to the foster child's behavior, the foster parents stopped making the threats.

The second metaphorical story involves two individuals standing on the edge of a cliff. I would use dolls or toys (or even a stapler and tape dispenser) and place them over an edge of the table. Then I would hold up the child doll and state, "You keep telling the child to jump, that she should behave and trust you (take a leap of faith), but she is saying, 'You first!'"

REFERENCES

Baumrind, D. (1971). Current patterns of parental authority. *Developmental Psychology Monographs, 4*(1, Pt. 2), 1–102.

Lewis, C. (2011). Providing therapy to children and families in foster care: A systemic-relational approach. *Family Process, 50*(4), 436–452.

Minuchin, S. (1974). *Families and family therapy.* Cambridge, MA: Harvard University Press.

Prochaska, J., & DiClemente, C. (1984). *The transtheoretical approach: Crossing the traditional boundaries of therapy.* Homewood, IL: Dow Jones/Irwin.

Raskin, N. J., & Rogers, C. R. (2005). *Person-centered therapy.* Belmont, CA: Thomson Brooks/Cole.

CHAPTER TWELVE

COLLABORATING WITH PROFESSIONALS

Therapists are not the only ones turning the kaleidoscope and making sense of its patterns. There are numerous professionals viewing and influencing the foster child's intricate, changing designs. Therapists must collaborate with the other professionals involved by both participating in and creating opportunities to make meaningful exchanges and decisions (Bischoff, Springer, Reisbig, Lyons, & Likcani, 2012). Whether such efforts are effective or stunted, the therapist's view of the kaleidoscope and its complex patterns will only ever be enhanced by collaborative efforts.

This chapter describes effective approaches to collaboration, relevant ethical guidelines, and specific advantages and methods for collaborating with child welfare, legal, educational, medical, and other mental health professionals.

EFFECTIVELY APPROACHING COLLABORATION

Therapists must spend time both in and outside of sessions participating in the multi-professional efforts to support children and their families, such as attending family team meetings and submitting reports and following up on court hearings and their outcomes. Roles of a therapist working in child welfare include gathering and sharing information, coordinating interventions, and advocating for clients' mental health needs. Whether therapists are treating 1 or 100 clients in foster care, effective treatment of these cases demands at least double the time commitment of a non–child welfare case (Lewis, 2011) due to the volume of treatment issues and relevant adults in the client's life.

Historically, child welfare professionals have operated from a "silo-thinking" perspective, that is, working in isolation, closed off from other professionals (Linden, 2015). High turnover rates, burnout, overwhelming job expectations, constant crises, and reactive coping patterns invite this type of insulated approach to treatment (Rossler, 2012). Fear and the need for self-protection breed these ineffective strategies and, interestingly, are similar to the way many children and families in the system are reticent to connect with helping adults. When therapists avoid or devalue the other professionals involved, they are modeling coping skills to deal with tension and stress that are contradictory to what they are supporting in their clients. However, when therapists show initiative and take responsibility in reaching out and connecting with the other professionals in these children's lives, the results can have a profound impact for all involved.

CASE STUDY 12.1

I had been working with 6-year-old Nicholas for a few months after he was abruptly removed from a preadoptive placement for unclear reasons. His new foster parent struggled with caring for him and his frustrating behaviors related to the loss and an insecure attachment pattern. Family and individual interventions did not result in the quick changes the foster parent wanted, and the placement was in jeopardy.

I called the teacher to see what was going on at school. She flatly denied that Nicholas had any behavior problems whatsoever and pointed out multiple strengths she noticed in the child. I thanked her for her time and tried to end the call. I felt relieved that Nicholas seemed to have found a safe refuge in school. But the teacher was angry. When I couldn't give her details about his court case or placement, she made it clear that any adult who spoke badly of Nicholas either didn't know him or was not in her right mind. I thanked her again for her positive work with Nicholas, but she was insistent: "Why can't you get this child in a good home? Why don't you just do your job?"

Now I was frustrated and inappropriately replied with, "Have you considered adoption?" She didn't respond. I didn't hear from her again. But Nicholas's worker did.

Within a year, she became licensed just for him, and when he was finally replaced there, it was like he had always belonged. The adoption was smooth and successful. Although I did not continue as his therapist, he and his adoptive mother stopped by to visit for years to come. I learned that reaching out and connecting with others invested in these children's lives can bring positive outcomes even when professionals make mistakes along the way.

When working in child welfare, cultural competency applies to more than just clients. The involved professionals span ethnicity, socioeconomic status, and religions (Hays, 2009). No one is free from tendencies to discriminate, stereotype, and judge others. Racial, sexual, religious, and socioeconomic status differences between professionals can create challenges in collaboration. These challenges can be opportunities to grow professionally and personally, or they can be obstacles to effective intervention for the client. Therapists must be aware of their own cultural contexts, own their biases, and strive toward competence. By remaining open to feedback and seeking trusted support when unsure of a new or stressful dynamic, therapists can continue to evolve and learn from mistakes along the way (VanderGast, Culbreth, & Flowers, 2010).

Countertransference is not just relevant to clients and their families; a therapist's personal feelings, thoughts, and behaviors based on past experiences, and often unresolved issues, can influence their work with case workers, judges, teachers, and the system itself. This can be a huge barrier to remaining open and constructive in collaboration efforts. Be aware of pulls to blame others or take sides with and against other professionals. Use supervision and self-reflection to increase awareness and care for the heavy reactions that are bound to arise. Everyone—children and adults—is doing the best they can with what they know and the resources they have. There is a difference between accountability and blame.

Many therapists working with this population view their role as an agent of social change—striving to make a difference in the child welfare system. With this mindset, there is a tendency for therapists to view the potential relationships with other professionals as adversarial, meaning that collaboration should be avoided or falsely engaged in—in other words, engaged in without ever believing it will help. As in most systems, there are a wealth of power imbalances in child welfare. Therapists who choose to see these imbalances as characteristics of a struggling system rather than unworkable barriers will be the true agents of change. The more hopeless, helpless, and unrealistic therapists become, the less effective they will be in serving the children, who, unlike therapists, did not make the choice to enter this system.

Ethical Issues

Therapists should consider collaboration with relevant professionals an ethical responsibility. However, collaborative efforts can easily become entangled in ethical dilemmas. When unsure of how to proceed with an ethical dilemma, therapists should consult a professional organization or a state agency. Do not do nothing. Most professional organizations provide free ethical consultation for members. Following are several major ethical areas therapists working in child welfare must attend to.

Confidentiality breaches occur frequently in child welfare, leaving children in foster care and foster families wary to trust anyone. The nature of the system means that the therapist is obligated to two parties: the funding agency and the client. The funding agency, which includes the state and the assigned private agency, has the right to see all reports and notes. Clients should be made aware of this fact before starting therapy. Consider allowing older clients and their parents to view notes and read reports before submitting them in an effort to build trust.

The Health Insurance Portability and Accountability Act (HIPAA) and Family Education Rights and Privacy Act (FERPA) apply to children in foster care, and violation is a serious offense (FERPA, 2015; HIPAA, 2015). Because the information boundaries are more complicated and confusing with this population, revisit employer policies and professional ethical guidelines. Remember, it is the therapist's responsibility to adhere, whether or not the employer is in compliance.

Other professionals involved are not necessarily bound by the same confidentiality rules as therapists, meaning that they may share information about a client without consent, whereas the therapist cannot. Therapists must ensure that appropriate releases are completed and kept up to date for all professionals contacted about the case. If the client is a permanent court ward, then the assigned foster care worker may sign as legal guardian. If the child is a temporary court ward, then the birth parent or assigned foster care worker may sign consents as legal guardian (Molin & Palmer, 2005). Releases should specifically identify what type of information will be shared or obtained, meaning that a written notice as well as verbal conversation about the exchange of information with both the parent/guardian and the child must occur. Although minors do not have the legal authority to refuse consents, receiving their input can offer an opportunity for empowerment and problem solving around their valid concerns regarding trust and privacy. Document the nature and timing of information released and obtained in progress notes. Besides being best and ethical practice, this will allow therapists to build trust and transparency in treatment.

Court Reports and Testimony

Many therapists are asked to submit court reports or recommendations concerning mental health issues as well as placement. Some therapists may be subpoenaed as the primary therapist for the client or family or as an expert witness if major mental health issues are involved in court arguments.

Some employing agencies restrict the type of recommendations therapists can make, whereas other agencies want specific recommendations related to a range of issues, from treatment to reunification or adoption. Regardless, therapists must weigh recommendations carefully and remember to report only on factual, observable items. For example, if a therapist has never viewed a child–parent interaction, the therapist cannot make a recommendation on reunification because the therapist has not witnessed the relationship between the parent and child. Therapists must be cautious about what they write and remember that all notes and reports can be subpoenaed into the court file at any time. Only document, report, and testify information that describes what happens in treatment and what the therapist has directly observed. Avoid putting impressions or judgments into any documentation or testimony. Focus on comprehension and application of major mental health diagnoses and solid understanding of child development, attachment, grief, and trauma. Use phrases such as "as evidenced by" when documenting specific behavior, and focus on observable terms only. Table 12.1 illustrates this type of documentation.

Table 12.1 *Effective and Ineffective Documentation*

Ineffective	Effective
The client is angry at her mother and shouldn't go home.	The client has made statements such as "I don't want to go home" and "I am scared to be alone with her."
The client is depressed.	The client appears depressed, as evidenced by his frequent crying during session. He reports that he cannot sleep or eat much during the day.
The client's father traumatized her.	The client identifies feeling afraid of seeing her father at visits. She describes believing her father will "find her and make her pay for telling" about the substantiated abuse.

Mandated Reporting

Abuse and neglect allegations are an integral part of treatment in child welfare. New allegations against the birth parent may arise after the child has been in treatment or removed from the situation. Children often make allegations against their foster parents for a myriad of reasons, including a belief that they will be able to go home or because they are actually being abused in the foster home. Each mental health profession has specific ethical codes that speak to the requirement to breach confidentiality when someone's safety is at risk. Every therapist is a mandated reporter and therefore legally required to report abuse; depending on the state, the penalty for failing to report suspected abuse or neglect could range from the therapist losing his license to criminal and civil penalties.

Prepare for potential reporting from the onset of treatment. Review informed consent with birth parents, children in foster care, and foster parents during the first session as well as throughout treatment. Use language about confidentiality that they understand. For example, say, "I need to let you know that if someone reports abuse or neglect to me I am required by law to report it. I don't investigate or make any judgment about truth. If I have to make a report, I'll let you know unless someone's safety is at risk."

When informing an adult or child about the need to make the report, remind her about the informed consent first, using empathy. Focus on being the messenger, not the message. In other words, do not personalize or defend actions. Allow the child or adult to be angry, validate the anger, and focus on the legal duty. If a child states, "I hate you; please don't do this," respond with, "I know you don't want me to do this, but I have to, and you have every right to be mad at me."

Therapists must be readily familiar with the already substantiated abuse or neglect of their clients and should not report any abuse or neglect that has already been substantiated. Only report suspected neglect or abuse prior to removal if it was not previously reported or substantiated. Additionally, the parameters of what constitutes suspected abuse or neglect are extended for children in foster care (Pecora, Jensen, Romanelli, Jackson, & Ortiz, 2009). Assigned foster care workers should always be informed when therapists are completing and submitting their state's child abuse/neglect reporting form. Additionally, for foster parents suspected of abuse or neglect, a written licensing complaint should be filed with the foster parents' licensing body, whether state or nonprofit.

OPPORTUNITIES FOR COLLABORATION

There are formal and informal ways to collaborate with other professionals. Examples of formal opportunities include case conferences, family team meetings, and court hearings, each of which will take place whether or not the therapist chooses to participate. Connect with the client's foster care worker to find out when these occur. If attendance is not possible, submit a therapy report to be shared at the meeting, and follow up on the outcome. Informal opportunities involve phone calls, e-mails, and sharing of information outside of conferences and court.

Child Welfare Staff

All children in the child welfare system will have multiple child welfare staff assigned to them: foster care worker (FCW) or supervised independent living/independent living (SIL/IL) worker (SIL/ILW), supervisor, licensing worker, and protective service worker. The FCW is the most significant contact for collaboration outside of the child's family. Keep the FCW involved in the treatment process, even if the FCW is reluctant to do so. Work with the FCW in a similar way that a therapist might work with a parent by building an understanding of the FCW's concerns, building empathy, and identifying ways to better support the child with the FCW's concerns. A mutually respectful dynamic between therapists and FCWs will have a tremendous positive impact on achieving goals of stability and permanence for children and families. For example, involve FCWs in the treatment planning process and progress reviews and make sure that they get the documentation of treatment that they require for their work.

Collaborate with the SIL/ILW in much the same way as with the FCW but with increased focus on addressing any communication concerns between the SIL/ILW and the client because of the tendency for the SIL/ILW to take on more of a parenting role. Dysfunction in this relationship is typical and can be a major concern and barrier for treatment progress. Be cautious of breaking trust with the client in collaborative efforts, and review all information and recommendations with the client before sharing with the SIL/ILW. Clearly identify treatment recommendations to both client and the SIL/ILW while empowering the client to choose which recommendations the client agrees to follow.

CASE STUDY 12.2

Sixteen-year-old Marie was placed with her maternal grandmother through the child welfare system due to parental neglect related to drug use. Although her birth father had not been active in her life before she was placed in care, he and his parents were working hard to "get her back" after Marie's mother's rights had been terminated. This meant competing with Marie's maternal grandmother—who had been a familiar and stable figure in her life since infancy and whom her younger siblings, who had a different father, were already adopted by—for guardianship/adoption.

Her worker informed me that in the past, family team meetings were largely attended and usually became complicated family feuds that Marie left from crying or screaming, with little progress in making decisions about her placement. As her new therapist, I worked with both the foster care worker and Marie to prepare for the dynamics of the meeting and to find ways for Marie to both care for herself and advocate for her wants and needs in safe and respectful ways. Role playing and planning "breaks" from the meeting when she became overwhelmed were major parts of getting through the 2 hours of intense discussion.

With our preparation and my presence as an additional support, Marie was able to clearly tell her father and paternal grandparents on the record for the first time that she loved them and wanted them in her life but was also sure that she wanted to have permanency through adoption by her maternal grandmother and stay with her siblings there.

Think of licensing workers as both monitors and case workers for foster parents. Therapists should make contact when a foster parent is not compliant or cooperative with bringing the client to therapy or following through on parenting recommendations or trainings for the client's mental health needs. Also be sure to identify foster parents' areas of strengths with particular age groups or types of behavioral health concerns to the licensing workers.

Become familiar with the FCW's, SIL/ILW's, and licensing worker's supervisors as well, because these professionals are typically the next in line for collaboration. High turnover rates and inexperience can make the supervisors more reliable team members in collaboration efforts, particularly in crises. Additionally, if therapists have any ethical or case-handling concerns regarding the assigned foster care worker, reporting said concerns to the supervisor is part of the therapist's role as advocate for clients. For example, if a therapist makes repeated efforts to contact the client's assigned foster care worker to gather birth family information, submit court reports, or make additional referrals without response from the worker, making contact with the supervisor is the next step.

Therapists will rarely have direct contact with the initial protective services worker on a client's case but can have access to parts of the protective services reports from the FCW. However, in the case of additional reports of suspected abuse or neglect after the child is already in foster care, therapists should have direct contact with protective services, whether they made the allegation or not. Cooperation with all requests for information and observations from protective services is mandatory.

Other Mental Health Providers

Chances are, if the client is in therapy, then there are other family members also in therapy, whether at the same or a different mental health provider or one assigned to the family through the courts. Collaboration with other therapists should focus on (a) sharing information and observations to improve case conceptualization and intervention strategies and (b) complementing rather than contradicting one another's treatment interventions. Schedule case conferences via phone or in person. Hold joint sessions and cofacilitate family or sibling sessions around major transitions or changes in permanency goals.

If a client completes psychological testing, request to case conference with the psychologist both before and after testing, either with or separate from the family, to share concerns and observations as well as clarify testing results and recommendations. Many times, parents walk away from completing psychological testing without a clear understanding of the results and implications. Explain the testing results and recommendations in language that the family and child can understand to make the findings relevant and helpful to them, which will increase their likelihood of following through.

Some clients may be assigned an in-home behavior aide to help increase placement stability. Behavior aides can be an incredible addition to a treatment team. Communicate with the behavior aide regularly and include the aide in treatment planning meetings. Compare observations and complement intervention strategies to work toward the same goals. For children with severe behavior problems in foster homes, this combination of services is especially advantageous and can free up therapy sessions greatly for other treatment interventions.

Medical Professionals

If a client is taking psychotropic medications, therapists must participate in regular case conferences by phone or in person with the prescribing psychiatrist to share the therapist's assessment results, treatment goals, recommended interventions, and progress made, even if any of these differ from the psychiatrist's recommendations and findings. Psychiatrists do not have the opportunity to observe and interact with the client and family to the extent that therapists do. The therapist's input to concerns around diagnosis and treatment is vital to effective complementary treatment. If the psychiatrist is not receptive to the therapist's input, be sure to document concerns in writing. Participate in psychiatric evaluation and medication reviews with the client either by attending appointments or by contacting the psychiatrist before and/or after any appointments with the client to share progress and emerging concerns as well as clarify and potentially disagree with the psychiatrist's recommendations. Some clients do not feel comfortable sharing accurate updates about their symptoms and may not ask treatment questions. Encourage clients to be more open with the psychiatrist.

Provide primary care physicians and any rehabilitation specialists with up-to-date treatment overviews, including current diagnoses, treatment recommended/received, and any prescribed medications.

Legal Professionals

Attorneys contact therapists primarily because they believe the therapist's testimony and insight will support their legal arguments, which may include subpoenaing the therapist. Unfortunately, therapists may be asked to make recommendations for permanency that they do not have the authority or information to make. A good rule of thumb for therapists to remember is that they should report only on direct observations or information already documented in assessment, treatment planning, and progress notes and avoid speculation at all times.

Unless the therapist is subpoenaed to testify in court, therapists will likely never directly interact with the client's judge. Collaboration with judges is done via court reports relayed by the FCW. Sometimes, clients have personal access to their judges, and therapists can help these clients know their rights in the courtroom and the different ways that they can advocate for themselves, such as by requesting a private conversation or writing a letter. These efforts can be profoundly empowering to the client and also affect the outcome of a case.

Educational Professionals

Reaching out to clients' teachers and other school staff can have a profound impact on treatment. Attend individualized education plan (IEP) meetings or school conferences if possible, or contribute to the meetings by submitting therapy reports as well as following up on meeting outcomes and recommendations.

Even if the child does not have an IEP, contact the client's teacher(s) if significant behavior problems are reported at school or when the child is reported to have problems in the home but not at school. Gather information about the child's presentation, including both strengths and concerns; identify types of support the client is responsive to; and advocate for the client's mental health needs using trauma-informed approaches to build empathy, understanding, and effective prevention and response efforts to behavioral concerns. This type of reframing and psychoeducation about a client's maladaptive behaviors can be profoundly influential to the way school staff manages behavioral concerns. Sometimes principals or assistant principals hold primary responsibility for all disciplinary actions at a school, and collaboration should extend to them. There are increasing training opportunities for school staff to take on trauma-informed educational approaches. Be sure to report any concerns with the way a teacher or staff member is inappropriately interacting with a client to the principal or assistants in order to advocate for the client (and undoubtedly many other children). It is possible that the concerns are a school culture issue, which is even more reason to speak up.

Some clients may already have a supportive relationship with their school social workers or counselors through their IEPs or their own initiative. Advocate for consistent contact and accessibility if the therapeutic support at school will be helpful to the client. Work to complement interventions with active school social workers and share relevant updates.

A paraprofessional educator, alternatively known as a para-pro, paraeducator, instructional assistant, educational assistant, teacher's aide, or classroom assistant, can be a key treatment team member if a client receives special education services or requires additional behavior management. Because this professional is the one who will be most familiar with the client's behaviors and is responsible for carrying identified preventative and responsive actions, include the individual in case conferences and treatment updates, along with the teacher and social worker.

CONCLUSION

An ethical mandate in all helping professions is to act as an advocate for clients. To advocate means to speak up for the concerns of others, but sometimes advocacy becomes misconstrued with the idea of speaking up for those without a voice. All children and families have voices; their voices are just often unheard. Through the act of effective collaboration, the therapist becomes an amplifier for the child and family, allowing their voices to be heard and recognized by the others around them.

RESOURCES

American Association for Marriage and Family Therapists (AAMFT) *Code of Ethics*: www.aamft.org/iMIS15/AAMFT/Content/Legal_Ethics/Code_of_Ethics.aspx
American Counseling Association (ACA) *Code of Ethics*: www.counseling.org/resources/aca-code-of-ethics.pdf
American Psychological Association (APA) *Code of Ethics*: www.apa.org/ethics/code/
National Association of Social Workers (NASW) *Code of Ethics*: www.socialworkers.org/pubs/code/code.asp

REFERENCES

Bischoff, R. J., Springer, P. R., Reisbig, A. M. J., Lyons, S., & Likcani, A. (2012). Training for collaboration: Collaborative practice skills for mental health professionals. *Journal of Marital and Family Therapy, 38,* 199–210.

Family Educational Rights and Privacy Act (FERPA). (2015, June 26). Retrieved from http://www2.ed.gov/policy/gen/guid/fpco/ferpa/index.html

Hays, P. A. (2009). Integrating evidence-based practice, cognitive–behavior therapy, and multicultural therapy: Ten steps for culturally competent practice. *Professional Psychology: Research and Practice,* 40(4), 354–360. doi:10.1037/a0016250

Health Insurance Portability and Accountability Act (HIPAA). (2015). Retrieved from https://www.hipaa.com/category/hipaa-law-administrative-simplification/

Lewis, C. (2011). Providing therapy to children and families in foster care: A systemic-relational approach. *Family Process,* 50(4), 436–452.

Linden, W. (2015). From silos to bridges: Psychology on the move. *Canadian Psychology,* 56(1), 1–5.

Molin, R., & Palmer, S. (2005). Consent and participation: Ethical issues in the treatment of children in out-of-home care. *American Journal of Orthopsychiatry,* 75(1), 152–157. doi:10.1037/0002-9432.75.1.152

Pecora, P. J., Jensen, P. S., Romanelli, L. H., Jackson, L. J., & Ortiz, A. (2009). Mental health services for children placed in foster care: An overview of current challenges. *Child Welfare,* 88(1), 5–26.

Rossler, W. (2012). Stress, burnout, and job dissatisfaction in mental health workers. *European Archives of Psychiatry and Clinical Neuroscience, 262,* 65–69. doi:10.1007/s00406-012-0353-4

VanderGast, T. S., Culbreth, J. R., & Flowers, C. (2010). An exploration of experiences and preferences in clinical supervision with play therapists. *International Journal of Play Therapy,* 19(3), 174–185. doi:10.1037/a0018882

CHAPTER THIRTEEN

BURNOUT, COUNTERTRANSFERENCE, ETHICS, AND WELLNESS

Providing treatment in the context of the child welfare system can be extremely rewarding, but there are perils that come with this work. No text on working with children and families in child welfare would be complete without discussing these concerns. Therapists will experience both positive and negative countertransference during the course of their careers. Therapists are also at risk for developing burnout and making poor ethical decisions. This chapter explores how to identify and counteract countertransference, reviews common ethical issues that arise when treating this population, discusses how to identify burnout, and reviews the tenets of wellness and the benefits of clinical supervision. Acknowledging each of these issues is paramount. Failure to identify burnout and countertransference often leads to unethical behavior, which harms both the therapist and the client. A lack of self-awareness can cause the kaleidoscope to over-focus on one color or shape. Perhaps the kaleidoscope even stops moving, and the therapist is unable to see any shapes or colors at all. The therapist's view becomes obstructed by the therapist's own kaleidoscope of needs and experiences.

COUNTERTRANSFERENCE

Countertransference is best defined as the therapist's feelings, thoughts, and behaviors that occur during the process of therapy. The therapist derives these feelings, thoughts, and behaviors from her own personal history of often unresolved issues (Gelso & Hayes, 1998). When these feelings are not acknowledged, they can be transferred onto the client, and the therapist acts toward the client as if the client is "making" the therapist feel the emotions. Countertransference exists as an ongoing part of therapy. Labeling the process as good or bad is counterproductive

CASE STUDY 13.1

I (Sheri) began my relationship with my coauthor, Heather, as a supervisor. She had been working with foster children for only a short time and struggled with the overwhelming sadness present in their lives. One day, she discussed the case of a disrupted adoption. Her 9-year-old client's mother returned her to the agency and terminated her parental rights. She didn't tell her child her plan and left it to the case manager and therapist (Heather) to spill the bad news. As Heather practiced what she would say to this child, she made statements such as, "We'll find you another home" and "We care about you." I challenged Heather to examine the reason behind her statements. Whom was she comforting? Were the statements true? Could she guarantee another home for this child? And why didn't the child have a right to be angry and sad about what happened? After processing the situation, we both acknowledged that this child's pain brought out feelings of hopelessness in Heather and, not wanting to feel them, she attempted to distance herself from the child by making statements aimed at making herself feel better.

because once countertransference is viewed as negative, the therapist might not want to acknowledge that it exists. Countertransference can be useful to treatment, as positive feelings of care and concern transfer to the client and allow the therapist to act in a nurturing way. The key to countertransference is to admit it happens; then it can be examined.

Countertransference occurs for several reasons. First, the therapist's culture, racial identity, spirituality, socioeconomic status, and sexuality all enter into the therapeutic environment and lead to countertransference. A therapist cannot divorce her own identity from the therapeutic process and, as a result, needs to be aware of how her own culture, socioeconomic status, and values will impact the session. For example, how a therapist feels about having children out of wedlock, using illegal substances, or alternative lifestyles might influence treatment. If the therapist has limited experience with different cultures, she may focus on stereotypes rather than learning about the nuances of culture. For example, a

CASE STUDY 13.2

I've had many incidents of countertransference over the course of my career, but one stands out because it so clearly prevented me from helping my client. As a young foster care therapist, I worked for an agency focused on family reunification, which resonated with me. I provided case management and therapy for an 8-year-old girl, Maggie, who came into care due to physical abuse from her mother. I provided family therapy and received clinical supervision from a supervisor who had only provided treatment to boys who had been charged with a crime and placed in a group home for treatment. He kept pushing me to recommend reunification, and I knew I should not. Maggie's mother had not made the necessary changes, had a history of mental illness, and could be unpredictably violent. However, I was afraid to confront my supervisor. I was worried that I would put my job in jeopardy if I confronted him, and I worried that he might become angry at me. These feelings were, of course, my issues and had no place in the decision-making process, but I did not have the self-awareness I needed then, and so I followed my orders. Maggie returned to care within 1 week of the reunification because of physical abuse from her mother. She suffered because of my inability to put her needs ahead of my own fears.

therapist who has no experience with a religious tradition that dictates specific roles for men and women might transfer feelings of anger toward a client who views women in a traditional subservient role. Similarly, a therapist who grew up in poverty might transfer feelings of judgment toward a wealthy client. Countertransference, when undetected, leads to serious lapses in therapeutic judgment. When the therapist's feelings become overwhelming, a therapist might shut down and distance herself from the client.

Next, working with this population can easily stir up the therapist's own attachment issues or history of trauma and lead to countertransference. While treating a child in foster care, the therapist might feel anger, disgust, judgment, pity, frustration, hopelessness, and helplessness.

Countertransference leads to feeling the need to rescue the child from the child's birth parent, or even foster parent (Kates, Johnson, Rader, & Strieder, 1991; Pollak, 1989), as well as feeling anger at the family members for their perceived shortcomings. Working with adults who have committed abuse or neglect against children brings up feelings of anger, hostility, and judgment, especially if the therapist has a history of abuse or neglect.

Imagine that the feelings the child and family bring into session are a deep lake, and to reach them the therapist has to travel a rickety untested bridge across the water (see Figure 13.1). The safe part of the bridge on one side is sympathy. The therapist on that side of the bridge feels sorry for the client but does not allow herself to feel the full extent of the client's pain. The therapist wants to protect herself from these feelings and makes statements such as, "I am sorry that has happened to you." On the other safe side of the bridge are both pity and judgment. On this side, the therapist views the client as beneath the therapist, believing that the client's situation is so tragic or so impossible that the client is poor and pathetic. The therapist views the

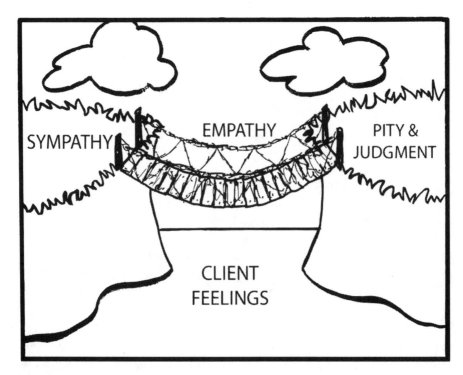

Figure 13.1 *Bridge of Empathy*

client with judgment, either believing that the therapist could handle the situation better or condemning the decision the client has made. Judgment can be either positive or negative. For example, the question "Why did you make that decision?" implies that the therapist thinks the client made a poor decision and expects the client to defend it. This type of judgment closes down conversation and builds defenses. However, saying "good job" to an adult is just as judgmental because the therapist is putting her personal values on the client, indicating that the behavior is "good" and should be continued. The message sent to clients is that they must please the therapist. This type of judgment leads clients to report feelings and behaviors to the therapist based on what they perceive the therapist wants to hear, rather than how they actually think and feel. This process slows down and blocks treatment. Both of these examples illustrate a situation where the therapist implies to the client that the therapist's worldview is more valid and "right" and that the client needs the therapist's approval. Pity and judgment also allow the therapist to keep emotionally distant from the client. By convincing herself that she would not behave as the client or would not allow herself to be in the same situation, the therapist creates a safe cocoon to protect herself from the reality of the client's situation.

In the middle of the bridge is empathy, the willingness to feel what the client feels and see the client's worldview from the client's perspective. Empathy requires a strong ego foundation and effective self-awareness. An empathetic therapist has the ability to identify when she is moving toward either side of the bridge, has the ability to tolerate imagining herself in the client's shoes, and has support to manage the feelings of hurt or despair. Unresolved countertransference forces the therapist to either side of the bridge and results in nontherapeutic treatment.

Self-awareness is the best tool a therapist can wield when providing treatment. Self-awareness allows the therapist to recognize feelings, examine them, and seek support if needed to prevent them from interfering with treatment. A competent therapist should always examine her positive and negative countertransferential feelings by being diligent and seeking support.

BURNOUT

When treating children and families in the child welfare system for a specific length of time, the therapist becomes at risk for burnout. Burnout refers to feeling emotionally exhausted, noticing a sense of depersonal-ization regarding clients, and feeling a lack of personal accomplishment (Maslach, Jackson, & Leiter, 1996). Other common terms are *compassion fatigue* and *empathy fatigue*. The therapist has feelings of failure and hope-lessness and can no longer muster empathy for clients. Symptoms of depersonalization include increased judgment of client actions and be-havior and anger expressed at clients for not getting better or appreciat-ing the help.

There are many causes for burnout. The constant exposure to sec-ondary trauma through hearing client stories wears on all child welfare worker professionals. Referred to as vicarious trauma or secondary trau-matic stress, the therapist might experience ongoing exposure to client crises; client pain; and client stories of violence, neglect, and abuse (Van Hook & Rothenberg, 2009). This exposure may result in the therapist demonstrating the same symptoms present in the client, such as recur-ring intrusive images of the traumatic event, depression, anxiety, and stress. Taking the case home happens often, and although the sense of stress decreases over time with experience, the ongoing thoughts and stories become emotionally exhausting. Research shows that therapists who work with caseloads comprised of clients with posttraumatic stress disorder (PTSD) report higher levels of compassion fatigue and burnout (Lawson & Myers, 2011).

Work-related stress also leads to burnout (see Table 13.1). Any pro-fessional working with this population witnesses the bureaucracy that at times impedes movement of a case. If the agency or organization the therapist works for puts demands on the therapist for specific results, the therapist can feel helpless and unable to affect change. The pressure to "fix" the child and family is often constant. Foster parents demand quick change, caseworkers want to move toward a resolution, birth parents want their children back, and judges want progress. Working with chil-dren and families in child welfare means acknowledging a fundamental

Table 13.1 *Signs of Countertransference/Burnout*

Emotional exhaustion	Stress interferes with sleeping/eating
Compassion fatigue	Inability to concentrate
Pitying clients	Increased work absences
Judging/condemning clients	Avoiding clients/work
Frequent anger at clients/system	PTSD symptoms from vicarious trauma

CASE STUDY 13.3

I experienced many issues of burnout during my career, but one yearlong instance stands out. In the eighth year of my career, I worked as a clinical supervisor at a group home for youth in foster care. The agency split responsibilities between clinical and case management staff, with the clinical staff able to make recommendations for treatment but unable to do much else. My direct supervisor ran the group home and implemented this separation of responsibility.

A 12-year-old Hispanic boy who had been placed in the group home for criminal conduct was assigned to my staff for treatment. None of the therapists I supervised had sufficient training to treat his offending behavior, so I found an outpatient program that treated offenders and recommended he be sent there for treatment. His caseworker had the responsibility to make the referral to a specialized treatment program, but I was not allowed to ensure the referral was made or confront the caseworker's supervisor.

The referral was never made, and the overseeing court referee condemned the agency for this failure. I had confronted my boss about this lapse, but she refused to let me make the referral myself yet blamed me for the error. I found myself shutting down at work, not providing the best care to my clients, and missing major treatment issues. I realized later that I suffered from emotional exhaustion and lack of personal accomplishment. Unable to feel as if I could effect change, I stopped trying. The burnout was easier to notice once I left the agency, but I felt angry at myself for allowing my burnout to impact my clients.

lack of control over the treatment. Child welfare agencies exist within a complicated and sometimes convoluted bureaucracy focused on rules and protocols. Demands placed on therapists and other professionals are often unrealistic and overwhelming. Other chapters in this text speak to the pressure from foster parents and birth parents to "fix the client," but this pressure also comes from the organizational structure of the agency. Some states have benchmarks for reunification that put pressure on the therapist to perform miracles. This pressure illuminates the differences between the power the therapist has to effect change and the responsibility the therapist has to effect change. Child welfare agencies bear the brunt of the responsibility for reunification and ensuring stable placements, but the courts have the power to enact change. Therapists become caught in the middle of this pull, receiving pressure to ensure a stable placement or ensure a successful reunification. So many other factors play a role in the success of treatment, and because the therapist does not have control over these factors, the desire to continue striving toward change wanes and then leads to burnout (Sprang, Craig, & Clark, 2011).

The therapist's own personal life also impacts burnout. Life goes on while treating children and families, including normal stresses and strains of life. When these stresses become overwhelming or just overtake the daily life of the therapist, burnout can occur. Although burnout impacts the quality of the therapeutic relationship, it also impacts the quality of the therapist's life. Burnout may lead to depression, anxiety, and somatic complaints such as headaches or stomach aches. The therapist suffers from poor work performance, and as the sense of personal accomplishment goes down, the depression and fear rise. Burnout may also lead to work absenteeism, which effects finances and could have an impact on the quality of the therapist's relationship with her own family and friends.

ETHICS

Ethical standards are the cornerstone of quality treatment. Therapists receive extensive training in ethics in their master's programs, but these ethical principles seem theoretical until the therapist is faced with real-world applications. A therapist working in the child welfare system is bombarded with ethical challenges from the onset of treatment. For example, the therapist is responsible to several factions: the court, the funding agency, and the child and/or families. The therapist must juggle her ethical responsibility to each of the "clients" while keeping the needs of the child and family at the forefront of treatment. These ethical issues become a quagmire when faced with writing court reports about a child's progress or being asked by a foster parent to disclose treatment issues. Review the codes frequently, and ask for help when unsure. All national mental health organizations provide ethical case consultation. This text addresses the most

CASE STUDY 13.4

I supervised a new foster care therapist, Samuel, who had good rapport-building skills but became easily overwhelmed by his clients' stories. He came to supervision one day to inform me that a female client disclosed that her father had taken off his clothes and slept next to her. The child begged her therapist not to report this incident, as she feared she would be placed back in foster care. Samuel promised his client he would not report the incident. During supervision I confronted Samuel on making an unethical promise. We processed his countertransference. He knew his promise was wrong but felt overwhelmed by the pain in his client's voice. Samuel had to report the incident and then tell his client he lied. The rapport never recovered.

common ethical issues that arise from working in the child welfare system, but all ethical standards apply to this practice and should be reviewed on a regular basis.

Poor ethical decision making often arises from countertransference and burnout. When a therapist becomes blocked by feelings, ethical judgment becomes impaired and might lead to problems with boundaries, failure to breach confidentiality when needed, or other ethical breaches. For example, the need to rescue a child might lead to feeding into negative comments about the birth parent or buying a child a lavish birthday present because the parents cannot afford one. Anger or feeling sorry for a child might lead to a failure to file an abuse report after the child begs to leave the abuse unreported.

Boundaries and Confidentiality

The clearest examples of ethical breaches in child welfare are boundary concerns. Because boundaries are so loose in the child welfare system, therapists often forget to maintain confidentiality with caseworkers or foster parents. The child's privacy is often not respected by all adults involved in the child's life, and information flows a bit too freely. Other boundary concerns can arise due to the length of time of the relationship. Although most therapeutic relationships have a clear end point, children and families in foster care can stay in therapy for years. The therapist watches the child grow and experience different developmental milestones, and even when treatment goals are reached, the court system may require the child or family to stay in care. Similarly, roles often shift in the foster care system, with therapists asked to supervise visits or transport their clients around town. These long-term relationships and boundary-crossing roles confuse both the therapist and child and make ethical breaches more likely.

Mandated Reporting

Therapists working with children and families often grapple with the difficulty involved in filing protective services complaints. This issue becomes specifically salient for therapists working with children and families in child welfare because abuse allegations are such an integral part of treatment. Emotions run high when faced with this task. Children may recant and beg the therapist not to report the allegation. Therapists fear losing the relationship with the child, family, and/or foster parent (Cruise & Horton, 2001). Therapists also fear making the situation worse for the child or fear that the protective services agency won't follow up. If the child makes allegations often, adults may view the child's allegations as inaccurate and fail to report them. Therapists may also fear the confrontation when telling a birth parent or foster parent about an allegation (Bryant, 2009; Herendeen, Blevins, Anson, & Smith, 2014). To cope with these stressors, therapists must identify the fears, own them, acknowledge them, and face them. Failing to admit fear of the reaction from clients might prevent the report. Failure to report suspected abuse is both an ethical and legal breach.

COPING STRATEGIES

The key to avoiding burnout is first to recognize when it is happening, to seek emotional support, and to develop sound coping strategies (see Table 13.2). The first coping strategy we recommend is gaining perspective on the situation. Remember that the therapist did not create the child welfare system, did not cause the abuse or neglect, and did not cause the foster care replacement. Try to focus on being the messenger instead of

Table 13.2 *Coping Strategies*

Seek peer support	Seek clinical supervision
Obtain your own personal counseling	Develop a wellness plan
Maintain a strong social support system	Take time off

the message. In other words, the therapist's job is not to defend the child welfare system, or even the agency or court decision. The therapist can validate feelings and help the child cope but does not have to defend the situation. The job is to relay information in an ethical way, and allow the clients to react as they choose. Focus on planting seeds or throwing pebbles rather than trying to build a forest or move a boulder. In other words, remember that the impact of treatment may not reverberate for years, and being a human being witnessing another human being's pain and experience is powerful unto itself.

The most effective method for ensuring that countertransference does not impact the therapeutic process, and to avoid burnout, is to seek out ongoing, consistent clinical supervision. Although this seems an easy task, it is not. Finding good-quality clinical supervision takes time. Once a therapist gains her full license, she may no longer want to pay for supervision if it is no longer required for state licensure. Agencies may provide administrative supervision but may not provide clinical support. A clinical supervisor will be able to identify areas for growth and provide support. Seek out clinical supervisors in your area and use the following checklist:

1. Ensure they have training in clinical supervision—for example, someone with an approved clinical supervisor (ACS) credential.
2. Interview your potential supervisor to determine the individual's theoretical orientation and supervision style. Ensure that it meets your needs.
3. Review the supervision contract and update as needed. If the clinical supervisor does not have a contract, do not use that individual.
4. Ensure you have regular and frequent access to your clinical supervisor for feedback and support.

The reason finding quality supervision remains imperative to a quality therapeutic relationship is because of the relationship between your supervisor and your client; often referred to as a parallel process, the quality of the relationship with the supervisor mirrors the quality of the relationship with the client (Bernard & Goodyear, 2009). A supportive but challenging supervisor will provide a safety net for the therapist to fall and bounce back, which allows the therapist to be more effective with her client. A poor supervisor, who adds stress or pressure, will similarly cause the relationship between client and therapist to be strained and unproductive. A therapist cannot help a child or family feel safe in a therapeutic environment if she does not feel safe. As we have demonstrated throughout this text, children in foster care, foster parents, and birth parents must feel safe in order to proceed with treatment.

Another method for obtaining clinical supervision is to seek out peer support. Finding other therapists who work with the same clientele and meeting at least monthly will also prevent burnout. Peers are able to identify problems and provide gentle feedback. Peer or clinical supervision is crucial to performing quality work.

Finally, seek out your own counseling when needed. Vicarious trauma exposure can lead therapists to suffer from symptoms of PTSD, including depression and anxiety (El-Ghoroury, Galper, Sawaqdeh, & Bufka, 2012). Ongoing exposure to issues in the child welfare system might lead to unseen countertransference. Seeking professional help should be the cornerstone of competent mental health treatment.

WELLNESS

The best way to prevent burnout and potential ethical breaches is to ensure that personal wellness remains a priority. Wellness refers to reaching an optimal state of well-being through the integration of the mind, body, and spirit (Myers & Williard, 2003; Barnett, Baker, Elman & Schoener, 2007). Myers and Williard (2003) described several models of wellness for a therapist to consider. Specific strategies found to be useful include ensuring a work–life balance, practicing some form of spirituality, maintaining good self-awareness, and focusing on physical health (Lawson & Myers, 2011). Effective wellness practices have also been found to mediate vicarious trauma (Williams, Helm, & Clemens, 2012). The key to wellness for therapists is the same as that for clients: Ensure a solid social support system, find effective coping strategies, maintain your physical health, and ensure time off.

Ultimately, remember that the kaleidoscope keeps turning and creating new images, regardless of how many therapeutic interventions work or fail. Being engaged in the act of treating children and adults during one of the most stressful times in their lives is both a gift and a burden. Children and adults allow the therapist to view their most painful and raw shapes and colors. Sharing their kaleidoscopes takes courage, trust, and a leap of faith. Remember to honor this gift by viewing their worlds with empathy and awe for their willingness to engage in the process. Honor the burden by acknowledging the sadness that comes from acting as a witness to this pain and caring for personal needs.

REFERENCES

Barnett, J. E., Baker, E. K., Elman, N. S., & Schoener, G. R. (2007). In pursuit of wellness: The self-care imperative. *Professional Psychology: Research and Practice, 38*(6), 603–612.

Bernard, J. M., & Goodyear, R. K. (2009). *Fundamentals of clinical supervision* (4th ed.). Upper Saddle River, NJ: Pearson.

Bryant, J. K. (2009). School counselors and child abuse reporting: A national survey. *Professional School Counseling, 12,* 333–342.

Cruise, T. K., & Horton, C. B. (2001). *Child abuse and neglect: The school's response.* New York, NY: Guilford Press.

El-Ghoroury, N., Galper, D. I., Sawaqdeh, A., & Bufka, L. F. (2012). Stress, coping, and barriers to wellness among psychology graduate students. *Training and Education in Professional Psychology, 6*(2), 122–134. doi:10.1037/a0028768

Gelso, C. J., & Hayes, J. A. (1998). *The psychotherapy relationship: Theory, research, and practice.* New York, NY: Wiley.

Herendeen, P. A., Blevins, R., Anson, E., & Smith, J. (2014). Barriers to and consequences of mandated reporting of child abuse by nurse practitioners. *Journal of Pediatric Health Care, 28*(1), e1–e7. doi:10.1016/j.pedhc.2013.06.004

Kates, W. G., Johnson, R. L., Rader, M. W., & Strieder, F. H. (1991). Whose child is this? Assessment and treatment of children in foster care. *American Journal of Orthopsychiatry, 61*(4), 584–591. doi:10.1037/h0079289

Lawson, G., & Myers, J. E. (2011). Wellness, professional quality of life, and career-sustaining behaviors: What keeps us well? *Journal of Counseling & Development, 89,* 163–171.

Maslach, C., Jackson, S. E., & Leiter, M. P. (1996). *The Maslach Burnout Inventory manual* (3rd ed.). Palo Alto, CA: Consulting Psychologists Press.

Myers, J. E., & Williard, K. (2003). Integrating spirituality into counselor preparation: A developmental, wellness approach. *Counseling and Values, 47*(2), 142.

Pollak, J., & Levy, S. (1989). Countertransference and failure to report child abuse and neglect. *Child Abuse & Neglect, 13*(4), 515–522.

Sprang, G., Craig, C., & Clark, J. (2011). Secondary traumatic stress and burnout in child welfare workers: A comparative analysis of occupational distress across professional groups. *Child Welfare, 90*(6), 149–168.

Van Hook, M.,P., & Rothenberg, M. (2009). Quality of life and compassion satisfaction/fatigue and burnout in child welfare workers: A study of the child welfare workers in community based care organizations in Central Florida. *Social Work and Christianity, 36*(1), 36–54.

Williams, A. M., Helm, H. M., & Clemens, E. V. (2012). The effect of childhood trauma, personal wellness, supervisory working alliance, and organizational factors on vicarious traumatization. *Journal of Mental Health Counseling, 34*(2), 133–153.

INDEX